In Defense of Asian American Studies

THE ASIAN AMERICAN EXPERIENCE

Series Editor
Roger Daniels, University of Cincinnati

A list of books in the series appears at the end of this book.

In Defense of
Asian American Studies

The Politics of Teaching
and Program Building

SUCHENG CHAN

University of Illinois Press

URBANA AND CHICAGO

1 2 3 4 5 C P 5 4 3 2 1
Library of Congress Cataloging-in-Publication Data
Chan, Sucheng.
In defense of Asian American studies : the politics of teaching
and program building / Sucheng Chan.
p.   cm. — (The Asian American experience)
Includes bibliographical references and index.
ISBN 0-252-03009-5 (acid-free paper) —
ISBN 0-252-07253-7 (pbk.: acid-free paper)
1. Asian Americans—Study and teaching (Higher).
2. College teaching—United States.
3. Curriculum planning—United States.
4. Education, Higher—Political aspects—United States.
I. Title. II. Series.
E184.A75C477   2005
973'.0495'0071173—dc22   2004030077

For Ling-chi Wang,
whose campaigns for racial equality and social justice
have been so unwavering and principled
that even his enemies respect him

Contents

Foreword

ROGER DANIELS

Sucheng Chan is one of the giants of the Asian American studies field. Since the appearance of her stunning first book, *This Bittersweet Soil: The Chinese in California Agriculture, 1860–1910* in 1986 she has produced a steady stream of books and articles, two of them, *Not Just Victims: Conversations with Cambodian Community Leaders in the United States* (2003) and *Survivors: Cambodian Refugees in the United States* (2004) in this series.

In Defense of Asian American Studies is a major theoretical but practical collection of essays about a controversial and embattled academic field by a scholar/administrator who has been a pioneer in the discipline. Although the focus is on her speciality, Asian American studies, the rhetoric and argument, by extension, also apply to the larger field of ethnic studies. What makes the essays particularly compelling is that these are not scholarly musings but were originally written for a specific purpose to gain a particular result. Thus they read like what they were: frontline dispatches from an intellectual war zone, written over a quarter of a century (1974–2003). Although the book describes struggles within one multiversity, the University of California—Chan was a scholar/teacher/administrator at three of its campuses, Santa Cruz, Berkeley, and Santa Barbara—the intellectual terrain they cover is similar to that existing at institutions all across the nation. In addition, parallel arguments continue to take place about what is now usually called African American studies and various incarnations of Hispanic American studies. At some institutions, the same kinds of issues are raised about the broader field of ethnic studies, which serves as an umbrella entity at some schools.

Chan has structured her essays into three topical groups whose titles generally describe the changing levels of debate within the academy: "Justifying Our Existence" (1974–93); "The Politics of Teaching" (1981–98); and "Empowering Ourselves" (1989–2003). In addition, the appended "Selected Bibliography" is, in itself, a demonstration of the expansion of a field which, when Chan began in the 1970s, hardly existed and now has a seemingly secure place in the curriculum of most major universities.

What gives the book its authority is the towering stature of its author. Unlike most of the academic administrators who have fought these battles, Chan is a major scholar of real distinction whose work has a secure place within a traditional discipline.

The essays themselves are combative, controversial, and comprehensive, ranging from, in the first section, an attempt to justify Asian American courses within the humanities curriculum (1974) to a successful proposal for a B.A. degree program in Asian American studies (1993). In the second section she deals not only with her teaching philosophy but also speaks about the vital importance of teaching Asian American students, both foreign-born and native, skills in writing and speaking English. The third section deals largely with the place of Asian American studies within the academy, ending with a speculative and intriguing exploration: "Whither Asian American Studies?"

These essays, taken as a group, are a holistic approach not just to Asian American or ethnic studies but to the whole problem of how to deal with minority students, their concerns, and their special problems within increasingly multicultural universities. Written with verve and passion, they will be must reading for everyone concerned with Asian American studies and its cognate fields.

Preface

At the 1997 annual meeting of the Association for Asian American Studies in Seattle, Kenyon Chan observed that historians of Asian America have not done a good job of documenting the history of our field. He is largely but not entirely correct. We *do* have publications that recorded the field's history as it was being made. Examples include *Roots* and *Counterpoint*;[1] several volumes of conference papers collectively edited by various members of the association;[2] several theme issues of *Amerasia Journal* that focused on Asian American studies; articles listed in the pertinent sections in two indexes published by that journal;[3] a special issue of *Change* magazine;[4] a chapter on Asian American studies in William Wei's study of the Asian American movement;[5] a collection of essays on Asian American pedagogy edited by Lane Hirabayashi;[6] some chapters in two volumes edited by Don Nakanishi and his coeditors;[7] and half a dozen essays in the *Journal of Asian American Studies*.[8] These provide glimpses of a complex story that took place at multiple locations in various parts of the country. Many criss-crossing currents in that history, however, have not yet been explored or analyzed.

To help flesh out a small part of the turbulent institutional history of Asian American studies, I offer here a selection of (mostly unpublished) essays written over a thirty-year period, from 1974 to 2003, as I attempted to defend the field. Even though they deal only with developments on various campuses of the University of California (UC) where I taught, they are of general historical interest because UC campuses played a significant role in the development of Asian American studies. Although the essays represent only one person's experiences, I believe they are useful because they recorded events and developments as they were taking place. For that reason, other scholars can use them as a small part of the documentary evidence generated over three decades.

Few aspects of the multifaceted and multistage history of Asian American studies have been treated in published studies, probably because the field's early days saw many conflicts among individuals who later learned to coexist. Some of us would rather not reveal what happened because we do not wish people and institutions still hostile to our endeavors to know about too many aspects of our past lest they use such knowledge to further attack us. (I, for example, toyed with the idea of writing a chapter entitled "My Enemies and Why They Hate Me." In the end, though, I decided not to write such a piece, not because I'm cowardly but because such a statement would probably whet the appetites of voyeurs more than it would elucidate complexities within the academic, political, and social formation called Asian American studies.) Conflicts continue to bedevil our field. As more and more new scholars join its ranks—individuals with little knowledge of, or sympathy for, our history of struggle and survival—it is becoming well-nigh impossible to agree about which aspects of that past are noteworthy and what the relationship of the past should be to the present and future. Thus, whatever one writer may say will surely be assailed by others.

The writings in this volume are neither "objective" studies of the history of Asian American studies nor "subjective" memoirs of my involvement in it. They represent, rather, my attempts to address various audiences in order to help them understand what Asian American studies was, and is, about. Indeed, some people may call the essays propaganda. I decided to publish them (chosen from several thousand pages of memos, letters, reports, and other ephemera cranked out over thirty years) because for three decades I worked hard to explain, defend, and reflect upon the field.

The essays in this volume served political purposes even though the *methods* I used to discuss, analyze, and present issues in public were more or less scholarly. My aim was to suggest to outsiders how they should view our field, in contrast to the misinformed notions they might have harbored. My language embodied a tension between justifying our existence to people who had the power to shut down our programs, on the one hand, and, on the other, searching for ways to enable myself and my colleagues-cum-comrades to stay on course as we negotiated our ways through treacherous terrain.

We encountered numerous pitfalls along the way because we had to fight for survival on two fronts: survival as an academic unit within the university, which meant that we had to institutionalize and professionalize ourselves to some extent, whether or not we liked doing so, and survival as a vehicle for social change, which required taking action from time to time in the hope of changing the world (or at least the communities) in which we lived. When I muted the political rhetoric that infused the field and its practitioners for many years, I "domesticated" our radical stance in order to win public acceptance but without betraying the objectives for which we fought so hard.

One tack I took repeatedly was to proclaim that the aims of ethnic studies need not contradict the basic tenets of a liberal arts education *if* that education is defined in a sufficiently inclusive way. "A liberal arts education" was the entering wedge I used to cut a path into the innards of the university. My approach differed from the visions and tactics of some of the field's other founders who preferred to do away with the university altogether or saw it only as a source of financial support for various political projects off-campus. Thus, from the point of view of some of the activists who created Asian American studies and other ethnic studies programs, I was a deviant. At the same time, from the perspective of the university I was a subversive. My personal story revolves around how I managed simultaneously to deviate from the militancy that prevailed *and* to subvert the university's power structure from within. It was necessary to do both because we had to fight a war on two fronts, against the academic establishment and against certain tendencies that characterized Asian American studies in its contentious formative years.

As a self-appointed publicist, I was a translator—talking to each intended audience in a language I thought its members would understand. I was not translating from one language to another, however, but from one mindset to another. Many of my essays contain a subliminal message: "Look, I know what you're worried about. You fear us because we look different and sound threatening, but you know, it *is* possible for you and us to find some common ground if you will only listen to us and treat us with respect before you react with the instruments of coercion that you possess." To get such a message across I had to decipher the attitudes of various people who dealt with us and find subtle ways to tweak their consciousness. Sometimes I was on target, but at other times I failed completely because "language games" are not always sufficiently powerful tools in the real-life struggles we wage.

Placatory language notwithstanding, the hard work of program building centered around countless battles to ensure the survival of Asian American studies and our cognate fields, African American studies, Chicano studies, and Native American studies. During the first decade of the existence of ethnic studies we fought every step of the way to have our courses approved as permanent offerings, to obtain additional faculty positions, to find grants to support program development and research, and to beat back myriad efforts to dismantle the programs. Those who participated in establishing the field worked long days and nights, and I hope that younger colleagues who have joined us (or are joining us), our erstwhile successors, will not be too dismissive of our legacy.

Life was difficult for the first two generations of Asian Americanists. (The first generation comprised faculty hired between 1969 and the mid-1970s, the second generation, those hired between the late 1970s and the late 1980s.) We had to spend much time doing what I call "invisible" work—efforts not deemed appropriate, much less worthy of reward, when campus committees evaluated us either as individuals undergoing tenure review or as units undergoing program review. Moreover, many of the faculty who taught Asian American studies in those years endured financially insecure existences as part-time lecturers and barely managed to piece together living wages from teaching a course here, another course there. The few full-time positions went to the first batch of faculty hired at San Francisco State University, the Berkeley and Los Angeles campuses of the University of California, City University of New York, and a few other institutions. Regardless of whether we were full-time or part-time faculty, our invisible work included functioning in various community organizations, engaging in intense political debates and internal struggles, organizing and attending mass demonstrations, and doing things with and for students outside the classroom.

Even though preparing and giving lectures in those early years, when virtually no usable text materials existed, took a lot of effort, as did grading examinations and papers, such tasks were the easy parts of our jobs. The most difficult thing I had to do was to deter certain students from harming themselves, whether psychologically or physically. The latter included self-mutilations, attempted suicides, and threats of "blood revenge." I once spent some seventy hours without sleep with a distraught student who held a loaded gun the whole time, threatening first to kill a young woman he claimed had "betrayed" him, after which he would commit suicide. He warned that should I try to call the police or force him to go to the campus counseling center, as I kept urging him to do, he would shoot me, too. Fortunately, by talking and listening to him, hour after fearful hour, I ultimately managed to disarm him, but it took months before my nerves calmed down.

Faculty members like me tried our best to help some Asian American young people deal with the anger and depression they felt as powerless members of racialized minorities and as subordinate members in families that were often patriarchal and sexist. We were not untrained therapists but rather teachers who used a radical analysis of Asian American history and contemporary life to raise students', and our own, political consciousnesses.

As a result of such time-consuming and emotionally draining activities that could not be listed on anyone's curriculum vitae, I had to postpone my tenure review not once but twice—until I finished a book manuscript. I could have tried to get tenure through militant means but chose not to. Even though I was a minority female faculty member working in a marginalized department, I had internalized the Berkeley ethos—the belief that scholarly distinction *does* matter—to such an extent that I did not wish to challenge the prevailing system of rewards and punishments. Unlike many of my fellow political activists in the 1960s and 1970s who shouted, "Shut it down! Shut it down!" when they held demonstrations at various institutions of higher learning, I have, instead, always demanded, "Open it up! Open it up!" Opening up the institutions where I was employed meant that even as I and like-minded colleagues sought to change them in fundamental ways, we also accepted some of their core features and values. This acceptance opened us to scathing criticism from those who saw the Asian American movement in a different light.

I moved from UC Berkeley to UC Santa Cruz in 1984 to become an administrator. In those years (1984–88), only about 5 percent of my time was given to research and writing (usually done between midnight and 2 A.M.), 10 percent to teaching, and 85 percent to bringing a highly politicized and dissident college back into the fold of the larger university of which it was supposed to be a part but was not. With the exception of one instance—a dispute I had with a dean about whether a candidate he favored, an Asian American who had no background at all in Asian American studies, should be offered the position supposedly allocated for Asian American studies—I did not deal directly with Asian American issues at UC Santa Cruz. That is why this book contains only one essay (chapter 11) about my years on that campus.

Only after I moved once again, this time to UC Santa Barbara in 1988, did I finally have the luxury of working on articles and books as a part of my daily routine. I still spent an enormous amount of time working on program building and serving on all kinds of committees as I turned a nearly moribund Asian American studies program into the first autonomous Asian American studies department at a major research university in the country. But I also resolutely reserved a few hours a day for scholarly pursuits. The books I produced in those years were more lightweight than my first tome, *This Bittersweet Soil*, because I simply could not afford to write another labor-intensive book like that one while I was trying to build an Asian American studies department at a time when we had only a handful of ladder-rank (tenure-track) faculty members but literally twice or even thrice as many students trying to enroll in our more popular classes as we had room.

More important than the books I wrote or edited is the book series I started, "Asian American History and Culture," published by Temple University Press. I established the series in order to demonstrate that Asian American studies is indeed a viable *field* of academic inquiry, that it contains a growing number of scholars doing innovative work, and that they are conversing among one another as well as with colleagues outside the field.

Someone once asked me why I have edited more books than I have written. The reason is simple. Compiling collections of essays that offer different perspectives on the same topic or explore its different aspects, such as those in *Entry Denied* (1991), *Claiming America* (1998), and *Chinese American Transnationalism* (2005)—what I call the "Chinese exclusion era trilogy"—shows more clearly than can sole-authored books that there is indeed a *community* of scholars in the field. In my view, a handful of scholars studying the same phenomena, however brilliant their work may be, does not and cannot constitute a discipline or a field. We need numbers.

This volume does not include commentaries on my work as a scholar; suffice it to say that publishing is also a highly politicized process in the sense that sometimes authors have to acquiesce to editors if they wish to see their work published. In several of my books, for example, copy editors changed what I had written in order to make my discussion of various topics conform to *their* views of the world. Although I always welcome alterations that make my prose smoother, I also refuse to go along with ideological censorship. Even a minuscule difference in word usage can be irksome. The person who wrote the back-cover copy for *Remapping Asian American History,* for example, used a word—"merely"—that was dismissive of earlier works. Although I requested that the word be changed to "mostly," no change was made, probably because the book was already on its way to the printer and the publisher thought such hair-splitting was unnecessary. Consequently, a word that I found objectionable, one that definitely does not represent my views, is now on the back cover of the book, which is the first thing most readers look at.

Why I and other scholars chose to write about certain topics, how we went about doing research, and the frameworks we used to analyze our findings are another part of the Asian American studies story—its intellectual history—that has not yet been written. It will not be easy to write such a history because Asian American studies, unlike such fields as women's studies, cultural studies, and postcolonial studies that also emerged around the same decades of sociopolitical ferment and likewise contained a liberatory or emancipatory impulse, did not begin with the production of certain texts that in time became canonical. Rather, our field began with two large student strikes that captured media attention and a series of less visible actions elsewhere.

We produced no potentially canonical texts during the early years in part because some activists involved in founding Asian American studies were contemptuous of intellectuals and their writings. Consequently, book-length studies by scholars who actually teach Asian American studies (a far smaller group than those who conduct research on and write about Asian Americans) did not appear until the mid-1980s, a decade and a half after the field's birth. As the volume of publications grows (a fact the bibliography makes abundantly clear), if we wish to track the intellectual history of Asian American studies we must take stock of pertinent writings in all the disciplines in order to plumb and explicate their patterns, meanings, internal contradictions, and long-term significance. Only when we are able to juxtapose the field's social, political, and intellectual histories will we finally gain the kind of in-depth, nuanced understanding that will enable us to turn our differences, past and present, overt and covert, into wellsprings of creativity.

Notes

1. Amy Tachiki, Eddie Wong, Franklin Odo, and Buck Wong, eds., *Roots: An Asian American Reader* (Los Angeles: UCLA Asian American Studies Center, 1971); Emma Gee et al., eds., *Counterpoint: Perspectives on Asian America* (Los Angeles: UCLA Asian American Studies Center, 1976).

2. Gary Y. Okihiro et al., eds., *Reflections on Shattered Windows: Promises and Prospects for Asian American Studies* (Pullman: Washington State University Press, 1988); Gail M. Nomura et al., eds., *Frontiers of Asian American Studies: Writing, Research, and Commentary* (Pullman: Washington State University Press, 1989); Shirley Hune et al., eds., *Asian Americans: Comparative and Global Perspectives* (Pullman: Washington State University Press, 1991); Linda A. Revilla et al., eds., *Bearing Dreams, Shaping Visions: Asian Pacific American Perspectives* (Pullman: Washington State University Press, 1993); Judy Yung et al., eds., *New Visions in Asian American Studies: Diversity, Community, Power* (Pullman: Washington State University Press, 1994); and Gary Y. Okihiro et al., eds., *Privileging Positions: The Sites of Asian American Studies* (Pullman: Washington State University Press, 1995).

3. *Amerasia Journal*, 15, no. 1 (1989), 16, no. 1 (1990), 21, nos. 1 and 2 (1995), 21, no. 3 (1995), 26, no. 1 (2000), 29, no. 1 (2003), and the listings in the index of volumes 1–13, pp. 1–2, and the thirtieth anniversary cumulative index, pp. 11–19.

4. *Change* (Nov.–Dec. 1989).

5. William Wei, *The Asian American Movement* (Philadelphia: Temple University Press, 1993), 132–68.

6. Lane Ryo Hirabayashi, ed., *Teaching Asian America: Diversity and the Problem of Diversity* (Lanham: Rowman and Littlefield, 1998). See also Lane Ryo Hirabayashi and Marilyn C. Alquizola, "Asian American Studies: Reevaluating for the 1990s," in *The State*

of Asian America, ed. Karin Aguilar San-Juan (Boston: South End Press, 1994), 351–64, and Lane Ryo Hirabayashi and Marilyn C. Alquizola, "Wither the Asian American Subject?" in *Color Line to Borderlands: The Matrix of American Ethnic Studies,* ed. Johnella E. Butler (Seattle: University of Washington Press, 2001), 169–202.

7. Don T. Nakanishi and Martha Hirano-Nakanishi, eds., *The Education of Asian and Pacific Americans: Historical Perspectives and Prescriptions for the Future* (Phoenix: Oryx Press, 1983); Don T. Nakanishi and Tina Yamano Nishida, eds., *The Asian American Educational Experience: A Source Book for Teachers and Students* (New York: Routledge, 1995).

8. Keith Osajima, "Pedagogical Considerations in Asian American Studies," *Journal of Asian American Studies* 1, no. 1 (1998): 269–92; Stephen H. Sumida, "East of California: Points of Origin of Asian American Studies," *Journal of Asian American Studies* 1, no. 1 (1998): 83–100; Mitchell J. Chang, "Expansion and Its Discontents: The Formation of Asian American Studies Programs in the 1990s," *Journal of Asian American Studies* 2, no. 2 (1999): 181–206; Kenyon S. Chan, "Rethinking the Asian American Project: Bridging the Divide between 'Campus' and 'Community,'" *Journal of Asian American Studies* 3, no. 1 (2000): 17–36; Shilpa Dave et al., "De-Privileging Positions: Indian Americans, South Asian Americans, and the Politics of Asian American Studies," *Journal of Asian American Studies* 3, no. 1 (2000): 67–100; Shirley Hune and Phil Tajitsu Nash, "Reconceptualizing Community, Pedagogy, and Paradigms: Asian American Studies and Higher Education," *Journal of Asian American Studies* 3, no. 1 (2000): 7–15; and Nancy I. Kim, "The General Survey Course on Asian American Women: Transformative Education and Asian American Feminist Pedagogy," *Journal of Asian American Studies* 3, no. 1 (2000): 37–66.

Acknowledgments

I thank Laurie Matheson, acquisitions editor, and Mary Giles, copy editor, for guiding this book through the production process. I am also grateful to Roger Daniels for accepting a manuscript that departs from the usual research monograph format. His flexibility is a testament to his broad vision of what comprises Asian American studies.

I thank my spouse, Mark Juergensmeyer, for always trying to make me laugh. When I am in a bad mood, his penchant to see the comic in even the grimmest situations really annoys me. When I am in a good mood, however, I understand his point that mirth has curative powers. We both thank Brandenburg, Rajah, and Cotufa, the furry members of our family, all of whom have gone to dog heaven, for showing us how sentient beings can greet each new day with boundless joy.

In Defense of Asian American Studies

PART 1

Justifying Our Existence

The seven essays in this section will undoubtedly seem dated. The conditions and population figures I discussed have changed since the 1970s, as have the analytical frameworks that scholars use to make sense of our world. For example, my use of the singular, "Asian American perspective," is no longer acceptable. Scholars in many fields now realize that in this postmodern age, multiple perspectives exist alongside one another, each occupying its own subject position while jostling for hegemony. If I were writing the same essays today, I would use the plural, "Asian American perspectives." Yet, in retrospect, the singular, "perspective," reflects historical reality because members of the first generation of Asian Americanists shared a singular vision. We were determined to bring about what we called "fundamental social change" (a euphemism for what we thought of among ourselves as "revolution") in the United States and its component institutions—especially schools, colleges, and universities—even as we fought bitterly over the *methods* to be used to attain our goals.

The essays in Part 1 address different audiences, which is why they contain subtle linguistic shifts even though they all are on the same topic. I address, in turn, a major funding agency in 1974 (chapter 1); members of local Asian American communities who watched in dismay and confusion as various groups struggled for control of the Asian American Studies Program at UC Berkeley in the 1970s (chapter 2); a faculty review committee at UC Berkeley that controlled the fate of ethnic studies in 1980 (chapter 3); fellow faculty members teaching Asian American studies around the nation in 1981 (chapter 4); the general public attending a forum hosted by the Department of Ethnic Studies at UC Berkeley in 1982 (chapter 5); a university press that established the first book series in Asian American studies in 1989 (chapter 6); and reviewers at the University of California, Santa Barbara, and in the Office of the President of the University of California in Oakland who assessed our proposal for a B.A. degree in Asian American studies in 1993 (chapter 7). These audiences represented the main groups that faculty and students in Asian American studies had to contend with in order to ensure the field's survival and growth.

With one notable exception (chapter 6), I am reproducing the pieces largely as I wrote and published them because they reflect the temper of the times during which they were written. The copy editor for this book did, however, make minor changes in the texts. In what follows, ellipses indicate deletions of sentences or short passages, and brackets tag additions made for the sake of clarification. The original punctuation and capitalization have been retained. All the pieces, as well as countless other memos, appointment letters, and reports that I wrote, aimed to win support for our overt academic and covert political projects. I justified our existence by explaining our objectives in terms that I thought each intended audience would understand, using a prose that I hoped would sound sensible and assertive yet nonmilitant. I believe that each essay did play a part, however minuscule, in ensuring the field's survival, because words *do* matter.

1 The Development of Asian American Studies Humanities Courses and Curricular Materials [1974]

This essay contains the opening sections of a grant proposal that I submitted to the National Endowment for the Humanities (NEH) in 1974. Even though I was trained as a social scientist, soon after I began teaching Asian American studies I realized there was an urgent need to develop humanities courses in our nascent, multidisciplinary field. I wrote the proposal and administered the grant but listed a tenured faculty member as my co-principal investigator (even though he did not participate in conceptualizing the work that the team I assembled planned to carry out) because I had to deflect attention away from the fact that I was an untenured faculty member who had received her Ph.D. only a year earlier. I did not want my lowly status to be flagged by the NEH or the office on the Berkeley campus that reviewed all grant proposals before allowing faculty to send them to funding agencies.

I turned to the NEH as a possible funding source because during the 1973–74 academic year I had an NEH postdoctoral fellowship for the study of U.S. minorities. Aware that "minorities" referred mainly to African Americans, before submitting my fellowship application I called the NEH and asked the program officer who spoke to me whether a study of Asian Americans would be eligible. He said he did not know, but, he mused, I would never find out unless I submitted an application. So, in my application, I discussed why I thought persons of color other than black Americans should also be counted as "minorities." Because I did receive the fellowship, I turned to the NEH again for a grant to develop Asian American humanities courses and curricular materials. The NEH funded the proposal at approximately $100,000—a large sum for a humanities project in those days. I believe it was the first grant that the NEH gave to a project in my field.

Keenly conscious of the marginal status of Asian American studies at that time, I slyly used the academic "weightiness" of the Berkeley campus, as well as the demographic visibility of Asian Americans in the San Francisco Bay area, to enhance the proposal's legitimacy, timeliness, and relevance.

* * *

The University of California at Berkeley is a recognized leader in many fields of higher education. It has the potential to become outstanding in yet another rapidly developing field: Ethnic Studies, and in particular, the Asian American Studies branch of Ethnic Studies. There are a number of reasons for such a potential.

First, demographically, the San Francisco Bay area has one of the largest—and growing—concentrations of Asians in the United States. Based on projections from the 1970 census and current immigration figures, the total number of the three major Asian American groups (Chinese, Japanese, and Filipino) is now close to three-quarters of a million in the San Francisco Metropolitan Statistical Area, comprising over 18 percent of the total population. If smaller Asian immigrant groups, such as Korean Americans and people from other Asian countries, are also counted, the percentage of Asian Americans is even higher.

This demographic fact dictates a special urgency to meet the educational needs—at all levels of education—of Asian American students. At the same time, it offers great opportunities for the development of viable Asian American Studies programs in colleges and universities in this region. Within the compass of a small geographic area, there exist several predominantly Asian American communities undergoing rapid social change. Beneath the tourist facade of Chinatown, Nihonmachi (Japantown), and Manilatown, there are socioeconomic conditions as squalid as those found in the worst urban ghettos in the United States. The deep-rooted problems that exist cannot be solved unless fundamental changes occur in the wider society. Who will formulate the policies and implement the needed changes is a matter of deep concern to Asian Americans. The location of the University of California at Berkeley allows students and faculty members to contribute to the process of social change in the Asian American communities in the area. Thus, academic development and community development can, and does, in fact, interact fruitfully with one another.

Second, just under 15 percent of the current undergraduate enrollment at Berkeley consists of students of Asian ancestry. (The exact breakdown of foreign-born vs. American-born is not available.) This large minority group of students not only has special educational needs . . . [but can make important contributions as citizens].... As current members and potential future leaders of their communities, they have opportunities to bring about changes that will be beneficial, rather than detrimental, to the overall long-term welfare of those communities' residents.

Third, in terms of institutional resources, the University of Califonia at Berkeley already possesses extensive library holdings and a group of capable, committed, and progressive faculty who furnish a sound foundation for the future growth and innovative development of Ethnic Studies. The Asian American Studies program at Berkeley is a recognized leader in this emerging area of academic endeavor. What is developed at Berkeley will undoubtedly be viewed with great interest by other Asian American Studies programs on campuses across the country.

Fourth, the potential for the dissemination of the materials, teaching methods, and educational perspectives we develop goes beyond the college level. Already, members of our faculty and some of our students are working with elementary, junior-high, and senior-high school teachers and citizens' task forces in projects to create suitable materials on Asian Americans for the public schools. The Berkeley Unified School District, to date, is the only school system in the United States that has established a pilot bilingual, bicultural program. Needless to say, for such a program to succeed—aside from financial support and adequately trained personnel—there is a great need for curricular development and the production of suitable texts. The kind of materials we intend to produce can be adapted for use at the primary and secondary school levels.

Lastly, there is also potential for benefitting the public at large. Much of the available information about Asian American history and current affairs is fragmentary or not easily accessible. The preparation of more accessible materials, though intended mainly for college teaching purposes, will be of interest to the general reading public as well, for the simple lack of alternative sources. Aside from content, we are also concerned with articulating a more cogent Asian American perspective—a perspective of which the public today is, for the most part, unaware.

Our Current Status and Projected Future Development

The Department of Ethnic Studies was established on the Berkeley campus in 1969. It began with four divisions: Afro-American Studies, Asian American Studies, Chicano Studies, and Native American Studies. At the beginning of the 1974–75 academic year, Afro-American Studies became a separate department. The other three divisions are also working towards departmental status.

Since its inception, the Asian American Studies program has tried to implement certain broad educational goals. . . . We aim to:

a. increase our knowledge of the history of Asians in the United States through the compilation, documentation, and analysis of historical data on Asian American communities;
b. create and develop an Asian American perspective in the study of Asian American history within the broader context of the historical development of American society, culture, politics, and economy;
c. search for the roots of the problems facing Asian American communities to-day through an analysis of the institutional structures and patterns of social stratification in American society;
d. generate innovative solutions to the above problems; and
e. train Asian American students—regardless of their choice of future occupations—to play constructive roles in Asian American communities by nurturing their sense of self-worth as individuals as well as their sense of responsibility with regard to the welfare of their communities.

Our efforts during the past five years of our existence (1969–74) have been directed towards the continuous implementation of these stated goals. We have developed a sound and educationally innovative curriculum and our success has been institutionalized by the fact that as of Fall 1974, undergraduates at Berkeley may elect to major in Asian American Studies. We are thus entering the second stage of our development—a stage that we hope will culminate in the attainment of full departmental status.

As we enter this second phase of our growth, we shall work to consolidate our curriculum, improve our teaching methods, and make Ethnic Studies courses an integral part of the liberal education of *all* students. We believe that the alternative perspectives presented in our courses offer healthy correctives to the predominantly Western-centric viewpoints found in most textbooks and lectures. Since the United States is a culturally pluralistic society, its educational system should reflect this pluralism to a far greater extent than it does at present.

The current transitional period is extremely crucial. As our objectives broaden, so will our student constituency. Accordingly, our course offerings must expand to meet new needs. At present, there are three alternative concentrations that students majoring in Asian American Studies at UC Berkeley may elect: the social sciences, community studies, and the humanities. The first two are relatively better developed. The area most in need of growth is the humanities. The humanities are in a more nascent stage of development in Asian American Studies because very little material suitable for classroom use exists. Most of the available or usable materials are studies written by non-Asians *about* Asian Americans. In social science and community studies courses, however unsatisfactory such texts may be, at least they *can* be used, especially when they are accompanied by appropriate qualifying remarks and discussions. They can serve as stopgap texts until more adequate ones are written and published. In humanities courses, however, social scientific studies by outsiders are inappropriate as assigned readings, so the need for first-person narratives is much more urgent. More than other branches of knowledge, the humanities have traditionally dealt with subjective self-expressions that capture the temper of an era or the struggles of individual sensibilities... We urgently need to find and make accessible Asian American voices in literature, in historical writings, in drama, dance, music, painting, sculpture, and other expressive art forms.

The Desirability of Humanities Courses in Asian American Studies

Journalistic stories of Asian Americans as "successful minorities" notwithstanding, the fact of the matter is that a *majority* of Asian immigrants who came to the United States in the nineteenth and early twentieth centuries were poor laborers who worked mainly in mining, agriculture, railroad construction and maintenance, and other kinds of manual labor in the Pacific Coast states. As the predecessors of today's migrant farmworkers, Asian immigrants suffered from both class and racial oppression. Since many of them were illiterate or literate only in their native languages, their history, until recently, has been a neglected, silent, or forgotten one. With the blossoming of ethnic-minority cultural and political consciousness, a powerful desire to reclaim our almost-lost history has emerged—not only to reclaim but also to correct, re-create, or express for the first time our historical experiences in order to come to terms with where we have come from, who we are, and where we should be going. This is the desire of activists, faculty, students, and citizens alike. Humanities courses are vehicles for such a process of historical reclamation and self-assertion.

The obstacles to the fulfillment of such a desire are many. Although we recognize that literature records many aspects of human experience that social studies cannot... we have a dearth of Asian American literature for several reasons. Many Asian immigrants could not find the time to write because of the harsh conditions of their struggles for survival. Moreover, during periods of upheaval, such as the anti-Chinese, anti-Japanese, anti-Indian, and anti-Filipino movements of the late nineteenth and early twentieth centuries, as well as the incarceration of Japanese Americans during World War II, letters, diaries, photographs, and other personal or community records were purposely destroyed or incidentally lost. Those immigrants who did write often wrote in Asian languages. So, what little has been preserved is usually inaccessible to their English-speaking-only descendants. Those who wrote in English faced additional difficulties. . . . Publishers were not interested in works by Asian Americans, or thought no Asian Americans could write well [enough] in English [to be published], or feared such works would not sell. . . . Valuable works such as John Okada's *No-No Boy*, Carlos Bulosan's *America Is in the Heart*, or Louis Chu's *Eat a Bowl of Tea* were printed in very small numbers; once sold out, they remained out of print for decades.

Small steps have been taken in recent years to fill the yawning gaps. Earlier works are being reprinted, promising new ones are being published. One or two anthologies of Asian American writings have appeared. What has been made available so far are works by second- and third-generation Asian American authors who write in English. To date, no effort has been made to collect the scattered writings of earlier immigrants [regardless of what language they wrote in]. Moreover, the writings of new immigrants from Korea, Taiwan, Hong Kong, the Philippines, and other Asian countries in their native languages are not yet considered a part of Asian American literature but should be.

Our humanities courses will be more than places in which students can *study* great "classics"; they will also furnish the environment in which hitherto unknown writings are made accessible and new writings by students themselves are produced. . . . We reject the elitist view that only the works of professional writers can count as "literature." Most of our ancestors were *not* professional writers; yet, what they wrote poignantly reveals their inner experiences. Their jottings expressed their loneliness, longing, hope. Such works are humanistic in the best sense of the word and provide important keys to understanding the social and cultural history of Asians in America.

[The remaining pages of the proposal discussed specific courses to be developed and curricular materials to be produced and are not reprinted here because they are too specific to be of general interest three decades later.]

2 "Revolutionaries" and "Reformers"
[1977 and 1978]

This chapter combines two brief articles from a newsletter, Asian American Report: An Occasional Publication of the Asian American Studies Program, University of California, Berkeley. *I wrote the first article with extensive input from my colleagues Elaine Kim and Merilyn Wong. It appeared in the* Asian American Report *no. 1 (1977). I wrote the second article, which appeared in* Asian American Report *no. 3 (1978), in my capacity as chairperson of the program's curriculum and development committee. Some of my colleagues and I started the newsletter in order to publicize our views and clarify our goals because the Asian American Studies Program was rife with conflicts in the 1970s. Competing groups churned out hundreds of flyers over the course of a year, accusing some faculty of committing all kinds of political sins. We felt compelled to rebut with our own publication.*

During the mid-1970s, several sectarian groups whose members had different visions about what "the revolution" should accomplish struggled for control of the program. Many members of these groups worked as teaching assistants, research assistants, and fieldwork assistants in the program, but people not affiliated with us could also attend our meetings and participate in making decisions affecting Asian American studies. In such an atmosphere of "ultrademocracy" there was no accountability whatsoever. Moreover, even though everyone claimed to be a Marxist or a Maoist in his or her ideology, in reality individual practices differed greatly.

Several of the groups saw the campus—specifically, the Asian American Studies Program—mainly as a source of funding for their activities off-campus and as a recruiting station for would-be adherents. Others, including myself, believed that an academic program had its own needs and should not be used to support groups that had other agendas. The never-ending struggles brought chaos to the Asian American Studies Program as hundreds, perhaps thousands, of people became involved and each individual or group staked a claim to the fragile academic turf.

I belonged to a group called the Faculty Seven, composed of Loni Ding, Elaine Kim, Oscar Sung, Ron Takaki, Ling-chi Wang, Merilyn Wong, and me. Because we argued that academic work was a form of community work, and hence not contrary to or apart from the latter, those who attacked us accused us of being "reformers" and demanded that we be ousted. That accusation made some colleagues flinch. We endured all kinds of harassment and intimidation. Strangers rang the doorbells of our homes in the dark of night to deliver anonymous threats. One letter I received in the mail said, "You WILL die." Below the words was an image of a clenched fist crashing through a yin-yang circle. Angry individuals, many of whom were not students, harassed the office staff, who felt so intimidated that they asked me to bring Rajah, my German shepherd, to work to protect them.

The protestors also disrupted our classes. One day, six Asian American students, along with the vice president of Berkeley's student body, who fancied himself a "White radical," marched into my large introductory course and started shouting, "The faculty have taken over! They must be removed!" Suddenly, a student in the class jumped out of his seat, struck a kung fu pose, ran down the aisle, and stood menacingly in front of the protesters. "Stop!" I called out. "I don't want any violence in my class. Let them speak." After listening for a few minutes to their tirade against the faculty who had allegedly "usurped" the program, I said into the microphone, "You've enjoyed the right of free speech in my class. Now you must leave." I left the lecture platform, walked to the row where the protesters were, and stared them down until they left. After their departure I said to the class, "Now that our rude visitors have left, shall we resume our discussion?"

After months of mass meetings, each of which took hours and hours during which nothing was resolved, the tide turned when, at a meeting attended by several hundred angry participants, Ling-chi Wang stood up and quietly said, "I am not ashamed to be a reformer." That unexpected declaration stunned the audience into silence. Ling-chi's fearless pronouncement imbued the rest of us with the courage to carry on. The changes we made—in our curriculum, in the personnel we hired, and in our general academic-cum-political direction—made it possible eventually for the program and its parent unit, the Department of Ethnic Studies, to create the nation's first Ph.D. program in comparative ethnic studies.

A Brief History of Asian American Studies at the University of California, Berkeley

Asian American Studies was established by a student strike on the Berkeley campus in 1969. We were set up as one of four programs in the new Department of Ethnic Studies. It was envisioned that our structure would be sufficiently flexible to evolve into an autonomous Third World College.

From our inception, we have been concerned with providing a relevant education for Asian American students. We exist in order to challenge and remedy the neglect of our history and the issues confronting our communities in the university curriculum.

The Asian American Studies Program at Berkeley has gone through a number of transformational phases since 1969. Between 1969 and 1971, we had no long-term plans for the survival and development of our program within the university. Our main emphasis at that time was community work.

From 1971 to 1973, attempts were made to stabilize our program. The emphasis, however, was on administrative means to improve our status. Problems connected with strengthening our curriculum and our teaching staff remained unresolved.

From 1973 to 1975, more systematic channels and procedures for decision-making were introduced. We designed, proposed, and got approval for a B.A. degree in Asian American Studies. More systematic recruitment of faculty and supportive staff was also instituted.

Unfortunately, during the 1975–76 academic year, problems arose due to poor administrative leadership. Then, in 1976–77, in the absence of agreement within the program on the long-term direction that Asian American Studies should take, endless discussions occurred which took little account of the concrete conditions and needs of our students and our communities. Certain opportunistic and dogmatic groups attempted to control the program through the proliferation of bureaucratic committees which were accountable to no one and accomplished little.

In June 1977, in response to these negative trends, [certain faculty members] voted to assume full responsibility for the program until the fall quarter, 1977. We felt it would have been an act of irresponsibility had we allowed the prevailing situation to continue, wherein persons who were neither students nor faculty dominated decision-making within the program. In the process of reorganizing the program, we have come to a clear understanding of what the long-term work of Asian American Studies should be.

The Long-Term Work of Asian American Studies

The long-term work of Asian American Studies is in three areas: educational work with students; the provision of research data and analysis with a Third World perspective; and participation in, and support for, community, national, and international movements for social change.

Educational Work with Students

There are approximately 4,500 Asian American students enrolled at the University of California at Berkeley. They constitute some 15 percent of the total student enrollment. Asian American Studies must serve the needs of a *majority* of these students, regardless of their majors or choice of future careers.

Our program must work to improve the communication skills of Asian American students. We must provide the training which will enable students to become effective spokespersons in public forums, particularly as advocates of Asian American concerns.

On the one hand, we must enable students to communicate effectively in English in their dealings with society at large. On the other hand, we must help train students to communicate in Asian languages, so that they can interact with all segments of our communities. . . .

We must also provide our students with skills for critical analysis, through which they may come to understand the true conditions of Asians—as well as other Third World people—in America. Such analysis includes learning about how racism and the patterns of development of American society have affected Asian American communities and individuals.

Courses designed to introduce students to comparative historical frameworks for analyzing the Third World experience include "Racism in America" . . . and "Colonialism and Imperialism." . . . Another course, entitled "Social Institutions and the Asian American Community," . . . analyzes the institutional structure of contemporary American society. Institutions such as education, the labor market, law, housing, health care, the mass media, and various governmental organizations are analyzed for their effects on Asian American communities.

Our history courses are designed to heighten our students' awareness of the historical conditions of Asians in America, and the social, economic, and political factors that were responsible for those conditions. . . .

Our community studies courses attempt to teach students to solve critical problems facing our communities. The introductory community studies course . . . is a survey of the key issues facing our communities today. We have a two-quarter course . . . that introduces students to community field research methods and sensitizes them to the ethical and political issues involved in doing community research.

Specific issues are covered in a series of courses . . . which will be taught on a rotating basis. In the past, we have covered issues such as law, housing, mental health, health care, junior high school curriculum, the mass media, and bilingual education. We intend to include other issues such as youth, the elderly, religious institutions, social welfare, labor, and immigration. The number of courses to be taught . . . depends on available resources during any particular quarter or year. All the instructors for the community issues courses are persons with proven dedication and competence in their areas of community work.

We want to learn about our communities, and the larger society in which we live, in order to change them. We want to learn methods to remove the institutional barriers that have been detrimental to the welfare of Third World people, workers, and women.

Part of our educational work involves the development of curricular materials that other Asian American Studies programs and community groups can use. We must experiment with innovative teaching methods. We must promote the exchange of ideas through oral, written, and visual materials. Finally, we must support other Asian American Studies programs whose existence may be in jeopardy.

The Asian American Studies Program at Berkeley is the largest and relatively most autonomous program in the nation. As such, we have a special responsibility to serve and support other programs. It is imperative that we be strong, innovative, and productive in our educational work.

Research for Social Change

If we carry out our educational work well, students will understand better what they can do to promote social change. Students, staff, faculty, and community workers must work together to find new approaches to solve difficult problems. Such work must be carried out in our communities, workplaces, campuses, and even our homes.

Persons who are involved daily in community work often do not have the time or the resources to carry out the research needed to provide data in support of community struggles. Since we are situated on a university campus, we have access to resources that others may not. Thus, we must not shirk our responsibility to compile accurate data and analyses about various community, national, and international issues of concern to us.

While our primary research focus should be on what our communities need, nonetheless, we must remember to view our communities within national and international contexts. Community research must illuminate the *linkages* that exist between the root causes of our minority status within the United States and the international position of the United States, especially in relation to Third World countries.

Ethnic Studies programs began as part of a wider movement for social change. Although our work is carried out primarily on college campuses, we would lose sight of our real significance if we do not see ourselves as part of the larger attempts by people at all levels of society to change the system of domination and subordination of minority and working people within the capitalist system, as it manifests itself locally, nationally, and internationally.

As a program, Asian American Studies has to determine how best we can provide support for movements for social change. While we cannot become embroiled in sectarian struggles among the different groups that make up the international progressive movement, nonetheless, we cannot set ourselves apart from that movement. The research we carry out, therefore, must be informed by sensitivity not only to the internal needs of our communities, but [also] to how those needs are related to conditions within the wider world in which we live.

Direct Participation in Community Work

While teaching and research are important work that persons connected with Asian American Studies must do, we would be acting in an elitist manner if we do not also participate directly in community work on a planned and responsible basis. Moreover, we must channel students into community projects that require the best human resources we have.

In American society, the educational system—especially higher education—serves as a "tracking mechanism" to channel people into different levels of our economic system. Asian Americans are heavily concentrated in service, clerical, and technical work. Employment in these areas of work tend to sustain the status quo, rather than challenge it.

Higher education, by channeling Asian Americans into certain sectors of our economy, in effect acts as a mechanism to drain away our human resources from work that will promote positive social change for our communities. Asian American Studies must counteract this negative aspect of our educational system.

The mutually supportive relationship between the community and the campus is a two-way affair. While students, staff, and faculty members are committed to contribute what they can to community growth, persons in the community also play important roles in campus developments. They serve as faculty members and as fieldwork assistants for our community [studies] courses. Moreover, there will also be systematic channels for community input through a Community Relations Committee.

Lessons We Have Learned

The most important lesson we have learned from our past struggles is that *Asian American Studies has its own work to do*. Moreover, our work must be planned and implemented over a long period of time. In short, while we can and must work cooperatively with others, we do not want to be used by other organizations as a resource base to carry out work that serves a different function from our own.

For many years, we were unable to make specific long-term plans due to a lack of clear understanding of the tasks we must carry out. Our internal failure to strengthen ourselves was exacerbated by our lack of full autonomy within the university structure. Much of our energy was spent simply to ensure our survival on campus.

Persons involved in the initial establishment of Ethnic Studies programs came from divergent backgrounds. Most of us were young and full of youthful exuberance. Many of us thought naively that the movement for social change began with our entry into that movement. Few of us realized that fundamental social change requires lifetimes of commitment, sacrifices, careful planning and analysis, and the step-by-step attainment of goals.

Because some of us thought social change was immediately attainable as conflicts within society sharpened, we had a tendency to view our program as a temporary phenomenon. We saw ourselves only as catalysts for the imminent changes to come. We tended to put our energies into those areas that promised the quickest and most visible results. Thus, due to the tendency to "go where the action is," our staff was, for the most part, transient.

Many of us also have certain erroneous views. We often perceive different aspects of our work as mutually exclusive, when, in fact, they are integrally related. We put more emphasis on form than content. Some among us had a tendency to assign value judgments to persons and events without careful investigation or analysis. And those of us who disagreed with such behavior often abdicated our responsibility by failing to speak out forcefully against what we believed to be wrong.

In retrospect, we now understand that some of the reasons for our weaknesses were:

1. a lack of precedence for the development of programs such as ours;
2. the transiency of personnel;
3. the haphazard development of a curriculum based more on the availability of personnel than on careful design;
4. anti-intellectualism and the false counterposing of "academic work" and "community work";
5. the erosion of community and student ties and the substitution of rhetoric for true, viable working relationships with our communities and students; and
6. the existence of a structure that allowed opportunists and dogmatists to control our program for their own personal or organizational ends.

We have by no means solved the above problems but we are working hard to improve our program. Asian American Studies must push forward to carry out the tasks which the original student strike envisioned: the provision of a relevant, quality education for Asian American students, and the provision of resources to aid in the solution of community problems.

Where Do We Go from Here?

Our first step in internal strengthening has already been taken. We have eliminated opportunistic and dogmatic elements from our program. We are fully committed to preventing such persons and groups from using and abusing our program in the future. We will always guard our autonomy, both with respect to the university, . . . [and with respect to] outside groups whose aims do not coincide with our own.

Our second step is to commit ourselves to building those sections of our curriculum that emphasize bona fide Asian American content. We want to offer the best courses possible in community analysis and research and in current community issues. Hopefully, community studies will become the core component of our program.

We are also improving our history courses. In the past, we had two series of history courses: one in Asian American history, and one in the history of Asia—primarily China. While courses on China enable us to learn about how a socialist society functions and serves the needs of its people, the contents of our courses on China would best contribute to our curriculum by being *integrated* into our Asian American history and community courses. With our limited resources, our highest priority must be given to courses and research projects that advance our knowledge of the Asian experience *in America*.

Third, we are maintaining an open and continuous faculty recruitment program. We must build a core faculty of persons who are committed and competent to carry out the work we outlined above. Only a committed and competent faculty can insure the long-range constructive and rigorous development of the Asian American Studies Program at Berkeley.

Fourth, we are establishing a Community Relations Committee to provide systematic input from the community in the development of our program. The instructors teaching our community courses, together with two representatives each from the Chinese American, Japanese American, Pilipino American, and Korean American communities will serve on this committee.

Fifth, we are broadening our student representation. In the past, members of only one or two student organizations claimed to represent *all* Asian American students on campus. We disagree with this claim and believe it is important that a wider spectrum of student groups be represented, if we are to be true to our desire to serve a majority of Asian American students.

Finally, we are setting up a decision-making structure that will be *both democratic and accountable.* Committee members will be identifiable as representatives of clearly delineated groups. There will be a separation of policy-making and administrative functions within the program.

Discussion of broad policy questions regarding our curriculum, our future direction, [and] our relationship to campus and community issues will be the function of the Steering Committee, which will consist of one representative from each workgroup, as well as student groups whose aims are compatible with our own. (A workgroup consists of all hired staff members teaching a course or performing well-defined functions such as secretarial/administrative work or library work.)

The coordinator of the program, together with the faculty, will be responsible for the administration of the program. The faculty will select the members of the Faculty Recruitment and Review Committee, the Curriculum and Development Committee, and the Community Relations Committee.

We are building a program that we hope will serve the needs of our community and our students more effectively. We welcome your comments, suggestions, and constructive criticisms.

* * *

The Asian American Studies Curriculum and Development Committee is engaged in four tasks this year. First, we are in the process of revising the degree requirements for the major in Asian American Studies in order to make our program of studies more relevant and useful to our majors. Second, we are exploring the possibility of establishing a minor in Asian American Studies. Third, we are seeking ways to tailor our curriculum to serve the needs of the hundreds of Asian American students who are not Asian American

Studies majors but who take one or more of our courses. . . . Lastly, we are negotiating with various departments on campus to get more of our courses accepted in fulfillment of the B.A. degrees in their majors.

Serving Different Types of Students

In carrying out the above tasks, we are faced with conflicting constraints. On the one hand, a well-designed major in Asian American Studies must be built on a solid foundation of prerequisites. Ideally, students should not be allowed to take our upper-division courses until they have taken our lower-division introductory courses. However, if we attempt to enforce our prerequisites too strictly, then many non-majors will be prevented from enrolling in our more specialized courses.

At present, we have approximately twenty-five students majoring in Asian American Studies, but twenty times that number enroll in our courses each quarter. We are thus faced with the difficult task of balancing the needs of those 5 percent of our students who are . . . majors against the needs of the other 95 percent . . . non-majors.

A significant portion of our teaching resources is devoted to lower-division courses which fulfill various graduation requirements, such as the American history and institutions requirements, the foreign language requirement, or the reading and composition requirement. Since we have had no budget increases for several years, a continued emphasis on lower-division courses means we have to find other ways to expand our upper-division course offerings.

Redesigning the Major

One way to address this dilemma is to design courses of study for our majors that include relevant offerings from other departments. For example, those students specializing in community studies can take courses from other departments that focus on urban problems, municipal government and finance, law and society, journalism and the mass media, [and] health care and social services.

Students with a concentration in the social sciences may benefit from taking courses in American economic history, economic theory, the sociology of race and ethnic relations, women (especially minority women) in the labor force, theories of social change, development and underdevelopment in Third World countries, the American role in world politics, and the functioning of the world economy—all courses currently offered by other departments and programs at Berkeley.

The area of the humanities has proven to be the most difficult to expand. Asian American culture—literature, the visual arts, the performing arts, philosophy, etc.—is still in the process of being defined and created. Moreover, it is not easy to find instructors who are practicing artists with a strong community orientation. Outside of our own program, we find very few courses which might enable our students to improve their communication skills and [develop their] creative talents. Students concentrating in the humanities will have to combine specific Asian American historical and contemporary content with practical skills learned in studio courses.

In the past, our students tended to shy away from courses in other departments because they thought most of those courses would not offer diversified views and critical approaches. However, a careful scrutiny of the syllabi of specific courses in certain departments indicated that the perspectives and concerns of some of the faculty members in other departments are quite relevant and complementary to our own.

Another way to expand our curriculum without any foreseeable budget increase is to rotate certain courses. For example, one year we can offer courses dealing with Asian Americans and the law, housing, the media, health and mental health, and the following year we can deal with immigration, youth problems, the elderly, and so forth. Such a rotation may help to increase the enrollment in these specialized courses if they are offered only in alternate years.

Establishing a Minor

For some years, we have contemplated the establishment of a minor in Asian American Studies. Such a minor will serve the needs of those students who cannot afford to take the full fifty units of Asian American Studies courses required of our majors but who would nevertheless like to take a coherent set of courses in our program that will help satisfy their desire to learn about their own history and communities.

An Asian American Studies minor will help to relieve the strain that some students now feel when they choose a "double major" in Asian American Studies and another field, . . . [which forces them] to satisfy unit requirements in both departments.

The Changing Composition of Asian American Students

The composition of the Asian American student body is changing due to the increased percentage of foreign-born Asian students on campus. The interests of the latter may not coincide with the interests and needs of American-born

Asian students. We hope that the enclosed undergraduate survey will enable us to see what kinds of students take our courses, why they do so, what they think of our courses, what they would like to see deleted from or added to our offerings, and, for those who have *not* taken any Asian American Studies courses, why they have not done so.

Our Continued Struggle on College Campuses

In the past few years, some Ethnic Studies programs across the nation have folded, and few new ones have been established. One reason is that our very existence constitutes a challenge to the status quo in the American educational system. Not only do we teach courses that enable us to reclaim our buried cultural heritage and history of struggle against racial and economic exploitation, but we [also] attempt to give students skills to challenge the established order of things. Not only are our curricular contents innovative, so are some of our teaching methods and perspectives.

Many departments on the Berkeley campus still officially or unofficially discourage their students from taking our courses. We have begun a survey of which of our courses are accepted on various lists made by different departments. Once this inventory is completed, we shall challenge those departments that do not allow their students to use our courses to fulfill certain general education requirements. This task is part of our continuing struggle to develop Ethnic Studies.

3   On Being Scholars in Ethnic Studies: Some Personal Reflections [1980]

By 1980 even though the Department of Ethnic Studies at Berkeley had achieved a degree of structural stability, faculty in other departments and campuswide administrators still viewed it with suspicion. In that year, the administration formed the ad hoc Committee to Review the Department of Ethnic Studies to examine all aspects of the three programs within the department. Having served on a number of academic senate committees—the organs through which faculty at the nine UC campuses exercise "shared governance" with the administration—during which I had become quite well versed in how Berkeley faculty members think, talk, and evaluate one another, I predicted that the area in which we would receive the harshest criticism would be our allegedly "low" scholarly productivity.

Of the five ladder-rank (tenure-track) faculty in the program at the Berkeley campus in 1980, only Ron Takaki had tenure. Elaine Kim was undergoing tenure review, Ling-chi Wang was busily writing a book in preparation for his forthcoming review, I had received permission to postpone my review, and Jere Takahashi still had some years to go before he would be up for tenure review. We all realized that should one or more of us be denied tenure, mainly because we had not written "enough" or reviewers thought our publications were insufficiently "academic," it would be well-nigh impossible to rebuild the program. I resented the fact that the accomplishment that still counted the most was the number and quality of our publications, despite all the hurdles we had cleared. Even though we were not asked to submit individual statements to the review committee, I wrote something anyway in an effort to help its members understand, however slightly, the difficult conditions under which we worked.

Note that I used the terms minority *and* minorities *in this statement, even though I preferred* third world people *or* people of color, *because I thought "minority" was a word reviewers would feel most comfortable with. I saw no point in rousing anybody's ire by using political terms that remain contested to this day. The goal at hand, I believed, was to get a favorable review and not engage in a debate over terminology.*

* * *

In a nascent field such as Ethnic Studies, the promotion of sound scholarship requires the performance of at least four tasks. As I see them, these tasks are:

1. establishing *conditions* conducive to the production of scholarly work,
2. clearly defining the *boundaries* of our field of study,
3. searching for, collecting, preserving, and cataloging the *primary sources* upon which sound scholarship can be based, and
4. doing the actual research itself and disseminating new knowledge through *publications* and other media.

In long-established departments, most of the junior faculty do not have to worry about performing the first three tasks. Their quality as scholars is measured mainly through evaluations of their publications. In a new field of academic endeavor such as ours, however, scholarship cannot proceed unless progress is also being made in the other areas outlined above. In the Department of Ethnic Studies at Berkeley, much of this work has fallen on the shoulders of untenured junior faculty. We have an anomalous situation in which those of us who are assistant professors *are* the senior faculty in our own department, while in the eyes of the campus as a whole we are considered as junior faculty like all assistant professors in other departments. Moreover, we have had to work under very unstable conditions, constantly worrying over the very survival of our department as a unit on the Berkeley campus. Putting as much energy and time into stabilizing the structural and organizational aspects of our department as we have done, plus our commitment to good teaching as well as to serving our communities, has meant that, *out of necessity,* doing research and publishing scholarly work have not always been our top priority.

The political legacy of the department—that is, the fact that we were established only as a result of a student strike—has also affected the internal atmosphere of the department. What this meant is that those of us who wanted to do rigorous scholarly work have had to work doubly hard: we have had to convince ourselves and our colleagues that it is *justifiable* to give top priority to scholarly activities, and we have had to carry out those activities with little, if any, financial and staff support. Moreover, we have to be accountable to several audiences. On the one hand, we have to face our colleagues on campus who ask, "Is what you do good, objective scholarship?" On the other hand, our friends in the community and our students ask us, "Is what you do relevant to solving the problems of our communities or meeting our educational needs?" Relevance here means identifying problems, working out viable solutions, and, most important of all, taking stands on issues. Because we *do* take stands, we are caught in a double bind. To take a stand is to be an advocate; it is, by definition, not "value-free" and "objective." For that reason, our work is often adjudged to be "nonscholarly."

As Thomas Kuhn has pointed out in his influential book *The Structure of Scientific Revolutions,* there comes a time in the development of every discipline when paradigm-building becomes the most important activity. The field of Ethnic Studies is now at such a stage of development. We have, for a dozen years now, criticized the existing literature, but we have had a clearer idea of what we are against than what we are for. We know that textbooks and studies about the experiences of ethnic and racial minorities in American society are full of biases; worse, most have ignored our existence altogether. Yet, after we criticize what "White scholars" have written, we have frequently floundered in what we ourselves would like to say about us. Some of us have looked for usable models from other disciplines. Some of us have adopted certain theories because they offer a critique of mainline scholarship. Up to this point, few minority scholars have been able to offer paradigms capable of encompassing all the major facets of minority experience (if such, indeed, were possible). Why has this been the case? Is it because we are incompetent scholars? No. The answer, I believe, is that we have been too impatient.

The activities of paradigm-testing and theory-building cannot occur in a vacuum. First, we must have building blocks to work with. In the social sciences and in certain kinds of historical studies, such building blocks consist of empirical case studies. Empirical case studies are not lacking in Ethnic Studies, but there are two problems with the ones that have been done. First, they reflect the preoccupations of the scholars who designed them, which are not necessarily the same concerns as what the subjects of the studies themselves may consider to be central to their lives. Since most Ethnic Studies scholars believe we have a responsibility to elucidate minority-centric points of view, we question the validity of the conclusions in many of the studies that have been done. Therefore, we are not only unwilling to build on them but we also have to expose the distortions contained in them before we can even begin our own work. Second, the distribution of existing empirical studies is extremely uneven. In the past, minority populations have caught the attention of the American public or the scholarly community only when we have been perceived as "problems." Thus, for example, in Asian American Studies, most studies on the immigrant generation debate the pros and cons of Asian immigration. As for studies of the immigrants' American-born children, a majority of them examines the degree and process of assimilation. Other aspects of the minority experience—aspects that reveal the inner lives of minority communities—are ignored altogether.

Ethnic Studies scholars, therefore, must engage in innumerable empirical studies of our own on all aspects of our people's histories and contemporary experiences. However, empirical studies—especially ones that employ sophisticated methodologies—are frequently expensive to carry out. That means research funds must be obtained. But because what we aim to do often falls outside the boundaries of established disciplines or areas of study, it is difficult to "match" what we wish to do with the available funding sources. Worse, empirical studies take time to carry out, and each case study can focus on only one small topic. Meanwhile, we feel pressured from many different quarters to provide answers—answers in the form of generalizations, paradigms, or theories. So, the shortcut way out is to use deductive reasoning (which many non-Ethnic Studies scholars also employ) instead of an inductive approach. Or, we are sometimes compelled to theorize on rather thin evidence. Unfortunately, paradigms constructed out of only a few case studies can be overturned easily. And so there is a tendency to discard a particular paradigm before it has even had a chance to be tested. One case in point is the so-called internal colonialism model.

One *sina qua non* of good research, especially in historical studies, is the availability of archival or primary sources. In Asian American Studies, such sources are virtually nonexistent. Or, what exists is scattered, inaccessible, uncatalogued, and hence unusable. There are few, if any, libraries eager to accept custodial responsibility for such sources even when they have been found. Therefore, potential researchers must venture onto uncharted seas and search for such materials with no guidance or help. Given this state of affairs, the choice of methodologies becomes problematic. Even when we know that a particular methodology would be most suitable for the study we have in mind, the lack of an adequate and reliable database may preclude our using the best methodologies we know of.

From the beginning, many Ethnic Studies faculty have advocated that we use interdisciplinary approaches—not only for methodological but also for philosophical reasons. We wish to see human beings and their societies studied as a whole whose parts are interdependent. We believe that the fragmentation of knowledge—necessitated by the disciplinary division of labor in academia—has affected minority populations adversely. (For example, few sociological studies of minority groups explore in depth the historical roots of their contemporary conditions. By failing to do so, the studies sometimes distort history or end up with conclusions that blame the "victims" for their miseries.) We believe that using an interdisciplinary approach provides *one* way to deal with scholarly biases because by calling into question the assumptions of one discipline from the perspectives of other disciplines we are better able to understand nuances and complexities in human social life.

An interdisciplinary approach, however, also poses dangers. By trying to deal with too many concerns from various disciplines simultaneously, we may encounter difficulties when we try to set the parameters of our studies. As in any other new field of academic inquiry, setting parameters means carving out academic turf. I do not agree with those of my colleagues who argue that *everything* is within our turf. I believe choices must be made and priorities set. It is better to start small, carry out clearly delimited enquiries well, and demonstrate the validity of our methods and perspectives before moving on to tackle larger issues.

Who will make those choices, set the priorities, and define the boundaries of our field depends on the distribution of political power within the university. Unlike more established disciplines, where such power struggles occur primarily within the disciplines themselves, in the case of Ethnic Studies many persons outside of our field, including all kinds of individuals who know virtually nothing about it, act as if they have a right to determine whether any particular study in Ethnic Studies is "legitimate." Legislators who appropriate funds, university administrators who adjudicate conflicts, colleagues outside of Ethnic Studies, as well as colleagues within our own ranks, students, members of minority community organizations, have all at one time or another voiced their views on what Ethnic Studies faculty can or cannot, should or should not, do. Minority scholars who survive in academia must constantly walk a tight rope between "scientific objectivity" and social responsibility. (I recognize that this problem is not one confronted by minority scholars alone. All of us who study "human subjects" have ethical responsibilities with regard to how we treat those who provide us with information and the uses to which we put such information.) Frequently, scholars in Ethnic Studies are accused of being too "political." It is alleged that it is *inherently* impossible for us to be good (i.e., "objective") scholars because we are too "close" to the subjects we study. Certainly, that can be true. However, being involved with the people and the communities we study can also enhance our insight into the experiences of those people and the workings of their communities. Indeed, having a stake in such communities opens up avenues of inquiry that might otherwise be closed to us. What minority scholars must develop is an ability to "step back" and reflect upon our findings. There is nothing to prevent us from applying the same rigorous standards as other scholars do. What we seek from our colleagues outside the field, therefore, is not hostile dismissal of our work but intellectual criticism—the same kind of constructive criticism they offer their nonminority colleagues.

4 Asian/Pacific American Studies
in the 1980s [1981]

In 1980 an energetic faculty member named Douglas W. Lee at the University of Washington founded the Association for Asian American Studies. He organized the first national conference of the association, which met in Seattle. He named himself president, appointed me vice president, and appointed Edwin Clausen as secretary-treasurer. The following year, much to my dismay, he showed up unannounced one day at my house lugging several cartons of material. He told me that he had been quarreling with the other faculty members in the Asian American Studies Program at the University of Washington and that he was fed up with Asian American studies as a field. He was leaving the field altogether.

Lee said he had sought the advice of several people, who all told him I would make a good president. He had driven all the way from Washington to California, he declared, to make me his successor. I protested that such a procedure was totally undemocratic and therefore unacceptable to me. He responded by pointing to the documents in the boxes, which included the association's correspondence, leftover copies of its program from the first conference, and an etching, made by a professional artist hired the year before, of the association's logo. I could, he said, do whatever I wanted with the cartons. He wished me luck and left. I have not seen him since.

I talked to a number of colleagues at Berkeley about the situation, but no one expressed much enthusiasm for keeping the organization alive. One even said it was too much of "an establishment thing." After giving the matter much thought, I concluded that such a body, if properly constituted, could play a constructive role in helping develop the field, particularly in many places without Asian American studies programs where faculty were trying their best to put together a course or two in response to student demand or conduct research on some

Asian American topic. The faculty at Berkeley or UCLA might not need such a social, political, and intellectual network, but faculty and graduate students elsewhere might find it nurturing.

Reluctantly, then, I decided to become a caretaker president and organize a second conference, during which a new slate of officers could be elected. I was relieved when Don Nakanishi and Gary Okihiro assumed responsibility for the association. I passed along the boxes from Doug Lee to Gary, who had space in his garage to store them. Such was the beginning of the Association for Asian American Studies.

While waiting for the second conference to take place, Ed Clausen and I put out the first issue of the Newsletter of the Association for Asian Pacific American Studies *in June 1981. What follows is the editorial I wrote for the inaugural issue.*

* * *

When Asian American Studies programs were established a decade ago, most students who enrolled in our classes were Asian Americans born in the United States. Today, at campuses such as the University of California at Berkeley and at Los Angeles, half of the Asian-ancestry students are foreign-born immigrants. The radical shift in the nativity of our students is a development that few of us involved in the establishment and development of Asian American Studies foresaw.

Ten years ago, also, there were few Pacific-Islander Americans except in Hawaii and southern California. Today, the Pacific American population is increasing in all West Coast states, although the number of Pacific American students is still very small in institutions of higher learning. Increasingly, Asian and Pacific Americans are being lumped together in federal and state programs, but questions are being raised about the nature of the ties between the two.

The changing composition of "Asian/Pacific Americans" is an issue that needs to be addressed by those of us who work in academia, in government agencies, and in communities. As a field of academic endeavor, Asian/Pacific American Studies is defined first and foremost by the *population* that forms the very foundation of our academic expertise, as well as of our social communities. Therefore, when the composition of our people changes it is our responsibility to document and elucidate the dynamics of our own history as it is being made. We must do the kind of issue-oriented and policy-oriented research aimed at finding solutions to some of the problems faced by our communities. We cannot afford to fall back on old dogmas about who we are, what we should be doing, or where we should be going.

In the dozen years since the establishment of our field, four issues have taken up most of our political energy. On many campuses today, these four issues are still the subject of hot debate. These issues are applicable to all Ethnic Studies programs. They remain unresolved on many campuses across the country. They are:

1. The issue of *governance:* Who should control Ethnic Studies or Asian/Pacific American Studies?
2. The issue of *"professional certification":* Who should be allowed to teach Ethnic Studies or Asian/Pacific American Studies?
3. The issue of the *boundaries* of our field: What should Ethnic Studies and Asian/Pacific American Studies cover or be about?
4. The issue of *educational mission:* What functions should we perform on campuses as well as within our communities?

No one can deny that the momentum to establish Ethnic Studies came out of the wider imperatives of the social protest movements of the 1960s and early 1970s. Yet as the years passed, a real tension arose between the desire to maintain what might be called the "ideological purity" of "the movement" versus the pragmatic needs to ensure our survival and development. I believe that in the 1980s, when financial stringency touches every area of socioeconomic life, it is of the utmost importance that we work out viable answers to the above four issues. In short, we must work towards our academic legitimation while maintaining the legacy of our original vision.

Local conditions differ on the campuses where Asian/Pacific American Studies programs exist. No monolithic pattern can be applicable to all programs. But certain basic commonalities *can* be underscored. This is precisely the dilemma that an association such as ours can help resolve and, in the process, make its greatest contribution to the field. Our association can and must become the forum in which issues are discussed honestly and openly in a rational and comradely manner. We can come together to share not only our curricular materials and research findings but also the political lessons we have learned.

In the foreseeable future it is highly unlikely that new programs will be established. Therefore, we must make sure that the ones that now exist will survive, consolidate themselves, and grow. In the past decade, Ethnic Studies and Asian/Pacific American Studies programs have sometimes been the arena in which entire worldviews were fought over. Because of this, the intensity of the internal struggles that have wracked some programs has been great, compared to the relative smallness of the material stakes. Perhaps a sign of our "maturity" will be our recognition that our field is *not* the whole world. Our field has boundaries. There are clear and specific functions we can perform. It is better in the long run that we take less upon ourselves but do what we are doing more effectively.

Social action is important. Teaching is important. But increasingly, research is also important. The time has come when we can no longer develop our courses any further by relying only upon secondary sources. If the frontiers of our field are to move forward, we must search for and make use of hitherto untapped primary sources [or create new databases]. It is no longer possible to rehash old materials to arrive at new insights. We must come to terms with the fact that doing good research is imperative not because "the university" demands that we do it, but because the internal logic of our own development [as a field] demands that we do it. Our association can serve as a clearinghouse of information and provide the channels of communication to enable us to pool our meager and hard-won resources for carrying out basic as well as applied research.

Unlike more established fields, there is very little room in our field for frivolity. Too many questions remain unanswered, too many problems await solutions. Applied social science research is an urgent need. Unfortunately, few of us can afford the luxury of picking research topics simply out of intellectual interest at this point in the development of our field, much as we may value the laissez-faire notion of academic freedom. We must continually ask ourselves: "*Whose* interests will the results of our research serve? How will our research findings affect the populations on whom we rely for our data?"

At our next national conference, let us come together to work out potential research agendas and share with one another our knowledge, convictions, frustrations, unarticulated questions and uncertainties, as well as our hopes and dreams. Through dialogue, sharing, and honest criticism, our field can and *will* develop in spite of seeming odds and our voices *will* be heard in academia, in government, and in society at large.

5 Asian American Studies, the Humanities, and a Liberal Arts Education [1982]

This chapter contains the text of a talk I gave at a conference on ethnic studies and the humanities held at UC Berkeley in 1982 that was supported by a grant from the California Council for the Humanities in Public Policy. Even though I repeated some of the points I made in the grant proposal I submitted to the NEH eight years earlier, I was addressing a different audience and for a different purpose. Whereas the grant proposal was read by only a handful of reviewers meeting in a secluded room, this speech addressed a larger audience in an open forum attended not only by students and faculty but also by the public. I had no way of knowing whether the audience would be sympathetic or hostile. Nonetheless, even though I am trained as a social scientist, I once again spoke as an advocate of the humanities, especially the relationship of Asian American studies to the humanities in general.

The conference represented a turning point in the development of Asian American and ethnic studies. Instead of being myopically focused on our students, communities, internal quarrels, and external struggles against administrators and reviewing committees, as we had done up to this point, we began to turn outward and face the world at large. We increasingly fashioned ourselves into spokespersons of the "truths" we felt people in American society should hear. Although I still used the term minorities, *I had also, by this time, begun to use* people(s) of color *in public discourse, often interchanging the two terms in the same sentence or paragraph. In this talk I used the pronoun* we *to refer not only to Asian Americans but also to Americans of all racial and ethnic origins. The process that Maxine Hong Kingston calls "claiming America" had begun in earnest.*

* * *

The central importance of the humanities in a liberal [arts] education is underscored in the very terminology we use to refer to four-year liberal arts colleges: we call them College of *Letters* and Science or College of *Arts* and Sciences. In a new field of academic inquiry such as Asian American Studies, we certainly recognize the importance of the humanistic components in our curriculum, but for a number of reasons there are many difficulties facing the growth of the humanities in Asian American Studies.

Until recent years, most of the available text materials have been written by non-Asians about the Asian American experience. While these could be used as stop-gap texts in social studies courses, they are inappropriate for humanities courses because in the latter . . . materials containing subjective expressions that capture the temper of an era or the struggles of individual sensibilities are needed. . . . Unfortunately, until recent years, few Asian Americans have pursued creative writing or the arts as careers. Because tangible products of Asian American creative activities are few in number, it has been difficult to develop a critical literature analyzing such outpourings of the imagination.

One reason that the Asian immigrant generation of the nineteenth and early twentieth centuries left few creative products is that most of them had come in search of work. Asian laborers toiled in mines, fields, construction projects, and manufacturing plants throughout the American West and, to a smaller extent, in some of the larger metropolitan areas of the Midwest and East Coast. Since most of our foreparents were either illiterate or literate only in their native languages, they wrote very little—especially not in English. Even those immigrants with the inclination to write seldom found the time to do so as they struggled for survival under harsh conditions. Although some writings in Asian languages were produced, very little has been preserved. In the anti-Asian environment of the early American West, in which Asian immigrants were sometimes driven out of towns and cities or physically attacked, whatever they might have written was lost or destroyed.

In the last two decades, however, Asian Americans in academia and in the community have taken steps to overcome some of these obstacles; we have created, for the first time, media for self-expression. Older works are being reprinted, writings in Asian languages are being translated, and promising new pieces are being published. A few authors, such as Frank Chin, Maxine Hong Kingston, and David Henry Hwang, have received critical acclaim.

With the blossoming of ethnic consciousness, there has emerged an urgent desire to reclaim our buried cultural and social history—not only to reclaim but also to correct false impressions and capture and present proudly, triumphantly, our historical experiences so that we can come to terms with who we are and where we should be going. Since the humanities are vehicles for such a process of historical reclamation and cultural affirmation, within colleges and universities—indeed, at all levels of our educational system—we must develop humanities courses that give parity to materials with ethnic minority content. These should be included alongside the products of the European and American cultural traditions. Such pluralistically oriented humanities courses must be promoted as part of a liberal arts curriculum because they can provide the environments in which hitherto inaccessible works are made accessible to all students.

Because some of the most vibrant expressions of this new cultural awareness are produced by nonacademics, we must reject the elitist view that only the works of professional writers and artists can be included in humanities courses. Most of our Asian ancestors were not professional writers or artists; yet, what they wrote, what they painted or sculpted, what they performed, revealed the poignancy of their lives. Such works are humanistic in the pristine sense of that word.

Our art and literature cannot be authentic if they are divorced from our historical experience. Since so much of that experience has been painful, there is little room for carefree, youthful insouciance in what we write, although there is ample room for humor. For the time being, at least, we cannot afford the luxury of practicing art for art's sake. Rather, we must create in order to remember and celebrate our past; we must create in order to authenticate and validate our present; we must create in order to find hope for the future as we wrestle with the human condition in these times of crises.

Grandiose as it may sound, our desire to recover and define our experience as it relates to our multiethnic heritage is, in a fundamental sense, a desire for the recovery of wholeness. Members of ethnic and racial minority groups in the United States have been oppressed in many ways. Children who grow up under the specter of racism suffer from a loss of self-esteem. Some find it difficult to become whole persons who can contribute productively to the progress of our communities. Adults who had repressed or oppressed childhoods tend to eschew the risks of self-expression lest the guts we place onstage for public scrutiny get thrown back at our faces to taunt us. At the same time, members of the majority society—being heirs to those who have discriminated against persons of color—also lack a sense of wholeness. As unwitting beneficiaries of this country's system of inequality, such persons carry with them a warped sense of superiority and perhaps possess distorted values. In short, racism has negative effects on the discriminators as well as on those discriminated against.

The development of the humanities in the United States, therefore, must include a firm commitment to the critical examination of our entire social, economic, political, and cultural histories. Then, we must use our heightened understanding to bring about changes in our individual as well as collective consciousness.

The educational system plays a profound role as an inculcator of values. That is why a more pluralistic educational approach must lie at the very heart of our efforts to come to terms with our history as a multiracial, multiethnic, multicultural, and polyglot people. We must all have opportunities to express ourselves in our own voices with our own special sensibilities. Disquieting as such introspection may be, it must be faced by all of us together. The burden of reclaiming the buried and distorted histories of minorities in this country should not fall on the shoulders of people of color alone. Programs of support for the humanities must include support for preserving, developing, and disseminating the cultural products of *all* the people who make up America. In this, our common endeavor, those of us in academia must play our part to provide leadership and vision.

6 Prospectus for a Book Series, "Asian American History and Culture" [1989]

After my first book, This Bittersweet Soil: The Chinese in California Agriculture, 1860–1910 *(1986), won three awards, I pondered how I might turn my newly acquired academic capital into a motive force for promoting Asian American studies as a scholarly endeavor. I wanted to launch a project that would go beyond efforts we had made to meet the emotional and intellectual needs of Asian American students. As I saw it, honors won by a handful of scholars are not sufficient to make an entire field of academic inquiry "legitimate." Rather, a significant number of faculty must produce works of enduring scholarship that open a forum for academic dialog and debate, and the quality of our work must be consistently high so that even the most disapproving critics cannot dismiss our writings out of hand. In pursuit of this dream, I decided to try and persuade a university press to establish a book series in Asian American studies.*

After talking to editors from several presses, I settled on Temple University Press because its senior editor, Janet Frandendese, showed great enthusiasm for such an undertaking. Janet and I had both attended William Cullen Bryant High School in Long Island City, New York, years earlier. We both had polio during our childhood and rode the same school bus that took physically handicapped students to and from school. Each weekday, the trip took several hours because the bus served dozens of students. During those long rides students chatted, told jokes and stories, did their homework, and got to know each other quite well. Our high school enrolled some four thousand students, which meant that an opportunity to spend several hours a day with the same friends was rare.

When I ran into Janet at an annual meeting of the Organization of American Historians three decades later, she reminded me of the camaraderie that had existed on that bus. Out of this single strand of an "old girls' network," the first book series in Asian American studies was born. Other university presses have since set up similar series, but it was Temple University Press that led the way.

I worked as an advisory editor for the series from 1990 to 1996. By then, post-polio syndrome was causing so many problems for me that I was forced to terminate all academic activities except teaching. (Two books I coedited were published in 1997 and 1998, but the work had been done before my physical condition became so poor. I did not resume publishing until 2003, after I had retired.)

During my six-year stint as advisory editor I vetted fifteen manuscripts that became books and a similar number of others that did not. Five of the works that became books won awards. Early on, I invited David Palumbo-Liu to join me because I did not feel competent to review manuscripts in literary, postcolonial, and cultural studies. Several years later, Michael Omi also became a member of the editorial team. David and Michael have carried the editorial load since my departure. In 2004 Scott Wong began to serve as a reviewer of history manuscripts for the series.

I have edited this chapter more than any other in this book in order to make it useful to readers interested in a capsule intellectual history of Asian American studies. I inserted numerous additional citations but kept the arguments I presented in the prospectus. I have also deleted an appendix that accompanied the original proposal, which discussed final manuscripts as well as not-quite-finished Ph.D. dissertations that Temple University Press might acquire, because not all of them became titles in the series. By comparing Parts 1 through 3 of the bibliography with Part 4, readers can see how the field has thrived (in terms of the number of books published) since 1989 when I wrote this prospectus.

* * *

Asian American historiography before the early 1980s may be divided into three stages: an initial period that began when Chinese first came in substantial numbers to the United States in the middle of the nineteenth century and that lasted until the early twentieth century; a second stage spanning the 1920s to the late 1960s; and a third that took shape in the early 1970s and ended in the early 1980s. This proposal to establish a book series in Asian American Studies will help consolidate a fourth phase that began to emerge in the 1980s with the publications of Roger Daniels (1981), Illsoo Kim (1981), William F. Wu (1982), Peter Irons (1983), Ronald Riddle (1983), Ronald Takaki (1983), Henry S. S. Tsai (1983), Lucy M. Cohen (1984), Won Moo Hurh and Kwang Chung Kim (1984), Edwin B. Almirol (1985), Edward D. Beechert (1985), Donald E. Collins (1985), Sandy Lydon (1985), Allan T. Moriyama (1985), Pamatma Saran (1985), Paul J. Strand and Woodrow Jones, Jr. (1985),

Sylvia Junko Yanagisako (1985), Sucheng Chan (1986), Roger Daniels and his coeditors (1986), Evelyn Nakano Glenn (1986), Henry S. S. Tsai (1986), James T. Fawcett and Benjamin V. Carino (1987), Thomas James (1987), and Paul C. P. Siu (1987). Last year, 1988, was a banner year: it saw the publication of significant studies by Roger Daniels, John Y. Fenton, Margaret A. Gibson, Yuji Ichioka, Joan M. Jensen, Peter Kwong, Ivan Light and Edna Bonacich, Pyong Gap Min, Wayne Patterson, and Raymond B. Williams. Only a fraction of these authors teach courses in Asian American Studies, but their intellectual labor definitely enriches and enlarges the field. This fourth phase is marked by works that no longer treat persons of Asian ancestry as unwelcome "perpetual foreigners" but rather as agents who made or are making history on American soil.

To take a backward glance, European Americans have written about the Asians in their midst since the 1850s. The first observers were not academics but individuals who wrote about Asians for partisan reasons. A few Protestant missionaries such as Otis Gibson (1877), a handful of diplomats who had served in Asia such as George Seward (1881), and an independent scholar such as Mary Roberts Coolidge (1909) defended the Chinese who came during the second half of the nineteenth century. In the second decade of the twentieth century the missionary Sidney Gulick (1914, 1917, 1918) likewise sought to cast a positive light on the Japanese presence in the United States. Almost all the other authors of that era, however, betrayed a deep phobia of, or hostility toward, the Chinese, Japanese, Koreans, Asian Indians, and Filipinos who arrived during the decades before federal legislation excluded them from America's shores. In addition to newspaper articles and dozens of pamphlets, several government documents—most notably the report of the U.S. Senate's Joint Special Committee to Investigate Chinese Immigration (1877), the report of the California state legislature's Special Committee on Chinese Immigration (1878), and the hearings on Japanese immigration before the Committee on Immigration and Naturalization of the U.S. House of Representatives (1921)—capture the flavor of the anti-Asian sentiments of their day.

During the second stage of Asian American historiography scholars entered the scene and produced the first substantial corpus of books on Asians in America. In 1928 William C. Smith, Eliot Grinnel Mears, and Roderic D. McKenzie each published a book on Asian Americans. The 1930s saw the appearance of books by Bruno Lasker (1931), Yamato Ichihashi (1932), Edward K. Strong (1934), Frank S. Miyamoto (1939), and Elmer C. Sandmeyer (1939). From the 1940s to the late 1960s, works dealt largely with Japanese immigration and the outcry against it, the degree to which Japanese immigrants and their American-born children were assimilating, and the confinement of more than 112,000 persons of Japanese ancestry in concentration camps during World War II. The first topic was the ken of Hilary Conroy (1953) and Roger Daniels (1962); the second was represented by William C. Smith (1937), Forrest La Violette (1946), and George De Vos (1954); the third was the concern of Carey McWilliams (1944), Alexander Leighton (1945), Dorothy Thomas and her coauthors (1946 and 1954), Morton Grodzins (1949), Leonard Broom and his coauthors (1949, 1956), Jacobus ten Broek and his coauthors (1954), Allan R. Bosworth (1967), Edward H. Spicer and his coauthors (1969), Roger Daniels (1972), and many others. A few studies of Chinese immigrants also appeared, including those by Milton R. Konvitz (1946), Fred W. Riggs (1950), Rose Hum Lee (1960), S. W. Kung (1962), and Gunther Barth (1964).

The above publications and their like formed the corpus of works available for classroom use when students demanded in the late 1960s and early 1970s that Asian American Studies courses be introduced and Ethnic Studies programs or departments—in one case, even a school—be established on college and university campuses. Seeking to expose and combat the deeply rooted racism that underpinned the misrepresentations of their people's history in the United States, the young radicals criticized many of the existing works in the most trenchant manner. To create a different body of literature more to their liking, undergraduate and graduate students, as well as junior faculty members, conducted oral history interviews, looked for Asian-language sources, and used a variety of mostly Marxist theories to interpret the experiences of their people. (A good number of pioneer Asian Americanists gravitated to Marxist analysis because it provided a ready-made critique of the dominant social science theories of the 1960s and 1970s in addition to its traditional dissection of capitalism and its exploitation of workers.) While such efforts provided much-needed correctives to earlier writings, they had problems of their own. The strident leftist rhetoric of some authors deflected attention from their otherwise insightful conclusions. Also, in some pieces the lack of "fit" between grand theoretical formulations and the far more modest empirical data presented allowed conservative critics to dismiss such writings out of hand.

The tone and orientation of the self-consciously politicized writings of the 1970s notwithstanding, there exists a very real problem that has limited the volume of publications in the field: there are relatively few qualified reviewers who can evaluate studies of Asian Americans—especially those that challenge the prevailing paradigms in the various disciplines—fairly. If a manuscript falls into the hands of an established scholar whose own work is under attack, the likelihood that it will receive a positive review is virtually nil. Were it not for the Asian American Studies Center at the University of California, Los Angeles, which published several anthologies—*Roots* (1971), *Letters in Exile* (1976), and *Counterpoint* (1976)—sponsored a collaborative project that resulted in a book edited by Lucie Cheng and Edna Bonacich (1984), and continues to put out *Amerasia Journal*, very little of the revisionist writings of this period would have appeared in print.

Tired of dealing with ideological censorship, some authors have published their writings themselves or under the aegis of community organizations, as exemplified by the volume of conference papers compiled by the Chinese Historical Society of America (1976), the collection of personal essays published by the Japanese American Anthology Committee (1980), and the pictorial history of Filipino Americans produced by Fred Cordova (1983). Although such works have contributed a great deal to our understanding of the history and contemporary conditions of Asian Americans, some of them do not contain the scholarly "apparatus"—reviews of the literature, citations, statistical tables, maps, and so forth—that picky reviewers expect to see. However, had community groups and small presses not stepped in, writings that attempted to unearth and recover our "buried past" would not have been made available to students, teachers, and the general public.

A number of Asian American authors, including Betty Lee Sung (1967), Victor and Brett de Bary Nee (1972), Michi Weglyn (1976), Frank F. Chuman (1976), Hyung-chan Kim (1977), Tetsuden Kashima (1977), Chia-ling Kuo (1977), Tamotsu Shibutani (1978), Bong-youn Choy (1979), Peter Kwong (1979), William T. Liu and his coauthors (1979), and Bill Hosokawa and Robert A. Wilson (1980) did find commercial or academic presses willing to turn their manuscripts into publications. European American scholars have also contributed to the literary output of this period. They include Stuart Creighton Miller (1969), James W. Loewen (1971), Brett H. Melendy (1971), William Petersen (1971), Alexander Saxton (1971), Hilary Conroy and T. Scott Miyakawa (1972), Ivan Light (1972), Stanford Lyman (1974), Roger Daniels (1975), John W. Connor (1977), Gail P. Kelly (1977), Delber L. McKee (1977), John Modell (1977), Darrel Montero (1979), Edna Bonacich and John Modell (1980), and Clarence E. Glick (1980). In general, the books published from the late 1960s to around 1980 were more sympathetic to the subjects they studied.

Despite this outpouring, materials are not appearing fast enough to meet classroom needs, not only because a good number of the original Asian American Studies and Ethnic Studies programs have survived—mainly on campuses in the West Coast—but also because new ones, such as that at Cornell University, are being set up on the East Coast. Students at many institutions across the country are calling for a more diversified, multiethnic curriculum. As faculty and administrators slowly come to accept, however reluctantly, the students' point of view, the demand for books and articles that deal with the histories, cultures, and contemporary conditions of people of color in the United States will increase. Dozens of titles on African Americans and Native Americans are appearing every year, while more and more books on various Spanish-speaking groups are also becoming available. In comparison, there are fewer books on Asian Americans, and they deal mainly with Chinese and Japanese Americans. Yet the fastest growing groups are Filipino, Korean, Asian Indian, and Vietnamese immigrants and their American-born children or grandchildren, about whom precious little has been written.

The series I am proposing is designed to remedy some of the ills identified above and to meet the need for usable texts—particularly narratives that present Asian American perspectives on the study of Asian American history, communities, and cultures. By "Asian American perspectives," I refer to conceptual frameworks that treat Asian Americans as agents of historical change and as creators of a new pan-Asian American culture. To transcend the strictures imposed both by the earlier assimilationist paradigm and the more recent, largely Marxist, assumptions, manuscripts containing a variety of theoretical orientations will be solicited and considered. Manuscripts will be chosen on the basis of solid scholarship, the significance of the topics they treat, the contributions they make to new ways of understanding the subject matter, and lucidity of expression.

These criteria are more difficult to apply than might appear at first glance because Asian American Studies has been intentionally multi- or interdisciplinary. The two terms are not synonymous. *Multidisciplinary* refers to the participation of scholars from various social science and humanities disciplines in the study of Asian Americans, while authors who aspire to be *interdisciplinary* must themselves be familiar with theories and methodologies from several disciplines so they can use ideas and approaches from one discipline to critique, modify, or enrich other disciplines. It does not take much effort to make a field multidisciplinary, but enormous diligence and dedication are required before authors can master the literature from several disciplines.

Despite the hurdles, a field that aspires to interdisciplinarity *can* produce pathbreaking works when the nexus between theory and empirical data or documentary evidence is handled judiciously. But there are pitfalls in interdisciplinary approaches as well. One peculiarity of Asian American Studies is that many of the historical studies have been or are being written by sociologists. When social scientists apply theoretical concepts to historical documents, some of which may be unique to a specific situation at a particular point in time, they may unwittingly make generalizations that erase the specificities, ambiguities, or nuances of historical reality. Unlike most historians who strive to assess the problematic nature of documentary evidence, some social scientists, especially those who use quantitative methods, sometimes accord too much significance to data that are really quite limited in scope. (For example, a sociologist once attempted a class analysis of an entire Asian immigrant community at the turn of the century by using information in a directory that listed the occupations of only about thirty individuals.) More than in other fields, a book series in Asian American Studies is one where an advisory/general editor can play a crucial role by setting up a carefully structured review process.

I think a two-step review will be needed for most of the manuscripts we shall consider for the series—a process that will involve far more work on my part than is done by most advisory editors. Before a manuscript is sent out to outside readers, I shall read it, edit fifty to a hundred pages both substantively and stylistically in order to suggest to the author what changes may be made, and return the manuscript to him or her for rewriting. Only if the revision is acceptable will I recommend that we send the manuscript out for external review. In most instances we should seek the advice of two kinds of outside reviewers for each manuscript. First, we need reviewers who are familiar with the minutae of Asian American Studies. They can offer detailed evaluations of the historical documentary evidence or social science empirical data presented and the appropriateness of the concepts authors use to interpret or analyze their findings. Second, we need scholars to assess the contributions the studies make to broader questions currently asked in the pertinent disciplines or interdisciplinary areas of academic discourse. If reviewers who simultaneously possess both kinds of expertise can be found, then only one outside reviewer is needed.

When the reviews are sent to the author(s), I shall include a cover memo suggesting the extent to which the issues raised by the anonymous readers should be addressed. Such a commentary on my part is needed because reviewers who are not familiar with the scholarship in Asian American Studies can easily misjudge it or show hostility to the perspectives and basic premises of practitioners in the field. It is important that we not allow obstructionist reviewers to veto manuscripts that are original and interesting but that do not pay homage to an existing "canon." I think the review process I am proposing is more stringent than that required by most university presses, but adopting it will result in a series that can stand up to close scrutiny.

To accommodate the variety of work being produced, four kinds of manuscripts will be considered for the series: research monographs, collections of research articles or essays, anthologies of creative writings, and collections of short autobiographies or oral histories. The third and fourth are intended primarily for classroom use. To avoid the submission of irrelevant writings, the advertisements announcing the series should make it clear that manuscripts dealing entirely with *Asia* will not be considered. Our goal is to publish writings that focus on the experiences of Asians *in America*.

I think I am uniquely qualified to serve as the advisory editor of such a series for several reasons. First, as one of the founders of Asian American Studies, I know the field well. I monitor new works as they are being written; I have met many of the graduate students and faculty in the field; and I know the problems that plague scholarly output in our area of specialization and have thought carefully about ways to overcome them.

Second, unlike most Asian Americanists who research and write about only one ethnic group, I am studying Americans of Chinese, Japanese, Korean, Filipino, Asian Indian, Vietnamese, Cambodian, Lao, and Hmong ancestries. I am writing a textbook that examines these groups thematically and comparatively instead of discussing each of them in a separate chapter as other authors have done. Also, I was asked to write the entries for five of these groups in a forthcoming encyclopedia of American immigration, and I penned the two latest bibliographies in Asian American Studies, which required intimate knowledge of writings about *all* the Asian ethnic groups.

Third, I am familiar with several disciplines. This is a crucial advantage because of the multi- or interdisciplinary aspirations of Asian American Studies. I majored in economics with a minor in political science during my undergraduate years and took seminars in economics, anthropology, sociology, and political science during my graduate studies. A decade after I completed my Ph.D., I decided—for aesthetic, philosophical, and political reasons—to become a historian. I took a year's leave of absence without pay in order to read all the articles published in the major history journals in the preceding decade. In this manner I learned, by osmosis, how historians think and write. The unusual trajectory of my academic career enables me to assess manuscripts that reflect the concerns and complexities of several disciplines.

Fourth, I am a reasonably experienced editor. In the last year and a half I edited two volumes of conference papers written by social scientists, whose technical prose I had to translate into plainer English so more people can understand their work. Because I stand ready to tackle even the most opaque prose, I intend to line-edit a substantial portion of each accepted manuscript before turning the job over to a professional copy editor.

In short, conditions are ripe for launching the kind of book series I propose, and I think I am the right person to undertake this task.

7 Proposal for a Bachelor of Arts Degree in Asian American Studies at the University of California, Santa Barbara [1993]

I did not write much about Asian American studies as an academic, political, and institutional phenomenon in the mid-1980s because I was busy revising the first draft of the manuscript that became This Bittersweet Soil *and administering a residential college on the UC Santa Cruz campus. I resumed my involvement with Asian American studies when I moved to UC Santa Barbara in 1988. When friends heard that I had accepted a job at that campus they told me I was crazy. "There's nothing there!" they exclaimed. But as I saw it, precisely because there was "nothing there," an opportunity existed to create something new—or, more accurately, to revive a program on the verge of extinction.*

In 1987, when the UCSB administration threatened either to shut down the program or merge it with Asian studies, about two dozen determined students mounted stiff resistance. In response, the provost decided to hire one faculty member—just one—to teach a few courses. When offered the job I said I would not accept it unless I was given the resources to develop a vibrant program that could ultimately become a department. The provost struck a bargain with me. If I would be satisfied with two ladder-rank (tenure-track) faculty positions as part of my "start-up package," he would support future requests for additional positions if I could demonstrate that the program was able to lure first-rate faculty to its ranks.

One peculiarity that made the UCSB program's quick growth possible was that on the UC Santa Barbara campus, unlike the situation at UC Berkeley, the academic senate committees that reviewed proposed courses did not require such courses to have the names of ladder-rank faculty attached to them. Thus, as soon as I arrived on campus I submitted a list of forty courses, each with a course description, for approval. Once those courses were on the books, I used their existence to argue why we needed additional faculty positions so that the courses could be taught. (Tautology is sometimes useful!)

As our enrollment grew apace I requested an early "external review" of the program in 1993. When we received a very positive review, I submitted a proposal for a B.A. degree. That was approved in record time, and then I requested that we be granted departmental status. Unlike programs, which in the UC system must report to some higher authority and can be dismantled easily, departments are more or less autonomous entities and cannot be "disestablished" without a lot of review. Upon receiving departmental status, we held a reception to which we invited many guests. As I looked over the party scene I could not help but wonder whether that occasion might be the high point in our development. My foreboding was prophetic, for in the years that followed we encountered many problems I never anticipated.

This chapter contains the proposal but without the sections that discussed bureaucratic matters. I was now making larger claims for my field than I had done in the 1970s and 1980s.

* * *

Introduction

Asian Americans are the fastest-growing minority group in the United States. The 1970 U.S. census of population counted about 1.5 million of them, the 1980 census some 3.5 million, and the 1990 census roughly 7.3 million. In the state of California, Asian Americans will become the second largest minority group by the year 2000.

Composed of immigrants from dozens of Asian countries and their American-born descendants, Asian Americans are a complex people. There are striking similarities as well as significant differences among the various ethnic groups now subsumed under the umbrella term *Asian Americans*. The similarities come mainly from their common experiences as racial minorities in the United States—the fact that American society historically has tended to treat all Asians alike, regardless of which countries they came from, what languages they spoke, or what their socioeconomic status might be. The differences arise from their diverse origins. Today there are divisions among people of different national origins speaking different languages or even among people from the same country who speak different dialects of their national or dominant language. People also differ in terms socioeconomic classes, religious beliefs, rural versus urban upbringing, whether they belong to the immigrant or American-born generations, are men or women, and are old or young.

Changes in the Asian American population have occurred so quickly that scholars despair of keeping pace with them. Whereas university administrators and faculty review committees used to look upon Asian American Studies and other branches of Ethnic Studies as programs providing compensatory education for minority students by offering them courses that enhanced their self-esteem, this view of the field is now outmoded. Today, there are compelling pedagogical and intellectual reasons to support the development of Asian American Studies.

What Is Asian American Studies?

Asian American Studies is an interdisciplinary field that examines all the relevant aspects of the historical and contemporary experiences of Asian Americans, including their histories, communities, and cultures (the word *cultures* refers to both patterned ways of behavior and to artistic and literary expressions). The history courses treat Asian American history as part of U.S. history, but they also highlight selected aspects of Asian history in order to show how homeland developments affected and continue to affect the lives of Asian Americans. Asian American communities are studied as examples of American ethnic communities whose internal structures and relationships to the wider society change from one historical period to another. Asian American cultures are viewed not as a simple "blending of East and West" but, first, as a process of social, cultural, and psychological self-definition through which Asian Americans construct identities and develop patterns of interpersonal relationships within the context of sociocultural interaction and, second, as artistic expressions that reflect the development of Asian American literary voices and the emergence of Asian American artistic sensibilities.

Why Should There Be an Interdisciplinary Major?

Some reviewers will no doubt ask why an interdisciplinary Asian American Studies major is needed. Why not simply ask departments such as Anthropology, Art Studio, Dramatic Art, Economics, English, Film Studies, Political Science, Psychology, and Sociology to each offer one or more courses on Asian Americans? To be sure, these traditional departments can indeed do that. However, those departments that do offer courses on various minority groups often tend to treat them as marginal embellishments and not as the central focus of the department's curriculum. Moreover, by compartmentalizing knowledge about Asian Americans in different departments, students may get a somewhat disjointed view of the experiences of Asian Americans.

Interdisciplinary programs, in contrast, offer the intellectual equivalent of stereoscopic vision or stereophonic sound—a fuller, more richly textured, and more finely nuanced understanding of the phenomenon (or, in this case, population) under study. By using the insights of one discipline to critique, interrogate, supplement, or complement those offered by other disciplines, both faculty and students will be forced to think more broadly and deeply as well as comparatively. The move towards interdisciplinary studies has been one of the more notable trends in American higher education in recent years. Efforts are being made nationwide to create new programs that cross disciplinary boundaries in order to escape the constraints imposed by each discipline. It is not a coincidence that some of the newest areas of academic endeavor—Ethnic Studies, Women's Studies, Environmental Studies, and Cultural Studies—are all interdisciplinary.

When they are in their nascent stage of development, many interdisciplinary fields are, in fact, only multidisciplinary—that is, each discipline investigates one aspect of a multifaceted topic while students are required to take a host of courses in different departments that do not necessarily engage one another analytically. A truly rigorous interdisciplinarity, in contrast, mandates a fundamental reevaluation of the assumptions and perspectives that underlie each discipline, its theoretical constructs, and its methodologies. The latter kind of interdisciplinary program is what the proposed B.A. degree in Asian American Studies will attempt to develop. Our majors will participate in this critical, interrogative, intellectual exercise in the junior seminar all majors must take and in their senior projects. In the process, they will become some of the most sophisticated thinkers UCSB will produce in the 1990s and beyond.

Contributions of Asian American Studies to Higher Education

As Asian American Studies develops as a discrete field of academic inquiry it is making important educational and intellectual contributions to American higher education in terms of pedagogy as well as research.

Educational and Pedagogical Contributions

ENLARGING THE BOUNDARIES OF THE LIBERAL ARTS Given the increasing visibility of Asian Americans in all walks of life in many areas of the United States, all students—and not just those of Asian ancestry—graduating from a good liberal arts college or university should know something about the histories, communities, and cultures of Asian Americans, who are an integral part of American society. Students who take one or more Asian American Studies courses will acquire knowledge about Asian Americans that is usually not yet available in courses offered in other departments. Just as important, they will learn to see and think of Asian Americans as central, rather than marginal, actors in society.

DEVELOPING A MULTIETHNIC/MULTICULTURAL PEDAGOGY In addition to gaining information about Asian Americans, students who take Asian American Studies courses will learn to perceive themselves and their multiethnic/ multiracial peers from a perspective that values equally people who have different ways of thinking and behaving and are from diverse backgrounds. Such courses enable students of Asian ancestry to come to terms with their ethnic identities and their relationship to their communities and to society at large on the one hand and open new cognitive vistas to non-Asian students who may not be fully aware of the multiethnic/multiracial complexities of American history and society on the other hand.

PROVIDING MENTORSHIP AND SERVING AS ROLE MODELS Since a vast majority of the faculty in Asian American and other Ethnic Studies programs/departments (up to this point) have been people of color, they serve as an important source of mentorship not only to students of color but also to European American students interested in pursuing certain subjects. Through conversations with students and by example, they offer students glimpses of the pressures, challenges, and rewards of academic life.

HELPING STUDENTS TO ACQUIRE USABLE SKILLS AND A SENSE OF SOCIAL RESPONSIBILITY Since its founding, Asian American Studies has placed great emphasis on training students to be of service to both their ethnic communities and to the larger society. Asian American Studies has always recognized and, wherever and whenever resources permitted, tried to develop students' language skills, both in English and in Asian languages. Being bilingual or even multilingual will enable future scholars to do better research and future social service providers to offer more culturally sensitive services. In some courses students engage in community-based internships or learn to write funding proposals. Students are encouraged to think critically not only about the world around them but also about how knowledge of that world is generated, validated, or debunked. Asian American Studies faculty are very concerned about doing research in a socially responsible way. Faculty ask themselves and teach their students to ask such questions as, For whom and for what purpose is this research being done? and, Who will benefit, in what ways, from the findings?

PREPARING STUDENTS FOR GRADUATE STUDY AND PROFESSIONAL TRAINING Committed to increasing their own ranks, Asian American Studies faculty encourage students to continue their education beyond college. As faculty in an interdisciplinary program or department, Asian American Studies professors can provide insight into many disciplines and professions. Students graduating with a B.A. degree in Asian American Studies are prepared for graduate study in a variety of humanities and social science disciplines—particularly Ethnic Studies, History, Literature, Psychology, and Sociology. Asian American Studies majors will also be able to prepare for professional training in Business Administration or Management, City and Regional Planning, Psychological Counseling, Education, Law, Library and Informational Science, Public Health, and Social Welfare. (Those who wish to enter medical school must, of course, have also taken the appropriate natural science courses.)

PREPARING STUDENTS FOR EMPLOYMENT IN A MULTIETHNIC SOCI-ETY The 1990 census showed that California is now the nation's most ethnically and racially diverse state. We have the largest percentage of Asian Americans (9.6 percent of the total California population) and Latino Americans (25.8 percent) in the country and the second-largest number of African Americans (2.2 million, second only to New York's 2.9 million) and Native Americans (242,164, second only to Oklahoma's 252,420). Almost three million persons of Asian ancestry, representing about 40 percent of all such persons in the United States, live in California today. Given this demographic reality, students graduating with interdisciplinary knowledge of Asian Americans, as well as with knowledge about other ethnic groups, will be well prepared for employment in many occupations—business and management, education, social services, the health professions, law, high-tech industries, and other lines of work that involve interaction with coworkers and clients from diverse origins.

Substantive and Analytical Contributions

CONTRIBUTIONS TO THE STUDY OF U.S. HISTORY Researching and teaching Asian American history can expand the boundaries and revise the conceptualization of U.S. history. Acquiring an understanding of how Asian immigrants and their descendants have been treated in American history and how they have responded to such treatment highlights many aspects of American society—what some scholars have called the "underside" of American history—not normally covered in U.S. history courses. The contribution that Asian American history can make to U.S. history is not just additive—in the sense of including bits and pieces of information about Asian Americans in U.S. history courses—but potentially revisionist and transformative. In other words, the way in which certain aspects of U.S. history is understood may be modified by the analytical insights gained from the study of Asians in America and how their presence revealed important cleavages in the social fabric of the nation.

CONTRIBUTIONS TO THE SOCIAL SCIENCES Asian American Studies can also make important intellectual contributions to the social sciences, both empirically and theoretically. Asian American social science scholarship is beginning to make an impact on the study of such subjects as 1) the restructuring of the world economy; 2) contemporary immigration into the United States; 3) changing patterns of race and ethnic relations; 4) the impact of demographic changes on American politics at the local, state, and national levels; 5) the influence of family dynamics, cultural values, and social support systems on personality and identity development; and 6) the interplay of micro and macro cultural developments within historical, institutional, and symbolic arenas.

1. The world economy is undergoing a process of globalization and restructuring made possible by the fluidity of capital, labor, and entrepreneurial talent. Trade and other transactions between the United States and countries on the other side of the Pacific Rim have become salient features of American life. From its early days, Asian American Studies has tried to place the study of Asians in America in the broader context of the international linkages between various Asian countries and the United States.

2. Contemporary Asian immigration is both an independent and a dependent variable in this process of global and trans-Pacific restructuring. Immigration from Asia is affecting how the restructuring is occurring while the process of restructuring itself is affecting the demographic composition of the Asian immigrant stream. Moreover, although the forces promoting contemporary Asian immigration into the United States resemble in some ways the circumstances surrounding Asian immigration in the nineteenth century and the first half of the twentieth century, in other ways they differ significantly. Scholars have only recently begun to study the relationship

between restructuring and immigration. Researchers in Asian American Studies are ideally situated, by training and research interests, to provide intellectual leadership in these emerging areas of scholarship.

3. The modes of incorporation of Asian immigrants into American society today also differ from patterns set in the past. In years gone by, scholars specializing in race and ethnic relations tended to examine only the binary or bipolar relation between two groups: the Euro-American majority and a particular nonwhite minority—in most instances, African Americans. Today, multipolar relationships among several minorities are becoming increasingly important, a fact that became very obvious during the 1992 Los Angeles civil unrest. Asian American Studies faculty are at the forefront of efforts to document and analyze this phenomenon.

4. While many studies have been done on the socioeconomic incorporation of Asian immigrants and their American-born descendants, research on how Asian Americans are affecting American politics is only beginning. Not only are Asian American activists engaged in voter registration drives, but researchers are also monitoring, documenting, and analyzing the patterns shown by Asian Americans in electoral politics at the local, state, and national levels. Scholars in Asian American Studies, however, have pointed out that the in-depth study of Asian American political activities must be broadened to include research on politics within the ethnic communities, the involvement of Asian immigrants in the politics of their homelands, and the protest politics of the 1960s, during which a pan-Asian ethnic consciousness emerged.

5. Research on the psychology of Asian Americans is leading to new insights about a variety of topics, including the conflicts involved in acculturation and ethnic identity development; variations in self-identities and their effects on emotions and behavior; the influence of identities, tokenism, and stereotypes on personality development; mechanisms that define "culturally responsive" therapy; cultural beliefs that affect outcomes in psychotherapy; and a host of other issues relevant to the understanding of the relationship between individuals and their social environment. Until recently, the study of African Americans has provided most of the bases for cross-cultural comparisons. However, the increasing numbers and salience of other ethnic/racial minority groups compel psychologists to stretch their conceptualization of what is universalistic versus what is particularistic and expand the domain of cultural variables, thus enabling a more extensive examination of sociocultural influences on human behavior.

6. The rapidly developing field of cultural studies has produced a great deal of theoretical work in social and cultural analysis, much of it stimulated by

European theories associated with new developments in poststructuralism, discourse analysis, and postmodernism. The new modes of theorizing question the epistemological presuppositions of any single discipline and argue for interdisciplinary models that span the micro and macro dimensions of cultural practices. Asian Americanists are beginning to tap this kind of theorizing that bridges the humanities and social sciences to help make sense of the burgeoning Asian American cultural productions in literature, film, and theater. Asian American Studies not only can benefit from such theoretical innovations but can also contribute to new insights, especially on the complicated relationship between race/ethnicity and cultural production.

CONTRIBUTIONS TO LITERARY STUDIES AND THE ARTS While the new field of cultural studies embraces both the social sciences and the humanities, the more traditional approaches to the humanities can also gain from bringing Asian American Studies into their fold. The critical acclaim that writers such as Maxine Hong Kingston, Amy Tan, David Henry Hwang, Philip Kan Gotanda, Jessica Hagedorn, and Bharati Mukherjee have received has helped to foster the idea that there is indeed such a thing as "Asian American literature"—writing worthy of serious study. The humanities component of Asian American Studies has, until recently, been rather underdeveloped. The first book-length work of literary criticism on Asian American writings was published only in 1982; to date [1993], only three additional books on Asian American literary studies have appeared, though more are in press. The critical study of Asian American films and other visual arts has barely begun. But this situation will soon change because Asian American cultural production is now one of the most dynamic aspects of Asian American communities. Once there is available a corpus of works to be explicated, the critics will quickly appear. Asian American literature and the expressive arts, as well as the scholarly study of them, will in time strengthen the movement to expand and diversify literary, cinematic, theatrical, and other artistic canons.

Contributions to UCSB's Academic Goals and Objectives

The UCSB Academic Planning Statement lists five goals and objectives:

1. to ensure a diverse faculty of exceptional excellence;
2. to increase the stature of research and creative activity;
3. to promote excellence in undergraduate and graduate instruction;
4. to continue UCSB's commitment to student diversity and quality; and
5. to enhance the quality of life on the campus and in the surrounding communities.

Since 1989, when the Asian American Studies Program at UCSB entered a new phase of development, it has contributed substantially to all of UCSB's goals.

GOAL 1: FACULTY DIVERSITY AND EXCELLENCE All the ladder-rank faculty who have been hired since 1989 are productive scholars and prolific writers. The best proof of this is that during the past year, three of the five ladder-rank faculty won national awards, while two received postdoctoral fellowships.

GOAL 2: INCREASING THE STATURE OF RESEARCH AND CREATIVE ACTIV-ITY The Asian American Studies Program is firmly committed to research and creative activity, not only among its faculty but also among its students. The proposed major is designed with this goal explicitly in mind.

GOAL 3: PROMOTING EXCELLENCE IN TEACHING All the Asian American Studies faculty—ladder-rank and temporary lecturers alike—are dedicated and effective teachers. The scores we have received in our teaching evaluations stand more than 20 percent higher than the mean for the campus as a whole. Over 1,400 undergraduates are taking our courses this year [1993]. Even though the program does not offer any graduate courses, all the ladder-rank faculty have nonetheless worked with graduate students from the departments of English, History, Sociology, and the Graduate School of Education by supervising reading courses, by training them as T.A.s, and by serving on their M.A. and Ph.D. committees. The two faculty who have joint appointments also teach regular graduate courses and seminars in the other departments to which they belong.

GOAL 4: STUDENT DIVERSITY AND EXCELLENCE By teaching students of color about their own histories, communities, and cultures and opening their eyes to the constructive roles they can play in society, the Asian American Studies curriculum is contributing to the retention of such students as well as promoting an increased appreciation of and a greater respect for diversity among *all* students.

GOAL 5: ENHANCING THE QUALITY OF LIFE By inviting outstanding Asian American artists, filmmakers, and writers to campus and by hosting two national conferences (in 1990 and 1991), the program has helped to enrich the cultural life of the campus and surrounding community.

The Study of Asians in the United States

To appreciate the innovative and unique aspects of the proposed B.A. degree in Asian American Studies at UCSB it is necessary first to review briefly the intellectual and institutional history of Asian American Studies. Although Asian American Studies emerged as a distinct field of academic inquiry only in 1969 as part of the political settlement of the student strikes at San Francisco State University and at the University of California, Berkeley, the study of Asians in America has a much longer history.

A great deal has been written about Asians in America since the Chinese—the first Asian immigrant group to set foot in considerable numbers on American soil—started arriving in the middle of the nineteenth century, but the quality of the existing literature is uneven, and many topics still await scholarly treatment. The early writings were, almost without exception, partisan in nature—either defending or attacking Asian immigration, a phenomenon that aroused intense hostility and controversy. It was not until the late 1930s that a number of "real" scholarly studies on Asian immigrants and their American-born children appeared. From the 1930s to the early 1970s, the four topics that received the most academic attention were the various anti-Asian movements, the assimilation (or lack thereof) of Asian immigrants and their descendants, the social organization—and, in the eyes of some, the social "pathology"—of Asian immigrant communities, and the internment of 112,000 persons of Japanese ancestry (two-thirds of them U.S.–born citizens) along the Pacific Coast during World War II.

Over the years, different paradigms have guided research on immigrants and ethnic/racial minorities. The most important has been the assimilation model. Immigrants are said to assimilate when they shed the cultures they have brought with them, adopt a new one, gain social acceptance, and participate in the institutions of the host society. In American higher education, the assimilation model held intellectual sway for a century because it reflected a basic development in American history. Wave after wave of immigrants from Europe were transformed into Americans—men and women who prized liberty, individualism, republican political institutions, and a market economy.

Left out of this picture, however, were Native Americans who perished in the so-called Indian wars, were removed from the regions where they lived, and were placed into reservations; mixed-blood Mexicans who were likewise conquered and subjugated; Africans enslaved and brought to the New World to perform the hardest labor under the cruelest conditions; and Asian immigrants whose toil helped develop the American West. As Benjamin

Ringer has put it, Americans of European ancestry drew a dichotomy between themselves—whom they referred to as "we, the people"—and darker-skinned "others," who were considered unfit to partake of the rewards of American society. So many social, economic, political, and legal hurdles were placed in the way of the racial "others" that even when they wanted to assimilate they could not do so. Unfortunately, scholars who have studied these minority groups have often overlooked that fact. Instead, they have blamed the victims for the injustices that people of color have suffered.

The grip of the assimilation model was finally loosened in the late 1960s and early 1970s when young Asian American activists on college and university campuses began agitating for the establishment of Asian American Studies programs just as their counterparts among African Americans, Chicanos, and Native Americans were demanding that other branches of Ethnic Studies be set up. During its first decade of existence the adherents of Asian American Studies severely criticized the assimilation model and proposed several alternatives to guide the study of Asian Americans. One was classical Marxist theory, extended to encompass Asian immigrants and other non-whites as workers exploited by a capitalist system. A second was the internal colonialism model developed by such black intellectuals as Harold Cruse, Kenneth Clark, Kwame Toure (known at that time as Stokely Carmichael), Charles V. Hamilton, and William Tabb and by such Chicano social scientists as Tomas Almaguer, Mario Barrera, and Carlos Munoz. European American sociologist Robert Blauner has identified five features—involuntary entry, destruction of culture, political control by outside forces, racism, and racial segregation in the labor market—that make the internal colonial model applicable to all peoples of color, including Asian Americans, in the United States. A third framework, adopted mainly by Asian Americans active in the anti–Vietnam War movement, depicted Asian Americans as brothers and sisters of people in Asian nations—in this instance, Vietnam—who were suffering from an imperialist American foreign policy.

The second and third models were closely related as they both sought to explain manifestations of the same phenomenon at different geographic sites. On the one hand, Europeans colonized places in Africa, Asia (with the exception of Japan and Thailand), the Americas, Australia, and other places in the Pacific Ocean, thereby abrogating their sovereignty. On the other hand, European settler colonies imported various nonwhite groups to serve the interests of whites. Thus, nonwhite minorities within the United States and in other countries that began as white settler colonies were a "Third World within" whose members share a common history of oppression with people living in the "Third World without." The struggles that Asian American activists engaged in were, in their eyes, simultaneously anticapitalist, antiracist, and anti-imperialist. In the process, they helped debunk the assimilationist paradigm.

In contrast to this first, rather abrupt, conceptual shift in the early 1970s, the second change in analytical framework that occurred in the early 1980s has elicited little notice. The new element that has crept into studies of Asian Americans published since the early 1980s is the concept of agency. Unlike the assimilationist and the internal colonialism paradigms, which are all deterministic in that they portray Asian Americans as the objects of other people's actions and victims of powerful structural forces, recent approaches emphasize the fact that Asian Americans possess agency and have been subjects in the making of their own history. As individuals and as members of groups, Asian immigrants and Asian Americans are depicted as people fully capable of weighing alternatives, making choices, asserting control over their own lives, and helping change the world in which they live. This approach is one of the salient features of the "new" social history that became popular in the 1960s and 1970s. The key question that new social historians ask is, Is human action determined more by economic forces and social conditioning or by human agency and subjectivity? Most scholars, including specialists in Asian American Studies, in fact have not adopted either of these polar positions. Rather, they have tended to use a dialectical approach. On the one hand, individuals are seen as possessing agency within the limitations set by larger structures, but, on the other hand, the scholars recognize that it is human actions that create those structures.

Not only historians but also social scientists have become interested in the concept of agency. For example, there is an increasing recognition among psychologists that psychosocial processes are constructed and shaped in an active and anticipatory fashion by individuals who act as agents within given sociocultural contexts. The "cognizing" of psychology reflects the influence of social constructionist thought in the study of individual differences and social relationships. More emphasis is now placed on how cognitive schemes underlie networks of associations that shape a person's construction of his or her experiences, which, in turn, determine his or her behavior in a particular situation. This theoretical shift underscores an individual's active role, as it is shaped by his or her culture, in constructing reality.

But even as excellent studies that emphasize the agency of immigrants, ethnic groups, and racial minorities were being produced, poststructuralist and postmodernist theories from Europe became fashionable in American academia, particularly in the humanities. Some of these theories call into question the very notion of "subjects" and are thus at odds with the concept of agency. Within Asian American Studies, the postmodernist influence thus far has been felt mainly in the literary studies component of the field.

At present, no single school of theoretical thought can claim to rule supreme in Asian American Studies, given the increasing heterogeneity within the Asian American population. Diverse paradigms are needed to explain different aspects of the experiences of Asian Americans. Empirically based theories of the middle range will prove more useful heuristically than grand theories that attempt to take in all of human existence. This proposal for a B.A. degree in Asian American Studies is thus being submitted at a critical historical moment that is pregnant with possibilities, when Asian American Studies is poised to "take off" both institutionally and intellectually.

The Institutional History of Asian American Studies

The students who pressured the faculty and administrators on various campuses in the late 1960s and early 1970s to allocate resources for Asian American Studies and other Ethnic Studies programs initially exercised great control over the curriculum and the hiring of faculty. On some campuses they continued to do so for many years. Their goal was to offer courses that would present the "true history of oppression" that peoples of color had suffered in the United States. They insisted that these courses be taught either by themselves or by faculty of color who embraced a pedagogy of liberation, a notion they borrowed from Paolo Freire. Then, as now, such a pedagogy is meant to empower students of color. That is why Asian American Studies programs place great emphasis on reconnecting Asian American students with the ethnic communities with which some have lost contact in their eagerness to assimilate. Finding ways to serve their communities—and, it is hoped, to transform them—has been an article of faith among students and faculty in the field.

A decade after Ethnic Studies—including Asian American Studies— emerged out of the tumultuous social movements that swept the United States in the 1960s, many of the programs still in existence began to take steps to institutionalize themselves under intense pressure from review committees and other groups monitoring their activities. Their curricula increasingly conformed to standard university criteria, while faculty possessing Ph.D.s began teaching more and more of the courses. Although the activist heritage of Ethnic Studies remains alive in myriad ways, Ethnic Studies faculty now recognize that doing good research not only does *not* undermine their other goals (as some people used to fear) but also may facilitate the latter's attainment.

A History of Asian American Studies at UCSB

The Asian American Studies program at UCSB was established some two decades ago, at the same time as Black Studies and Chicano Studies. While the latter two programs long ago evolved into departments, the growth of Asian American Studies remained stunted for a variety of reasons until 1989. . . .

During the 1987–88 academic year, campus administrators suggested that the Asian American Studies program be merged with the Asian Studies program. Asian American students strongly opposed the merger. So did faculty in Asian Studies, who thought Asian American Studies courses were more like encounter groups and functioned more as the hotbed of student activism than "real" university courses. When the administration conducted a search in 1988 for a new director, I was offered the job. Upon my appointment, I requested that my title be changed from director to chair to symbolize UCSB's commitment to support our evolution from a program into a department in several years' time.

Given this second lease on life, the Asian American Studies program at UCSB expanded rapidly. Enrollment in Asian American Studies courses increased from 472 in 1989–90, to 616 in 1990–91, to 1,052 in 1991–92, and 1,442 in 1992–93. In these four years, the number of courses offered has doubled from thirteen to twenty-six. The number of ladder-rank faculty has increased from one to five.

Unable to wait for a major in Asian American Studies to be approved, half a dozen students petitioned for an "individual major" in the field. Students find our courses interesting and meaningful. The teaching evaluations that faculty receive have been extremely positive. Numerous students have claimed that the Asian American Studies course(s) they are taking is/are the best course(s) they have had at UCSB and the faculty members teaching them are the best instructors they have ever had—anywhere!

[The remainder of the proposal discussed the budget and the need for new faculty positions and additional staff. Because the requests were specific to the situation at UCSB, they are not reproduced here.]

PART 2

The Politics of Teaching

Developments on the Berkeley campus in the early 1980s forced
me and my colleagues to add a new dimension to our jobs.
Instead of simply teaching courses *about* Asian Americans to
(mainly) students of Asian ancestry we also had to *defend* the
right of Asian Americans to a Berkeley education. As Asian immigration increased in the 1970s, more and more college-age
Asian Americans began to apply for admission to Berkeley and
other highly competitive and prestigious universities around the
country. Their heightened visibility elicited fear and hostility. A
new form of racism reared its ugly head as individuals floated
proposals to put a ceiling on the number of Asian American
students to be admitted. It was not just their growing numbers
that disturbed campus decision-makers; rather, the antagonism
focused on the Asian-ancestry students' low verbal scores on the
Scholastic Aptitude Test (SAT) of the College Entrance Examination Board and their inability to write coherent English.

Serving on multiple campuswide committees, I interacted
frequently with senior faculty who participated most actively in
UC's practice of "shared governance." In those settings, I began
to sense, viscerally, a growing alarm over the rising number of
Asian American students. While Ling-chi Wang organized community activists to oppose potential efforts to curb the students'
numbers, I used a more research-oriented approach to deal with
the troubling developments.

I thought it would be important to have an "objective" database
upon which policy decisions could be made. So, I approached the
director of the campus office that conducts research on the student population to see if he could help me compile the statistics
I desired. He urged me to apply for a grant so that he could hire

additional, temporary staff to do the computer runs I needed. I applied for and received a grant of $10,000 from the Metropolitan Life Insurance Company and presented my findings at a seminar hosted by the Center for Studies in Higher Education at Berkeley and attended by many campus VIPs. The center's photocopies of my report were available under its Occasional Papers imprint. Chapter 8 reproduces that report minus the statistical tables and graphs it contained.

A related project I undertook was to figure out ways to teach English language skills more effectively to Asian immigrant students. I had no training whatsoever in teaching English, but that did not stop me from proposing a multipronged approach to the task at hand (chapter 9). In order to speak authoritatively about the topic, I decided to acquire some hands-on experience teaching language skills to Asian immigrant students and asked the Asian American Studies Program to allow me to teach one section of the Subject A–equivalent course that our program offered. (Subject A is a basic writing requirement that all students must fulfill, either by passing an examination or taking a course.) Chapter 10 discusses my experience in that labor-intensive endeavor.

A second important development also took shape in the 1980s. Even though the existence of Asian American studies programs was still precarious and the number of faculty had barely increased since our founding, my colleagues and I dared to look for new worlds to conquer. In addition to catering to the "special" needs of students of color, we pondered how we might help change the worldviews or mindsets of non-Asian students and colleagues. Accordingly, we began to form coalitions with all kinds of people. In the process, our original international perspective became more U.S.-centered, particularly when we saw how the neo-conservative revolution fueled by the Reagan administration was negatively affecting more and more people of color, women, and workers.

Students and faculty in ethnic studies thought that establishing an "ethnic studies graduation requirement" would be an effective way to combat some of the "isms" that hampered our aspirations. We wanted to open the eyes of students, regardless of their origins, to alternative ways of relating to one another across ethnic, racial, class, and sexual boundaries. We realized no single course can change students' ideas fundamentally, but we had to begin *somewhere.* Chapter 11 describes how I responded when large numbers of European American students enrolled in my Asian American history class at UC Santa Cruz (where I taught from 1984 to 1988) in order to fulfill the new ethnic studies requirement. Chapter 12 discusses briefly how the same requirement worked out at UC Santa Barbara.

A commencement speech I was asked to give at UC Santa Barbara—which the committee overseeing graduation exercises insisted I must write out so that they could see whether or not it would sound "divisive" or "offensive"—offers a glimpse of how I had learned to address a largely non-Asian audience, getting my message across as "softly" as possible while sounding pleasantly wise (chapter 13). Chapter 14 summarizes my teaching philosophy, which I followed consistently over the years, regardless of who I taught.

8 Contemporary Asian Immigration and Its Impact on Undergraduate Education at the University of California, Berkeley [1981]

Ever since I started teaching Asian American studies I have tried to use scholarship itself to combat racial discrimination against Asian Americans in higher education. Initially I did so by speaking and writing an academic prose that was relatively free of political rhetoric. Beginning in 1980, however, I began to conduct research on issues that negatively affected either my field or Asian American students.

Through much of the 1980s, Asian American studies faculty members at Berkeley fought against efforts to reduce the growing number of Asian-ancestry students on that campus. I used statistics in the Student Information system and collected by the campus itself (but which I analyzed) to show that even though many Asian immigrant students had problems with English, they were not "lowering Berkeley's academic standards" as some alleged.

As I went around campus, talking to faculty members in other departments who had many Asian-ancestry students in their classes, I discovered two opposing views. Those who taught writing and other language-based courses expressed great exasperation with the students, but many engineering and science faculty members praised their academic performance and diligence. "What about their inability to speak and write good English?" I asked, playing devil's advocate. "Ah, yes," they responded, "that. . . . But what matters to us is that they can think!" *My report on the changing demographic composition of the Berkeley student body—and what that change portended—is reproduced here but without the twenty-one statistical tables it contained.*

I began on purpose with the words jet black hair and yellowish skin. *Those words were my implicit way of saying to those who opposed the students' growing numbers, "I know what's bothering you. Our appearance makes you squirm."*

Later I also used the word abatement *to suggest a desire to turn back the tide or minimize the inundation because I sensed that the "abatement" of Asian and Latino immigration, in the world outside academia, was becoming a goal among anti-immigrant groups. I knew the questions I posed in the second, short paragraph were questions that many people were asking. I used the seminar to teach a little Asian American history to an audience that included individuals who had power to affect our future.*

* * *

This paper is a preliminary attempt to provide some sociological analysis of a visually noticeable phenomenon at the University of California, Berkeley. As one looks around the campus, one sees large numbers of students with jet black hair and yellowish skin. These students seem especially evident in the buildings housing the engineering, physical sciences, and biological sciences departments. At lunch time, one also sees a lot of them on Dwinelle Plaza.

Who are these students? Where have they come from? What are they like? Why are there so many of them?

Historical Background

The Berkeley campus has always had a sizable number of students of Asian ancestry. From the late nineteenth century to the 1920s, most of the Asian-ancestry students were foreign students who had come from various Asian countries to pursue higher education. Few of them were born in the United States. By the 1920s, however, an increasing number of the Asian-ancestry students at Berkeley were the American-born children of immigrants.

Chinese immigrants first came to California during the Gold Rush. Most of them came without their wives and children. In 1882, Congress passed the Chinese Exclusion Act, which barred all but a handful of Chinese from entering the United States for permanent settlement. It was not until the first three decades of the twentieth century that these immigrants produced a second generation. So it was not until the 1920s and 1930s that a second generation came of age to attend college.

Japanese immigrants started arriving in the late 1880s. Restrictive legislation was first enacted against them in 1907. The 1924 Immigration Act ended Japanese immigration altogether. The Japanese began forming families, however, at an earlier stage in their settlement history than the Chinese had done. Thus, by the 1920s and 1930s, many Japanese Americans, known as *Nisei* (second-generation persons of Japanese ancestry), also began to appear on university campuses in Pacific Coast states.

Immigrants from Korea, the Philippines, and India came in smaller numbers, which meant that few Korean, Filipino/a, and Indian American children showed up in colleges and universities before the 1960s. Therefore, when one spoke of Asian or Asian American students, one referred primarily to students of Chinese or Japanese ancestry. In 1966, when the first ethnic survey was carried out on the Berkeley campus, it found that, of the twenty-six thousand students then registered, 2.7 percent were of Chinese ancestry and 2.5 percent were of Japanese ancestry. Fourteen years later, almost a fifth of Berkeley's undergraduate population is of Asian ancestry. How did this phenomenal rise occur?

Contemporary Asian Immigration

In 1965, Congress passed the Act of October 3, 1965 (79 *Stat.* 911), which terminated the "national origins" quota system of immigration. President Lyndon Johnson signed this act in the era of the civil rights movement, partly as an attempt to rectify the historical injustice of having restricted immigration from Asian countries into this "land of the free and home of the brave."[1] The law took full effect after July 1, 1968. It set up a visa allocation system based on six preferences plus an additional non-preference category for other qualified applicants.[2] The Eastern hemisphere was allocated an annual ceiling of 170,000 immigrants, with an annual per country limit of twenty thousand persons based on a labor clearance requirement. The Western hemisphere received an annual ceiling of 120,000, with no country limitation or numbers based on specific preferences, but with a labor certification requirement.[3] Under the new law, Asian immigration began to increase dramatically. In the 1971–78 period, while Mexico and Cuba ranked first and third in terms of the numbers sent,[4] immigrants from the Philippines, which ranked second, constituted 7.9 percent of the total immigration into the United States, while immigrants from Korea comprised 6 percent. The Chinese, who came mostly from Taiwan (since the United States had no diplomatic relations with the People's Republic of China during those years), made up 4.3 percent.

In 1975, as a result of communist governments coming to power in Vietnam, Laos, and Cambodia, large numbers of refugees began landing in America. To date [1980], over four hundred thousand Indochinese refugees have settled in this country, adding to the astonishing rise in the Asian-ancestry population in the United States.

The U.S. Census Bureau counted 3.5 million persons of Asian ancestry living in the United States in 1980. This represents an increase of 128 percent in one decade. (These figures do not include Indochinese refugees.) In 1980, there were 1,253,987 non-refugee persons of Asian ancestry in the state of California, which has the largest number of such persons in the fifty states.[5] The most numerous group in California is Filipinos (357,514), followed by Chinese (322,340), Japanese (261,817), and Koreans (103,891).[6] Many knowledgeable persons in Asian American communities believe these figures are under counts. Officially, 5.3 percent of California's population is of Asian ancestry. In the city and county of San Francisco, 21.7 percent of the population is of Asian ancestry.[7] There are almost half a million Asian immigrants and Asian Americans in the nine counties comprising the San Francisco Bay area, who make up approximately 9 percent of the total population. Obviously, the increasing number of Asians in California will be reflected in the ethnic mix of its major institutions.

Asian Immigrant Students in Higher Education

California's public higher education system has been one of the institutions in the state that has felt the impact of contemporary Asian immigration most clearly. The phenomenon has affected all three segments of the public higher education system. At the community college level, San Francisco Community College has probably had to make the most profound adjustments since an estimated 50 percent of its enrolled students today are non-native speakers of English. Within California state colleges and universities, San Francisco State University and the campuses of California State University at Los Angeles, Long Beach, and Sacramento now enroll the largest absolute numbers, as well as highest proportions, of Asian-ancestry students. Within the University of California system, the Berkeley and Los Angeles campuses contain the largest number of students of Asian origins.

The concentration of such students on the campuses located in the San Francisco and Los Angeles metropolitan areas is understandable for two reasons. First, Asian immigrants today tend to have come from urban settings and desire to remain as urban-dwellers. Employment for those who do not speak English well is more readily available in large urban areas. Second, Asian immigrant families are highly conscious of the academic standing and prestige of different colleges and universities. In the old days, foreign students from well-to-do families in Asia favored the Ivy League schools on the East Coast; if they came to study on the West Coast, they chose Berkeley or Stanford. Today, few immigrant families can afford to send their children to private institutions. The University of California, therefore, has become the number one choice of Asian immigrant parents in the state. Their children may sometimes, in fact, prefer to go somewhere else where they think they do not have to work as hard or where some of their high school friends are headed, but episodic evidence suggests that parents place extraordinary pressure on their children who get admitted into Berkeley to enroll there.

It has become something of a cliche to say that Asian-ancestry families are willing to make great sacrifices to secure higher education for their children for "cultural" reasons. It is argued that due to the historical importance accorded the educated elite—who were, indeed, almost synonymous with the ruling class in societies steeped in Confucianism (China, Japan, Korea, and Vietnam)—persons from all socioeconomic levels desired an education. Education and literacy did not always bring wealth and power, but they inevitably conferred status and elicited respect. It is argued that the cultural value placed on education has been so deeply ingrained that no matter where Asian emigrants settle, they carry this cultural baggage with them.

No doubt this cultural legacy is important, but it cannot explain the entire phenomenon. A situational factor also has to be taken into account: being an immigrant, in and of itself, has sociological significance. There are several aspects to this question.

One has to look first at the kind of Asian immigrants who have been coming. They are not a random sample of the overall population of the sending countries. Rather, they are a select group, both in terms of their motivation and the built-in constraints in U.S. immigration laws. During the first decade after the country's gates were reopened, a significant proportion of the immigrants had professional or technical occupational backgrounds. These are persons who care about career mobility and who seek professional environments that will allow them to make the best use of their education. For its part, due to manpower needs the United States has welcomed such professionals because the country gets thousands of highly trained workers per year without having to bear the cost of raising and educating them.

Analytically, contemporary Asian immigrant families can be divided into four groups.[8] The first is families in which the income-earners are from professional backgrounds and who manage to retain their former occupational status after arrival. Parents in such families push their children or younger siblings to seek higher education as a means to *maintain* their families' socioeconomic standing.

The second group consists of families with professional backgrounds and whose breadwinners do not succeed in finding jobs of comparable status after they arrive. Due to their inability to overcome barriers created by the legacy of racial discrimination, the persistence of linguistic discrimination, and the difficulty of meeting American certification standards, these persons have to accept either entry-level jobs in the fields in which they were trained or change occupations (usually to a lower-status line of work) altogether. Parents in such families push their children to achieve academically in order to *compensate* for their downward social mobility.

The third group consists of businessmen and other persons with financial capital. Though these families possessed wealth in their countries of origin, they did not always enjoy high social status. After entering the United States they pressure at least some of their children to attain professional status in order to gather unto the families both wealth and prestige. Higher education is thus a means to *enhance* the overall well-being of such families.

The fourth are immigrants from working-class backgrounds. Their desire to see their children perform exceptionally well is just as strong. For them, the United States retains its image as a land of opportunity. They know that in their countries of origin, higher education is available only to the rich or extraordinarily bright. In America, on the other hand, even mediocre students can gain admission to a tax-supported institution of higher learning. Trans-Pacific migration in search of higher education for their children is one of the few channels available to such families to *attain* upward social mobility for the first time.

If these hypotheses are correct—they remain to be tested empirically—it is not surprising to find that 19.7 percent of Berkeley's undergraduates during fall 1980 were of Asian ancestry even though only 9 percent of the Bay Area's population is Asian or Asian American. Asian-ancestry students have the highest eligibility rate for admittance into the UC system,[9] while the propensity to seek higher education is high *across all socioeconomic levels.*[10] Unless there is a dramatic change in U.S. immigration laws in the near future, the Berkeley and Los Angeles campuses can expect little "abatement" in the number of Asian immigrant students knocking at their doors. The nationality mix will, however, change, as the number of Filipinos and Koreans seeking admission will probably continue to climb. As for Vietnamese students, much will depend on our government's refugee policy.

Asian-Ancestry Undergraduates at Berkeley: A Statistical Profile

In fall 1980, the Berkeley campus had 4,782 undergraduates of Asian and Pacific-Islander ancestry. There were 2,798 Chinese; 933 Japanese; 372 Filipinos; 372 Koreans; 115 Asian Indians;[11] sixty-three individuals born in Iran (a country mistakenly included as part of "Southeast Asia" in UC Berkeley's campus statistics) and in Southeast Asian countries other than Vietnam and the Philippines; and sixteen Pacific Islanders.[12]

Among the different Asian ethnic groups,[13] those of Chinese and Asian Indian ancestry show the most diverse geographic and national origins. Persons of Chinese ancestry—regardless of whether they were born in the United States, Hong Kong, Taiwan, the People's Republic of China, various countries in Southeast Asia, islands in the Pacific, Europe, or Canada—continue to identify themselves as Chinese. The same is true of Asian Indians, who count among their numbers people born in India, Pakistan, Bangladesh, Africa, the Middle East, Europe, Canada, the United States, and various Pacific islands such as Fiji.

Rate of Increase

The different ethnic groups have increased at different rates since 1976, with students of Vietnamese ancestry showing the most dramatic increase since they started from the smallest numerical base. Koreans have increased by 250.9 percent, while Filipinos and Asian Indians show substantial gains at 87.9 percent and 76.9 percent, respectively. Although the growth of Chinese is less dramatic, they increased by the largest absolute number. Japanese-ancestry students showed the smallest rise. Overall, the four-year period saw an increase of 35.3 percent for all the groups taken together. This is equivalent to an annual growth rate of about 8 percent. If we project a similar rate of increase into the future, by fall 1985, there will be approximately seven thousand Asian-ancestry undergraduates at Berkeley. If the total undergraduate population remains more or less constant, then Asian-ancestry students will form about 30 percent of the total undergraduate population by 1985.[14]

American-born versus Foreign-born

The American-born and foreign-born are almost evenly divided, with 52.9 percent having been born in the United States and 47.1 percent abroad. The foreign-born segment has increased rapidly over the last ten years as a result of immigration. It will continue to expand in the future. Unfortunately, it is not possible to calculate precisely the rate of increase of the foreign-born group using official campus statistics because in earlier years large numbers of students failed to put down their place of birth, which makes it impossible to categorize their nativity.

The percentage of American-born is highest among those of Japanese ancestry because immigration from Japan has been low—less than five thousand persons per year compared to approximately twenty-five thousand a year for Chinese and about thirty thousand a year for Koreans as well as for Filipinos. The percentage of American-born among those of Chinese ancestry is 50.5 percent; that for Filipinos is 50.3 percent. This set of statistics is a direct reflection of Asian immigration history. The only three groups of Asians to have come in large numbers before the mid-1960s were the Chinese, Japanese, and Filipinos. That is why these are the only groups with large second-, third-, and even fourth-generation members. In contrast, 86.6 percent of the Korean-ancestry undergraduate population are foreign-born, and 80 percent of the individuals of Asian Indian origin are foreign-born. All of the Vietnamese students enrolled at Berkeley [in 1980] were born in Vietnam.

Citizenship/Visa Status of the Foreign-born

Statistics on the citizenship and visa status of the foreign-born Asian students indicate that the immigrant students and their families have come to settle in the United States. Sixty percent of the Filipino immigrant students have already acquired American citizenship, while 46.4 of the foreign-born Japanese, 38.4 of the Chinese, 27.2 percent of the Asian Indians, and 22 percent of the Koreans have also become U.S. citizens. Only 5.4 percent of Vietnamese undergraduates, however, have done so. It should be noted that these figures do not necessarily reflect any particular group's *propensity* to become citizens. Rather, the data point to the relative recency of a particular group's arrival. That is, since current immigration laws give preference to the entry of close relatives, those groups which had formed communities before 1965 were able to make use of the preferential quota system to bring relatives over as soon as the restriction was lifted. Thus, Chinese and Filipino immigration revived as soon as the new law went into effect, whereas it took Koreans and Asian Indians several years to build up an influx. With the exception of the Japanese, about 90 percent of each group (combining the number of already naturalized U.S. citizens, those with permanent residency status, and the immigrants) are now permanently settled in the United States.

Home Location

Data on the home locations of Berkeley's undergraduates of Asian ancestry show two things. First, Berkeley's Asian-ancestry undergraduates hail predominantly from the nine San Francisco Bay–area counties. While this is true for the undergraduate population as a whole, the concentration of Asian Americans from this region is higher. Bay-area residents range from 56.3 percent among Japanese Americans to 79.3 percent among Filipino Americans. Korean Americans are divided about evenly between the Bay area and Los Angeles, which has the largest Korean population outside of the Republic of

Korea. So it is not surprising that Korean American students from the Los Angeles metropolitan area find their way not only to UCLA but to Berkeley as well. Approximately 90 percent of every Asian-ancestry student group are California residents. What is most impressive, statistically speaking, is the fact that the San Francisco Bay area sends over two thousand Chinese American undergraduates to the Berkeley campus. Historically, San Francisco has been the heart of "Chinese America." Campus statistics indicate that San Francisco continues to, and will continue to, occupy a dominant position as a Chinese American population center.

Second, the home location data corroborate the fact that all the groups have come to settle permanently. With the exception of Asian Indians, the other groups all show that only about 5 percent of their members list an Asian country as their home location. While 11.6 percent of the Chinese, 34.5 percent of the Japanese, and 10.9 percent of Asian Indians are on F-1 or non-immigrant visas, only 5.4 percent of the Chinese and 8.7 percent of Asian Indians list an Asian country as their home location. The discrepancy between the two sets of figures can be interpreted in one of two ways. Either those on non-immigrant visas hope to find ways to remain in the United States and thus have mentally already adopted California as their "home," or it could mean they interpret "home" to be whatever place they are living in at the moment. The high percentage of stateless persons among Vietnamese undergraduates is directly related to their refugee status.

The permanent-settler status of these students means they *are* Americans or are fast becoming Americans. They *have* to learn to function in American society. Whatever problems they encounter, or whatever problems their presence creates, are not going to go away. The issue that such a fact raises is, To what extent is it the responsibility of the University of California to help such students adjust academically and socially to the American environment so that they can become productive members of their adopted country? What does, or what should, higher education mean to these students?

Academic Characteristics

Students of Asian ancestry show some peculiar academic characteristics. It is a well-known fact that they are "good" students. At least, the ones who have made it into the institutions of higher learning have been good students. They have high grade point averages and the highest retention rate of any group within the UC system. Yet these students do suffer academic handicaps. The most pronounced one is their limited proficiency in English. This is especially true of recent arrivals. Their lack of verbal facility may be an important factor that limits the range of subjects they major in. It may also limit the number, as well as the kind, of elective courses they take.

In terms of the distribution of Scholastic Aptitude Test (SAT) verbal and math scores of Berkeley's Asian-ancestry undergraduates, overall those who are American-born tend to be slightly "better" students than their white peers. Their SAT verbal scores hover around the same median as those of white undergraduates, while their SAT math scores are higher than those of their white counterparts. These scores reinforce the stereotype that Asian students are good in math. Among the American-born, 20 percent of the Chinese, 21.1 percent of the Japanese, 24.3 percent of the Koreans, and 33.3 percent of the Asian Indians have math scores above 700. If we look at the percentage who scored 600 or higher in the math test, then 61.4 percent of the Chinese, 62.5 percent of the Japanese, 67.5 percent of the Koreans, and 61.1 percent of Asian Indians are included. Filipino American students appear to be the only group among the American-born whose members do not seem to be "mathematical geniuses"; only 4.4 percent of them scored 700 or above in their math test.

The SAT math scores are even higher among the foreign-born. Math scores of those who have acquired naturalized citizenship and therefore have been in the United States for at least five years are roughly comparable to those of the American-born. Those who have been in this country for a shorter period of time—the permanent residents and immigrants—do almost uniformly better. Among Chinese undergraduates born in Hong Kong, 63.6 percent of permanent residents, 68 percent of immigrants, and 79.4 percent of those on non-immigrant visas scored 600 and above. Among Chinese born in Taiwan, the respective percentages are 87.2, 75.5, and 90. Students born in the People's Republic of China did less well on their math test, however, probably because of the general breakdown of the educational system in China during the Great Proletarian Cultural Revolution (1966–76). Moreover, they probably did not receive any compensatory education after they left the Chinese mainland. The math scores of Chinese-ancestry undergraduates born in various Southeast Asian countries and elsewhere in the world are not as spectacular, either. Only 55.9 percent of those who have acquired citizenship, 47.2 percent of the permanent residents, and 36.4 percent of the immigrants scored 600 and above. Students who received at least a part of their education in Taiwan did best in their math aptitude test.

Koreans and Vietnamese also did very well in their math SAT. Among Koreans, 51.5 percent of those who have acquired citizenship, 68.8 percent of permanent residents, and 73.2 percent of immigrants scored above 600. One hundred percent of the Vietnamese undergraduates who have become citizens, 75.1 percent of the permanent residents, 39.3 percent of the immigrants, and 72.7 percent of the refugees scored above 600.

If we look at the verbal scores of these students, a mirror image emerges. There is direct correlation between the length of residence in the United States and how well students did. The American-born among all the groups had a median verbal score in the low 500s. Taking all the ethnic groups together, the percentage of American-born who scored between 400 and 600 ranges from 50 to 70 percent. In contrast, the foreign-born did dismally in their verbal test. Among the Chinese born in Hong Kong, 5.7 percent of those who have acquired citizenship, 28.8 percent of permanent residents, and 27.8 percent of immigrants scored *below* 300. Chinese undergraduates born in Taiwan had even more trouble in their verbal test; 11.8 percent of the naturalized citizens, 27.9 percent of permanent residents, and 33.3 percent of immigrants scored below 300. Those born in the People's Republic of China did least well of all; 11.1 percent of those who have acquired citizenship, 41.9 percent of the permanent residents, and 25 percent of the immigrants scored below 300. Ethnic Chinese undergraduates who had been born in Southeast Asia and elsewhere show a similar pattern; 2.9 percent of the naturalized citizens, 11.1 percent of the permanent residents, and 36.4 percent of the immigrants scored below 300.

The lack of verbal facility is even more pronounced among the undergraduates of Korean and Vietnamese origins. For Koreans scoring below 300 on their verbal test, the respective percentages for naturalized citizens, permanent residents, and immigrants are 17.8, 42, and 58.5. Among the Vietnamese, the respective percentages are 25, 50, and 25. In contrast, only six of the foreign-born Filipinos and a lone Asian Indian scored less than 300. English is used as a medium of instruction and daily communication in the Philippines and in most parts of India, so these two groups of students do not suffer from the same linguistic handicap as the Chinese, Koreans, and Vietnamese do. If we take the 200–399 range, then a shockingly large percentage of the foreign-born among the Chinese, Koreans, and Vietnamese are barely functional in the English language; 60 to 80 percent of students from these three ethnic groups scored below 400 in their SAT verbal test.

It should be pointed out, however, that high achievement in quantitative subjects, along with poor verbal skills, is *not* an inherent, ethnically linked "Asian" characteristic. The test scores of the American-born students of Asian ancestry attest to this fact; the distribution of their scores is quite "normal." The reason that foreign-born Asian students at Berkeley and elsewhere show an inverse set of math versus verbal scores has to do with the way that admissions criteria are set. Since a *combined* SAT math and verbal test score is used to determine admission, those who do poorly in their verbal test *must* obtain extraordinarily high math scores to balance out their overall score. Asian-ancestry high-school students who scored poorly in English and not so well in math do not make it into the UC system.

Asian-ancestry students also differ from their white, black, and Spanish-speaking peers in the distribution of their majors. The different engineering departments draw the largest percentage of Asian-ancestry undergraduates. While approximately 10 percent of the non-Asian undergraduates are in engineering, 17 percent of the American-born Asian students are in engineering, while among some groups as high as 40 percent of the foreign-born are aspiring engineers. The concentration in engineering is least pronounced among Japanese Americans (the group with the largest percentage of American-born) and among Filipino Americans (the group with the lowest math scores).

The natural sciences also draw a large concentration of Asian-ancestry undergraduates. Here, there is a divergence between the American-born and the foreign-born, with the former favoring the biological sciences and the latter clustering in the physical sciences. As in engineering, the proficiency of the foreign-born in math proves useful in quantitative-oriented fields. In fact, the divergence between the biological and physical sciences can be used to underscore the argument that the students' choice of majors *is* influenced by verbal ability. The medical professions probably have the highest status of all, and many Asian-ancestry biology majors are aspiring doctors, dentists, or other health professionals. But the fact that the biological sciences require somewhat greater verbal skills than do the physical sciences means that the foreign-born Asians are less able to excel in the former than in the latter fields.

In contrast, among non-Asian undergraduates at Berkeley, 30 percent are majoring in the social sciences compared to only 16 percent among the American-born Asians and only 10 percent of the foreign-born ones. The only two exceptions are students of Filipino and Korean ancestry, many of whom are probably aspiring law students. Law is a highly regarded profession in the Philippines—a country with an overabundance of lawyers. Among Western-educated Koreans, political science is a favorite field, especially for males. A very large percentage of Korean-ancestry professors with full-time appointments in American colleges and universities teach political science.

There are hardly any Asian-ancestry students in the humanities, whereas almost 16 percent of Berkeley's non-Asian undergraduates major in one of the humanities. Among American-born Asians, only 6 percent are humanities majors; among the foreign-born, only 3 percent are so declared. Many among this minuscule number are majoring in a foreign language—mainly an Asian language or French.

Why Are There So Many Asian-ancestry Engineers and Scientists?

While poor verbal communication skills restrict the choice of majors among Asian-ancestry undergraduates, I do not believe this is the only factor responsible for their career choices. I would like to argue that there are at least three other sets of reasons that must be considered.

Historical Factors

Two kinds of historical factors come to mind. One has to do with the modern history of various Asian countries. While it is true that studies of occupational status around the world indicate that certain professions such as medicine, law, and engineering receive uniformly high rankings across all societies and cultures, these modern scientific and technological fields have a special status in Asian countries because of the history of European colonialism and its impact on Asia. The loss or partial loss of sovereignty, power, and prestige that many Asian countries suffered during the height of European colonialism was a source of profound distress to many political leaders and intellectuals in those countries. Some of modern Asia's most prominent leaders and intellectuals saw science and technology as the basis for the economic, political, and military superiority of the West. As part of a movement to "strengthen" and "modernize" their nations, they sent some of their brightest young people to Europe and the United States to study science and engineering. The view that science and technology represent "modernity" has persisted. Coupled with this is the fairly widespread concomitant belief that Western civilization is inferior to Asian ones in terms of moral and humanistic concerns. More important, many Asian immigrant parents think the creative arts are synonymous with a degenerate life-style. They do not understand that most humanities majors do not become writers and artists living Bohemian lives. Their fear that their children will become hippies is so great that they would do anything to prevent such an eventuality.

A second set of historical circumstances is related to how Asian immigrants have been treated in the United States. Until World War II, with few exceptions, many managed to earn a living only as laborers or servants. One of the very few sources of upward mobility was small-scale entrepreneurship. Restaurants, laundries, grocery stores, and curio shops are prime examples of Asian-immigrant small-scale enterprises. Few of the second-generation Asian Americans who received college degrees were able to find employment in the fields in which they had been trained in the 1920s, 1930s, and early 1940s.[15] However, after the United States entered World War II, Asian American engineers, scientists, and technicians found employment in their fields for the first time because the country experienced a shortage of manpower, especially in defense-related industries. They performed so well that they broke down many of the discriminatory barriers that had hitherto existed and made it possible for those who came after them to find work in these areas. In the late 1940s, as the Nationalist regime fell in China, many Chinese students studying in the United States applied for and were granted political asylum. In the 1950s, U.S. legislation on refugees enabled tens of thousands of Chinese to enter. These individuals were extremely well-trained, and many came from high socioeconomic backgrounds. They swelled the number of Asian-ancestry technical personnel in American industries and higher education. The belief that Asians are competent in engineering and the physical sciences became a "tradition" after the 1950s. Today, students go into these fields because they believe that employers in these sectors of the economy are more willing than those elsewhere to hire them. It appears they are right.

Economic Factors

Immigrant families usually are driven to earn a good living. Parents want their children to work in what they consider to be "desirable" professions as soon as possible. Education is seen in highly pragmatic terms. An undergraduate degree in computer science or engineering or business administration is much more marketable than one in art history or comparative literature or sociology. Market forces are making undergraduates of all ethnic origins across the nation more job-oriented than students graduating a decade ago. Asian-ancestry undergraduates merely show a greater awareness of this fact than their non-Asian peers.

A related consideration is that many Asian immigrant families are unfamiliar with the American concept of a liberal arts education. Rather, many know the British or European model of higher education, which involves direct entry from secondary school to formal professional training. Although the American system of higher education is a two-tiered one, with the undergraduate years designated for a general education while reserving graduate or professional school for formal professional training, Asian immigrant parents and their progeny *de facto* treat American higher education as a single-tiered system. They pressure their progeny to choose those majors that provide job-related training and certification with a bachelor's degree. Certainly, many do go on to graduate school; nonetheless, they still tend to choose majors that lead directly to careers that will pay well without further study.

Psychological Factors

Because Asian-ancestry students experience so much pressure to do well academically, there is a natural tendency for them to major in fields in which they believe they *can* do well. The lack of communication skills, it can be argued, generates a sense of powerlessness in social situations. To compensate for such feelings of inadequacy, they may choose to study subjects that allow them to compete effectively in order to acquire a sense of potency. When someone has to adjust to life in a society and culture in which he or she is not completely accepted, or in which he or she has to excel constantly to prove his or her worth, then comfort may be found in that person's ability to manipulate and control the physical world as a means to compensate for the inability to deal effectively with the social world.

After one completes one's schooling, one's professional career can become the focus of one's identity. That is to say it becomes possible to think of oneself as a physicist or an engineer first and as a Chinese or Korean second. This tendency need not be seen as a form of self-denigration because individuals are defined in relationship to others. If others with whom one interacts esteem one's professional standing more than one's ethnic identity, then it seems wise to present oneself in the most readily acceptable mode of social interaction.

Years ago, C. P. Snow argued that culture can be as significantly defined by the ethos of one's occupational calling as by linguistic, artistic, or social measures based on ethnicity. The cultural world of the scientist differs from the cultural world of the humanist. Given linguistic barriers and other problems arising from cultural/ethnic differences, it can be argued that Asian immigrants with professional training find it easier to gain entry into the cultural world of science than into the cultural world of the humanities. By becoming scientists, they place themselves into a social stratification system based more on merit related to technical competence than on the ability to deal with human relationships in settings informed by values and norms that may be alien. Had the United States not had a history of racial discrimination, such forces may not have come into play. The fact of the matter is that residual manifestations of racial discrimination do remain. Asian immigrants and even the American-born therefore continue to use professional status as a means to overcome racial inequality in America.

Notes

1. The 1882 Chinese Exclusion Act prohibited the immigration of laborers for ten years. Acts passed in 1884, 1888, 1892, 1902, and 1904 tightened the restrictions on the entry of even those who were technically exempt from exclusion. In 1907 a so-called gentlemen's agreement between the United States and Japan ended the immigration of Japanese laborers. The 1924 Immigration Act, which was directed mainly against aspiring immigrants from Eastern, Central, and Southern Europe and which did not name the Japanese explicitly, nevertheless ended Japanese immigration altogether. The 1917 Barred Zones Act prohibited the entry of people from India, while the 1934 Tydings-McDuffie Act contained a clause that reduced the number of Filipino entrants to fifty a year. As a token gesture, the U.S. Congress rescinded Chinese exclusion in 1943, when an annual quota of 105 persons of Chinese ancestry, regardless of their nativity or citizenship, was allotted. In 1946 the exclusion of Filipinos and Asian Indians was lifted, but the restriction against Japanese and Koreans did not end until 1952. For all these groups, however, the number allowed entry each year was less than two hundred. It was not until 1965 that "national origins" ceased to be used as the basis for setting immigration quotas.

2. The Select Committee on Immigration and Refugee Policy recommended certain changes in the preference quota system that will lump visa applications into two broad categories: a) those wishing to immigrate here for the purpose of family reunification; and b) persons who are independent immigrants. [Ten years would pass, however, before these recommendations became law in the 1990 Immigration Act.]

3. The labor certification requirement allows the United States to peg the kind of immigrants admitted to economic and manpower needs in the United States. There is, of course, a time lag between changes in economic conditions in the United States and changes in the type of individuals admitted.

4. As of January 1, 1981, there were 380,191 active visa applicants from Mexico and 21,060 active visa applicants from Cuba. These numbers do not include refugees or undocumented entrants.

5. California is followed by Hawaii, with 583,660, and New York, with 310,531 officially counted persons of self-declared Asian ethnicity. *Los Angeles Times,* July 27, 1981, pt. 1 p. 4.

6. Ibid.

7. U.S. Bureau of the Census flyer, June 1981.

8. In this section I am referring to immigrants who come as members of whole families; I am not talking about individuals who come to join existing families.

9. In a study of the high school graduating class of 1975, it was found that Asian-ancestry students (not counting Filipinos) have a UC-eligibility rate of 39 percent compared to a white rate of 16.5, a Filipino rate of 6.6, a black rate of 5, and a Chicano rate of 4.7. University of California Systemwide Administration, Office of Outreach Services, *Beyond High School Graduation: Who Goes to College?* Berkeley, May 1978, p. 17.

10. This hypothesis differs from the assumption made by the authors of the *University of California, Berkeley, Long-Range Academic Plan Statement, 1980–1985* regarding the college participation rate of Asian-ancestry students. Commenting on the high rate of college participation, the study stated, "It assumes that the college participation rate for

Asian high school graduates will continue at its present extremely high level (about three times that for Anglo). This is dubious. That rate reflects the college attendance propensity of [the] existing Asian high school population which are [*sic*] predominantly native Californian in origin. There are indications that the sharp increase in [the] grade school Asian population now taking place is a result of a large influx of immigrants. If this is the case, the Asian college participation rate *may begin to fall* when this group reaches the high school senior class" (Appendix G, p. 2, emphasis added).

For reasons outlined in this paper, I am arguing that the propensity to seek higher education among Asian immigrants is not only as high as, but may be higher than, that shown by American-born Asians. It will be difficult to determine which hypothesis is more accurate because admissions criteria and economic conditions may change in coming years, and these, along with other factors, may interact with the propensity to attend college to determine the actual number of Asian immigrant students who will enroll at University of California campuses.

11. Formerly the term *East Indian* was used for persons from the Indian subcontinent. This was a misnomer. In European colonial history the "East Indies" referred to the British and Dutch East Indies (Malaysia, Singapore, and Indonesia) and *not* to the Indian subcontinent. In the 1980 census the term *Asian Indian* was adopted following the successful petition by the Association of Indians in America for this new term.

12. Iranians, miscellaneous Southeast Asians, and Pacific Islanders will not be included in my discussion because their small numbers are statistically insignificant, although, obviously, such individuals are important in human terms.

13. Ethnicity and national origins do not always coincide. Official campus statistics employ ethnicity as a variable; I have tried to refine this by also using nativity as a variable. Unfortunately for those students who have not yet acquired U.S. citizenship, no data are available on their citizenship.

14. This projection is a ceteris paribus assumption. Some of the remarks in note 10 about eligibility rates also apply here.

15. For a detailed study of employment problems faced by second-generation Japanese Americans, many of whom were college graduates before World War II, see Edward K. Strong, *The Second-Generation Japanese Problem* (Stanford: Stanford University Press, 1934).

Appendix: A Comparison of Asian-ancestry Undergraduates at the Berkeley and UCLA Campuses

Within the University of California system, the Los Angeles campus has the second-largest number of Asian-ancestry undergraduates. In fall 1980, while Berkeley enrolled almost five thousand such students, UCLA had almost four thousand. The ethnic mix is somewhat different at UCLA, however. Approximately a third at the southern campus are of Chinese ancestry, while another third are of Japanese origin. The two campuses have about the same number of Filipinos, while the number of Koreans and Vietnamese is greater at UCLA.

The difference in the ethnic mix on the two campuses reflects the ethnic composition of the two regions from which they draw the bulk of students. Los Angeles has never attracted as large a Chinese-ancestry population as has San Francisco. On the other hand, since the 1920s Los Angeles has been home to the largest Japanese American community in the United States. In more recent times it has also drawn the largest number of Koreans, while neighboring Orange County has become home to the largest group of Indochinese refugees in the United States.

Being a large metropolitan area with more employment opportunities, Los Angeles has further attracted a larger percentage of recent immigrants. This fact shows up in the nativity of the Asian-ancestry undergraduates at UCLA. Due to a change in the data collection form, new students entering UCLA after fall 1980 did not have to declare their place of birth, so we have no data for freshmen. Among the Asian-ancestry sophomores, juniors, and seniors, 51.6 percent are foreign-born. If entering freshmen could have been included, no doubt an even higher percentage would have been shown to be foreign-born.

The proclivity of Asian-ancestry undergraduates to major in engineering is less obvious at UCLA than at Berkeley. At UCLA there is a greater concentration in biological sciences, perhaps because there is a medical school on that campus. There is also a larger percentage of UCLA Asian-ancestry undergraduates in the physical sciences than at Berkeley. In fact, if we aggregate engineering and the physical sciences the proportion of students in these quantitatively oriented fields are about the same on the two campuses. Among the American-born and those who have become naturalized citizens, a slightly greater percentage of the UCLA students major in the humanities.

In terms of SAT scores, Asian-ancestry undergraduates at UCLA have, across the board, lower scores on both the verbal and math tests than their counterparts at Berkeley. The differential is especially noticeable at the high end of the math scores. Among some groups, 30 percent fewer of the UCLA students scored above 600 in their math test. The pattern of lower SAT verbal scores shown by Berkeley students is even more pronounced among UCLA students. While almost half of the foreign-born Chinese students at Berkeley received less than 400 in their verbal test, the comparable figure at UCLA is 60 percent. Of the Korean-ancestry students at UCLA, three-quarters scored below 400. Almost 70 percent of the Vietnamese students had scores lower than 400 in the verbal test.

Correlations between SAT scores and cumulative GPAs were computed using the UCLA data. There is a greater correlation between high verbal scores and high cumulative grade point averages than between high math scores and high cumulative GPAs. Only slightly over a quarter of those students with math test scores above 700 are A- to A students, whereas more than half of those with verbal test scores above 700 are A- or A students. SAT scores between 400 and 600 have little predictive value. Most of the students in this middle range are C to B students.

If the demographic trend of the past decade continues it is likely that the absolute number of Asian-ancestry students at UCLA will soon surpass that at Berkeley. The challenges facing UCLA in the years to come will be great indeed.

9 An Integrated Approach to Teaching Verbal Skills to Limited English Proficiency (LEP) Students [1981]

This essay was presented as a position paper at the Conference on Semester Conversion and the Lower-division Experience at UC Berkeley in 1981. In the late 1960s, campuses of the UC system changed from a two-semester to a three-quarter academic year, with summer session counting as a fourth quarter. Each quarter consisted of ten weeks of instruction plus a week for final examinations. The aim was to make fuller use of the university's facilities on a year-round basis. Many faculty members disliked the change because they had to redesign all their courses, either by deleting large chunks of material or somehow cramming in as much as they did under the semester system. Students, however, loved the quarter system, but the reasons they gave for doing so did not flatter the faculty. As one of my former students put it, "Yeah, we love the quarter system 'cuz if a class is boring or the professor is a windbag, at least we can get the course over with in ten weeks."

In 1981 a Berkeley administrator who strongly favored a return to the semester system formed a committee and asked it to convene a conference on semester conversion and the lower-division experience. What the committee hoped would happen was that strong academic arguments in favor of returning to a semester system would emerge from the dozens of position papers that faculty were asked to submit. I responded to the call for papers by proposing an alternative approach for improving the verbal skills of limited English proficiency (LEP) students than those being used at the time.

I thought my ideas, which came from reading a great deal of the social linguistics literature, had merit, although several faculty members in English as a second language (ESL) reacted angrily to my proposal. Not only was I infringing on their turf, but I was also indirectly questioning their teaching methods. I purposely used the word freaks *to signal that I knew how some people viewed Asian immigrant students.*

Nothing came of the discussions on English-language teaching methods because, in the end, the goal of enhancing the educational experience of lower-division students was less important than building support for the calender change. The campus did return to a semester system—the only UC campus to do so. The following is included because it shows how far an Asian American studies faculty member like me had to move from my graduate training in order to defend the educational rights of Asian-ancestry students.

* * *

The Changing "ESL" Student Population[1]

A decade or so ago most of the students enrolled in English-as-a-Second-Language (ESL) classes were foreign students who had come to the United States for higher education. U.S. immigration laws required them to return to their home countries after they had completed their studies or, in some cases, after they had received a number of years of practical training in their fields. To be sure, there were also some immigrants on campus whose mother tongue was not English and who required help to improve their English verbal skills, but these immigrant students were mainly of European origin and their number was relatively small.

Since the late 1960s, as a result of changes in U.S. immigration laws there has been a steady increase in the number of Asian immigrants. Children from these immigrant families are now enrolling in increasing numbers in institutions of higher learning. Their presence is especially noticeable in colleges and universities in California and in major metropolitan areas around the nation. In fall 1980, almost 20 percent of the undergraduates at the University of California, Berkeley, and almost 17 percent of the undergraduates at UCLA were foreign-born, and between three-fifths and three-quarters of them have been in the United States for less than five years. Today, a majority of students who enroll in ESL classes are no longer foreign students who will return home after their studies but are immigrant and refugee students who will settle permanently in this country.

The sociological distinction between a foreign student and an immigrant student is crucial. The latter, having come to live permanently in the United States, needs to become proficient in English not only to perform well academically but also to become a productive member of American society. For educators like myself who believe that one of the true strengths of American society is its multiethnic, multicultural, and, one hopes, multilingual population, finding ways to improve the immigrant students' English proficiency while *simultaneously* helping maintain their cultural integrity and proficiency in their mother tongues becomes a true pedagogical challenge.

Factors Contributing to the Immigrant Student's Limited English Proficiency

For the purpose of this discussion, "English proficiency" refers to the ability to read, write, and communicate orally in English *for the purpose of academic discourse.* I am concerned primarily with a student's ability to read college-level texts and to write college-level expository essays, reports, and research papers, not with his or her ability to chat with friends or family members outside the classroom. Second, I am concerned about a student's ability to relate meaningfully to his/her professors, teaching assistants, tutors, counselors, and staff members in the process of getting an education.

As I see it, based on my teaching experience there are six analytically distinct although sociologically and pedagogically related factors that contribute to a student's limited oral and written communication skills. They are:

1. an inadequate knowledge of English grammar, vocabulary, and modes of rhetorical organization;
2. an insufficient mastery of college-level study skills;
3. a lack of practice in particular styles of verbal and nonverbal communication specific to college-educated Americans;
4. a lack of familiarity with some commonly assumed "basic knowledge" of American history and contemporary society;
5. a lack of acquaintance with the organization of knowledge in American liberal arts colleges, whether these colleges exist independently or within larger research universities; and
6. the persistence of linguistic "racism," which manifests itself in subtle forms of discrimination against those who do not speak English well.

Factor 1 is unique to students whose mother tongue is not English; factor 4 is applicable to all foreign or immigrant students; factor 6 is experienced by "language minorities," particularly those who are nonwhite; while factors 2, 3, and 5 are becoming increasingly applicable to undergraduates in general. Therefore, the limited-English-proficiency (LEP) student's situation is just a special manifestation of a much larger problem—the declining level of basic skills found in high school graduates who are admissible to college. The LEP student differs only in that he/she is not a native speaker of English and does not know certain things about American society.

LEP students are not freaks to be kept out of the UC system lest their presence leads to a lowering of traditional "academic standards." Neither will isolating LEP students in ESL classes or tutorial sessions in Student Learning Centers solve the problem. The fundamental fact that administrators, faculty members, and providers of student services must recognize is that LEP students who make it into the UC system are exceptionally good students. We shall never see those students whose verbal skills are so poor that they cannot get into the UC system. Those we *do* see and will encounter in increasing numbers in our classrooms are students who have compensated for their "language handicap" by high scores in quantitative tests or high GPAs.

It is *not* an inherently Asian, ethnically linked characteristic for Asian-ancestry students to possess poor verbal skills along with excellent quantitative skills. Rather, the abnormal distribution of SAT scores among Asian immigrant students is a *direct result* of the way admissions criteria are implemented in the UC system. That is to say, because a *combined* or average SAT score is used, the only way that students with low SAT verbal scores, or low English Achievement Test scores, or poor grades in high school English courses become regularly admissible is to compensate for, or average out, their low verbal scores with high scores in nonverbally dependent subjects. These students have well-developed cognitive skills. If their reading and writing levels at the time they are admitted are inadequate for college-level academic work it will not take several years of "remedial" language instruction for them to catch up to the expected level of verbal competence if faculty members will encourage them to use their intelligence to get over the hurdle.

The Number of LEP Undergraduates at UC Berkeley and Why We Should Help Them

A majority of the LEP undergraduates at Berkeley are of Asian ancestry. In the foreseeable future, Asian immigrants will continue to form the bulk of LEP students. Therefore, projections based on data pertaining to Asian-ancestry students will tell us a great deal of what we need to know.

In the last five years Asian-ancestry students have increased at the rate of approximately 8 percent a year, using data for 1976 as the base year. If the same rate of increase continues, and if the overall undergraduate population at Berkeley remains stable, then by 1985 it is likely that 30 percent of the total undergraduate population will be Asian. More than half of this population will be foreign-born. About three-quarters of the foreign-born will be recent immigrants who have been in the United States for less than five years. Among the recent immigrants, some 60 percent will probably have limited English proficiency at the time they are admitted.

To put it another way, today, in 1981, there are probably slightly over a thousand LEP undergraduates at Berkeley.[2] By 1985 there will be 1,500 to 1,700 of them. A great majority of these LEP students, however, will be regularly admissible students, not special-action students, because their overall academic records will be good.

At present, given the wide leeway that undergraduates have in choosing their majors and satisfying graduation requirements, the LEP students *will* have high retention rates and good overall academic achievement. Many will even graduate with honors in the "difficult" majors. Why, then, worry about them? After all, the needs of the truly educationally disadvantaged students are more urgent.

I think what is at issue here is something more fundamental than persistence and retention rates or GPAs. As supporters of a liberal education we should be concerned about whether all students will graduate as well-rounded individuals or simply as well-trained technicians. The bottom line is this, Do we want to do something to prevent the erosion of the foundations of a liberal arts education?

In recent years undergraduates in general seem inclined to enroll in majors that give them direct, job-related training and certification. Asian-ancestry immigrant students, in particular, tend to major in engineering, computer science, the physical and biological sciences, and business administration. The Asian-ancestry students did not create this proclivity towards professional training; they merely exacerbate a nationwide trend. Fewer and fewer undergraduates seem to see the value of a liberal arts education. The philosophical foundations of such an education are peculiarly nineteenth-century and early-twentieth-century American. They inhere in the belief that individuals with a well-rounded education form the requisite "base" for a democratic society. Perhaps what today's undergraduates perceive is that in our post-industrial age there is little room left for individual autonomy. That is to say, the ideal of educating individuals who can think independently and communicate effectively is precisely just that: an ideal. What seems more important to today's college graduates is the acquisition of marketable skills. LEP students from immigrant families probably feel the pressure to acquire marketable skills even more urgently. Do we want to dissuade them from this tendency?

Pedagogical and Organizational Implications

The increasing size of the LEP undergraduate population has widespread implications. Those who do not wish to deal with this issue on campus will argue either that we should change admissions requirements to keep them out or relegate "remedial" instruction to high schools or summer programs. A second approach would be to beef up those units that already deal with LEP students by giving them more resources. Yet another approach is possible, and it is one I am advocating. This third way has a number of premises:

1. In general, LEP students are good students with well-developed cognitive skills; what they lack is a *conglomerate* of skills that go beyond remedial language instruction.

2. If we accept premise 1, it follows that it is a waste of teaching resources, as well as a waste of the LEP students' time, to teach them the English language in a vacuum. What is needed is an integrated approach that will simultaneously teach English grammar and vocabulary, college-level study skills, academic styles of discourse and rhetorical organization, a basic knowledge of American society—particularly the organization of its educational system—and ways to cope with linguistic discrimination.

3. No single instructor can handle the multifaceted pedagogical challenges that LEP students pose. Moreover, there is very little pre-packaged curricular material suitable for the purpose at hand. Therefore, teamwork is required. New curricular materials must be developed.

4. Ladder-rank faculty members—especially those with experience in teaching the large introductory lecture courses in their departments—must play a key role in developing new curricular packages and integrated teaching methods. There seems to be a growing trend on some campuses for a division of labor in the academic enterprise. Ladder-rank faculty do research and give lectures; part-time faculty and teaching assistants teach the introductory courses, grade papers, and lead discussion sections; and tutors and counselors in student learning centers aid students with their homework and teach them study skills. This division of labor would make sense if there were constant communication and feedback among the different kinds of teaching personnel. Unfortunately, such does not always seem to be the case. It has been said that if what students need are reading and writing skills, ladder-rank faculty who are experts in their fields in terms of substantive content cannot be expected to teach reading and writing. Yet if the faculty members themselves cannot determine and define what *kinds* and what *level* of logical thinking and analysis are acceptable in their own areas of expertise, who can? If faculty members are able only to tell students what we consider to be a good piece of work without being able to explain *why* it is good or are unable to instruct students on *how* to produce something of comparable quality, then we fail as teachers. There is no reason that we cannot become more *explicitly conscious* of what we expect of our students.

5. Faculty involvement in this effort should be considered a legitimate *research* activity and not simply an aspect of teaching. We are conducting research into the teaching and learning process as it applies to a special group of stu-

dents with clearly definable characteristics. The work involved is *not* remedial and is worthy of the attention and effort of the best researchers. Financial support for such applied research will yield dividends that are immediately applicable to the solution of one of the major dilemmas facing the Berkeley campus in the 1980s.

Implementation

To implement the integrated approach advocated here we shall need a team of ten to twelve faculty members to design, select, and write a curricular package for lower-division LEP students, as well as a new or modified course series in which the curricular materials will be used. Faculty members can be selected from impacted departments experiencing increases in LEP students and from academic units employing personnel with some experience in working with LEP students. For example, the following faculty/staff team might be assembled:

> three or four faculty members teaching lower-division courses in engineering and the natural sciences;
> three or four faculty members teaching lower-division courses in the humanities and social sciences; and
> one faculty/staff member each from ESL, Subject A, English 1A–1B, Asian American Studies 6A-B-C, and the Student Learning Center.

The course series to be created will be a one-year sequence that will fulfill certain breadth requirements while inculcating verbal skills that enable students to fulfill the Subject A and English 1A–1B requirements. The topics to be covered will be divided evenly among the humanities, the social sciences, and the natural sciences. Students will learn how to think, read, write, and communicate orally in the expository modes required (in general) in each division of knowledge. Students will be made to understand that the course series is a package and they must make a commitment from the beginning to complete the whole sequence. LEP students will receive differential hours of instruction in English grammar and vocabulary-building, depending on their initial level of competence. At the end of the year, however, all the students who have completed the sequence will have been brought up to more or less the same level of linguistic competence. (There will, of course, still be differences, which will show up in the grades they receive.) The faculty team will carry out the following tasks:

1. They will determine, through consultation with their colleagues, the expected or acceptable level of verbal competence among lower-division students in various disciplines.

2. They will anthologize three packages of readings: one in the humanities, one in the social sciences, and one in the natural sciences. These packages can be organized either thematically or as general introductions to the divisions of knowledge or as examples of academic discourse in particular disciplines. Selections may be from published materials or be written especially for the packages.
3. They will prepare questions, exercises in grammar, synopsis, vocabulary-building, and analytical thinking for each reading.
4. They will devise teaching methods most suitable for LEP students, such as teaching them how to monitor and self-edit their own work.
5. They will pilot-teach the materials to a selected group of LEP students.
6. They will monitor the performance of members of the pilot group throughout their undergraduate career and carry out a continuous process of evaluation.

Conclusion

The proposed project can serve as a vehicle through which the value of a liberal arts education can be demonstrated. Students can learn basic skills that are applicable across many disciplines, many professions. By offering the proposed course sequence to freshmen, the hope is that LEP students, who may need help the most when they first enter college, will receive the kind of help that will prove useful beyond their freshman year. Moreover, they will get a more systematic understanding of the structure of knowledge in American universities, which will help them understand why we have breadth or general education requirements. A more careful *sequencing* of courses instead of the current laissez-faire approach will provide these students—indeed, all students—with a firmer foundation upon which to build coherently designed courses of study. The intensive inculcation of verbal skills will give at least some of these LEP students greater confidence to explore more diverse majors and future careers. We can hope that they will find the courage to take more risks instead of finding shelter only in fields in which they are certain they will do well.

I believe there will be faculty members who would like to participate in this experiment if a) some of us are given release time to develop the curricular materials; b) there is financial support for the project; and c) the products of our efforts are accorded the same esteem as the products of "real" research projects. There are faculty who care about students and enjoy teaching. All that needs to be changed is a slight reordering of priorities in the reward system!

Notes

1. In this paper, the term *limited English proficiency* will be used in place of the term *English as a second language*. LEP describes an objective characteristic of the student, whereas ESL connotes an entire pedagogical approach—a field with its own educational philosophy, teaching and research methods, curricular materials, and body of literature. The premise of this paper is that ESL is *one of several* approaches that can be used to deal with the learning situation faced by LEP students. Therefore, the two terms are not synonymous. ESL is not the only method available to improve the English verbal skills of nonnative speakers.

2. This estimate is arrived at by counting the number of Asian-ancestry undergraduates at Berkeley in fall 1980 who scored below 400 in their SAT verbal test. There is no magic to the cutoff score of 400: it is used only as a very rough measure of the approximate size of Berkeley's LEP undergraduate population. If we add non-Asian LEP students, the number is, of course, larger than one thousand.

10 They *Shall* Write! Anthropological Observations on Teaching Verbal Skills to Asian-Ancestry Students [1982]

I wrote this essay to record what happened in a composition course I taught during the 1981–82 academic year. I characterize what I did as "anthropological" because I was a participant-observer engaged in an ethnographic exercise. I never published the essay, but I did circulate it among a handful of colleagues. Some people who read the paper said, "Oh, what you did was too labor-intensive! We can't afford to adopt the approach you used in a huge campus such as ours." They were right. A faculty-student ratio of one faculty member and two teaching assistants (T.A.s) to only thirty-four students (as was the case in this class) was indeed out of line. Administrators concerned with budgetary matters would never have consented to this kind of labor-intensive teaching in a large public research university.

But the main reason I gave up lobbying on behalf of LEP students was that I was up against the clock in terms of my tenure review. I had already postponed the review from my sixth year as a UC faculty member (the normal time-table) to the seventh. I could not take a year off to complete the book that I planned to submit for my tenure review because the Asian American Studies Program at UC Berkeley had only five ladder-rank faculty at the time, which meant I had to continue teaching while my colleagues Elaine Kim and Ling-chi Wang (whose "tenure clocks" ran ahead of mine) took leaves, in turn, to complete their book manuscripts. When I still had not finished writing This Bittersweet Soil *by my seventh year, I postponed the review again to my eighth—the last possible date before my contract would be terminated once and for all. Because Elaine Kim and Ling-chi Wang had received tenure by then and our senior colleague, Ronald Takaki, had also finished* Pau Hana, *the book he was writing during those years, I was finally able to take an unpaid leave to finish my book. This was the second time I had to take an unpaid leave. In those days there were no programs similar to the ones available in the 1990s that aimed to enhance the "tenurability" of junior faculty, particularly faculty of color.*

Looking back, the "problem" described in this chapter eventually took care of itself due to a number of developments. Asian immigrants seem increasingly to be coming to the United States when their children are still quite young—young enough to pick up English easily. I also think that many faculty members simply gave up trying to help students write grammatically correct prose. Even more important, Asian immigrant students are no longer the only group of students who cannot write well. Sad to say, many students of all ethnic origins and at all levels of education are no longer as literate as students of bygone years used to be. Nowadays, the abbreviated and slangy language used in e-mail rules.

* * *

Why a Social Scientist Decided to Teach Composition

Curiosity and despair drove me, a social scientist with no training in teaching composition, to offer one section of a reading and composition course in the Asian American Studies Program at the University of California, Berkeley, in the Winter quarter of the 1981–82 academic year. This course is one of nine different courses at Berkeley that fulfill the first half of the freshmen English requirement. I felt compelled to find ways to improve the verbal proficiency of Asian-ancestry undergraduates because I wanted to do what I could to counter negative reactions against this group of students who are getting admitted into Berkeley in increasing numbers despite the fact that many of them can barely function in the English language. How such students manage to do quite well academically was a puzzle to me. I hoped that by satisfying my own curiosity I could help other instructors find better ways to teach language skills to such students.

I first became concerned about the poor verbal performance of Asian-ancestry students in the Winter quarter of the 1980–81 school year, when I taught the introductory history course in Asian American Studies. Having been on leave the preceding academic year, I had forgotten that little could be expected of lower-division students in essay exams. The course in question enrolls approximately 250 students per quarter. Since it is taught every quarter, more than seven hundred students take it every year. I had taught this course once a year since 1974. The students in it are fairly representative of the Asian-ancestry undergraduates at Berkeley. So, I usually try to find out something about them as they provide a window through which changes in the Asian American population in the outside world may be observed.

I usually assign two short essays, an in-class midterm essay examination, and an in-class final essay examination in this history course. Even though I usually have several teaching assistants (T.A.s), I like to read the first set of essays, as well as the midterm exams, myself in order to standardize the grading and get an idea of how well the students were learning the course material. Besides, reading what the students write is one of the few ways to get to know them in a large lecture course such as this. My students' performance on the midterm exam that I gave in Winter 1980 was dismal; more than a third of the class received a D or F. This had never happened before.

I was as dismayed as my students were. In a soul-searching session, they told me that most of them had never written an in-class essay exam before. I also discovered that most of them did not know what "analyze," "discuss," "evaluate," and "compare and contrast" mean. After I explained what intellectual operations are expected in answering questions containing such words, some students asked why I had not explained any of this to them before. They were both anguished and angry. They said I had no right to ask them to analyze anything when I had not taught them what that process entails. "But," I protested, "you're supposed to have learned all that in high school!" They insisted they had never been taught such skills in high school. Not knowing whether or not to believe them, I became equally anguished and angry.

Feeling sorry for the students, I proposed to hold four hours of reviews per week for the remainder of the quarter to teach basic study skills to students who needed to learn them. Attendance would be voluntary. However, I promised the students who came to the review sessions that if their performance on the final exam improved by one grade or more, I would weigh their midterm grade only half as heavily as I had originally announced. For those who did not bother to come, their midterm grade would stand. In the ensuing four weeks, approximately forty students showed up each time at the review sessions.

I made two startling discoveries during these sessions. I was wrong in assuming that most of those who needed help would be foreign-born students. American-born students were equally in need of pre-college-level instruction. I also found that my students could not write coherently because they did not know how to read college-level texts. There were two kinds of poor readers in my class—the lazy ones whose eyes scanned the pages but who did not absorb the information or ideas behind the words and non-native English-speakers who had such a rudimentary knowledge of syntax and vocabulary that they got completely bogged down by their incomprehension.

I conjectured that the xerox machine and the colored highlighter were twin culprits in causing the first group of students to develop poor reading habits.

I told the class that in the "old days," when I was a student, we did not have access to copy machines, so we had to take notes on what we read, especially if the assigned readings were on reserve at the library. Since it was time-consuming to take lengthy notes, we had to learn to write succinct summaries. In the process of thinking about what to write down, we "processed" the information and made it our "own." These days, in contrast, if no adequate texts are available for a course, a faculty can easily compile an anthology of reading materials that students can purchase in photo-copied form. Owning a copy allows a student to highlight the readings instead of taking notes. Indeed, some students seem to think that merely possessing a copy of the required readings is sufficient. I told the class that highlighting fragments of sentences is not the best way to learn the material because it requires little active thinking. To force them to think more deeply, I forbade my students to use highlighters. Instead, they had to take notes on the following week's reading assignment. I encouraged them to use only one phrase or, at most, a sentence, to summarize each paragraph. Before sending them off to do this on their own, we practiced with several excerpts. I asked each student to pick words or phrases that best captured the main ideas. Then we discussed why particular words or phrases were more apt than others. I instructed them to do the same thing with each paragraph they read at home.

The following week, much to their surprise, they found they could remember that week's reading more clearly. To make this newly acquired skill "stick," they practiced writing a synopsis of each reading. The students complained that doing their reading assignments this way took longer, but they admitted it made them more conscious of the learning process. Consequently, they could recall the information far more readily.

The non-native English-speakers had an opposite problem. They read too closely, feeling compelled to look up in the dictionary every word they did not know, of which there were many. When I told this group of students that it is not always necessary to understand the meaning of *every* word, they refused to believe me. Though many of them had received years of instruction in English-as-a-Second-Language (ESL), most had little sense of the relative importance of different parts of speech. They did not know how to locate key words in sentences. Neither were they sure which sentence in a paragraph was the topic sentence. So I tried to convince them that sentences, paragraphs, essays—indeed, entire books—contain elements or parts that differ in importance. If they knew the structure of English, they would soon be able to pick out the key words in sentences, looking *those* up in the dictionary if they did not know their meaning. But, I pointed out, it is not necessary to look up *all* unfamiliar words. The most important challenge, I thought, was to get these students to overcome the fear that gripped them as they looked at page after page filled with words they did not recognize. For those students who had the courage to follow my advice, this discovery was a liberating experience: they overcame a major psychological barrier.

Although the problems encountered by the two groups of poor readers differed, learning to discern the structure of sentences, paragraphs, and essays was central to improving both groups' ability to read and write better. To make the ideas that words embody less mysterious, I taught the students how to guess the most likely questions that might be asked on exams. That they could do such a thing was a novel idea. Formulating possible questions on assigned readings became something of a game. I am certain several students must have been very happy that a number of the questions on the final exam were thinly disguised versions of questions they themselves had proposed.

The review sessions gave me a lot of extra work, but the students' improvement was so extraordinary that I felt my time had been well spent. Almost all who came to the reviews improved their performance. For the most part, their scores on the final exam were about two grades above what they had received on their first midterm. This experience showed me that it *is* possible to have high expectations of student performance even when one has to teach basic skills along with substantive content.

Meanwhile, a survey I did revealed that approximately 70 percent of that class were freshmen. Compared to previous years, this was an abnormally high percentage. Even though the course is a lower-division one, it fulfills the American history requirement, so many upper-division students also enroll in it. Before 1980, the distribution had been about 20 percent freshmen, 30 percent sophomores, 30 percent juniors, and 20 percent seniors. The unusually large percentage of freshmen in the Winter 1980–81 class helped explain part of the discrepancy between my expectations and the students' initial performance.

However, I was also convinced that the class level of the students did not explain fully why the class as a whole had done so poorly on the midterm. Three things puzzled me in particular: how students with such poor study skills get into Berkeley; how these students manage to stay in college; and why, after only four weeks of tutoring, they could improve so dramatically. I wanted to know if my class was representative of the new generation of students now entering college, but no one seemed to have any answers.

I added the insights I had gained in this course to those I had garnered a year earlier when I had offered a course about Vietnamese refugees who had been resettled in the United States. This course did not have its own course number and title because it was offered under the rubric of "special topics."

I used word of mouth to spread the news that such a course would be available. Even though I emphasized that all students would be welcome, those enrolled were all Vietnamese who had been in the United States for less than five years. Most of them still had great difficulty with oral and written English. I decided to teach these students English by having them write about their experiences as refugees. I knew that the flight of their families from South Vietnam had been traumatic; I thought it was important that they be given a chance to write their own history. Several Vietnamese students who had been in my introductory history course had told me that faculty members in Asian American Studies do not seem to understand what they had been through. In particular, they thought that my colleagues and I—radicals from the 1960s—were unreasonably intolerant of their anticommunist attitudes. I told them it was their responsibility to educate us. I believed that by getting them to write about topics they considered important, they would be motivated to learn to express themselves as well as possible.

Each of the fifteen students enrolled in the course "Special Topics: Vietnamese in America" had to write a long term paper in which they were to analyze their personal experiences within the larger contexts of U.S.-Vietnamese relations and of Asian American history. Over the course of the ten-week quarter, they wrote six short essays on related topics, which were revised to become sub-sections of the long paper. I scrutinized each interim essay to try to figure out what their writing problems were, then I designed lectures and in-class exercises to address those problems. The results were once again gratifying. About half the class produced essays of twenty-five pages or longer that were eloquent and poignant. While the other half did not write outstanding essays, they nevertheless improved their writing skills significantly. Almost all of them continued to make basic grammatical errors, but by the end of ten weeks few of them had any trouble finding words to express what they wanted to say.

There was another problem I tried to deal with in that class. Like other recent immigrants, quite a number of the Vietnamese students could not pronounce English words in a manner intelligible to English-speakers. From previous experience I knew that such students become acutely embarrassed if someone tries to correct them in public. Yet I felt it would be sad to allow such bright individuals (who were certainly capable of doing better) to continue speaking heavily accented English. Moreover, I did not wish to see my students using their "poor English" as an excuse not to take certain courses or choose particular careers.

I *had* to find a way to demonstrate to them that proper pronunciation is important, that it is *not* embarrassing to be corrected in public, and that hearing a foreigner speak one's mother language well is a pleasure. I thought the best way to get my point across would be by example, so I announced that I wished to learn a little Vietnamese. I first asked the students to teach me how to say their names correctly. This was no easy task since Vietnamese is a tonal language. As we progressed, some of the students lost their shyness and became quite impatient with me whenever I mispronounced certain words. As we discussed why they reacted with such annoyance, they began to understand how language is a filter or prism through which we perceive and judge people from other lands. It was extremely important that they learn to speak English as well as possible, I pointed out, because linguistic discrimination is a fact of life in the United States. They would be doing themselves a disservice by speaking poor English while living here. More important, having given them an opportunity to correct me they now felt less embarrassed when I corrected their own mispronunciations.

To find out whether the students now showing up in my courses were representative, I analyzed the distribution of the scores on the SAT verbal test taken by all Asian-ancestry undergraduates at Berkeley. The picture that emerged was disturbing. Data from the Student Information System computer tapes for Fall quarter, 1980, revealed that 48 percent of the foreign-born Chinese, 65 percent of the foreign-born Koreans, and 69 percent of the foreign-born Vietnamese undergraduates had scored below 400 on the SAT verbal test. Yet such students seemed to be doing all right academically. A campuswide language-background survey that I did during Spring quarter 1981 showed that foreign-born students of Asian ancestry as a group had a higher GPA than the rest of the undergraduate population. Moreover, an unusually large proportion of these students majored in the "difficult" majors such as engineering and the physical sciences. Obviously, they managed not only to get through their four years at Berkeley but also to do quite well academically.

The more I read these students' written work (which was poor), and the more I examined their overall academic performance (which was good), the more curious I became. The academic behavior of Asian-ancestry students became not only a pedagogical issue I wanted to fathom but also a research topic that piqued my curiosity. I decided to use anthropological methods—in addition to sociological ones—to investigate this new and fascinating subpopulation on the Berkeley campus.

I thought a good way to carry out this investigation would be to teach a "real" composition course. I believe the classroom can be used as a sociolinguistic laboratory to study the language background, language behavior, and language-learning potential of Asian-ancestry students. Academic purists may be outraged that a social scientist such as myself should have the gall to teach a composition course. Fortunately, I teach in an interdisciplinary department, so none of my colleagues was affronted by my proposal. I persuaded them that not only was I qualified to teach reading and composition but also that it might be an advantage to have a composition course taught by someone who had not been an English major. My argument was simple: since most of our students are aspiring professionals, teaching them to analyze the world around them will be just as useful as introducing them to a body of creative writings.

The "Yellow English" Problem

Treating my forthcoming course as a research project, I conducted a literature search and found that most of the existing research on Asian-ancestry students had been done in the late 1960s and early 1970s. Important changes have occurred since those years when a majority of the Asian-ancestry students were second- , third- , or even fourth-generation Chinese and Japanese Americans. Students born abroad in Asia, who became numerically important on American college campuses in the late 1970s as a result of renewed immigration from Asia, now constitute about half of all Asian-ancestry undergraduates at Berkeley. Thus, few of the findings of earlier studies are applicable to the current generation, who differ both sociologically and psychologically from their predecessors.

Besides nativity, the ethnic composition of Asian-ancestry students has also changed. Whereas Chinese and Japanese American students predominated in the earlier era, there are now more and more Filipinos, Koreans, Asian Indians, and Vietnamese. While the number of Chinese-ancestry students has continued to increase, the number of Japanese-ancestry students has declined. Unlike other Asian emigrant countries, each of which sends between twenty and forty thousand people to the United States every year, Japan sends only about five thousand because Japan's economy is robust enough to provide enough jobs for its people. Meanwhile, the Japanese American birthrate is falling while their rate of outmarriage is rising.

In a state such as California the public's perception of, attitude toward, and degree of interaction with minority students have all changed considerably in the last decade. Consequently, both the self-perceptions and the objective experiences of Asian-ancestry students have shifted as well. Unlike Asian Americans of earlier generations, fewer now feel like outcasts; neither do today's students try as desperately to conform to European American norms. They show more self-confidence and act more at ease—these being behavioral changes that observant faculty members and teaching assistants have all noticed.

Most of the available writings on Asian-ancestry students deal with their sociopsychological characteristics. The persistence of Asian cultural values and norms and the consequent conflicts between Asian and American cultures have been offered as explanations for the students' observed behavior. Little has been written about their verbal proficiency. There is, however, a body of unpublished studies—mostly doctoral dissertations—that focus on the language problems of *foreign* students from Asia, but such students face circumstances different from those encountered by *immigrant* students, who are also foreign-born but many of whom spend part of their childhood and adolescence in the United States.

Colin Watanabe and Elaine Kim wrote the only articles linking the verbal performance of Asian American students to larger social and cultural factors. Both authors have taught reading and composition to Asian American students at Berkeley. Watanabe argues that the cultural background of Asian American students is responsible for their verbal reticence. In traditional Chinese and Japanese cultures, he states, the social relations within families were so authoritarian that even after several generations in America the dominant position of the parents—especially the fathers—leads to a one-way flow of communication from parents down to the children. The concept of filial piety legitimizes such a pattern. Since children are supposed only to listen and obey, they are given few opportunities to talk, much less express their individual opinions. Within the home also, the special position accorded the eldest son tends to minimize the amount of verbal exchange among siblings. The eldest son, who is expected to set an example for his younger siblings, is alienated from his brothers and sisters, who are both fearful and jealous of him.

Watanabe further hypothesizes that the expectations of Asian parents and teachers also hinder the verbal development of Asian-ancestry children. Since many parents make considerable sacrifices to enable their children to obtain a higher education, they exert great pressure on them to do well academically, with the result that Asian American students do not like to take risks and tend to choose only subjects in which they can get A's. They do not speak up in class lest they say things that might subject them to ridicule from their classmates or cause them to receive poor evaluations from their teachers. Moreover, many teachers tend to stereotype Asian American students, falsely perpetuating the belief that such students are good in math but poor in language skills. Children on whom such stereotypes are repeatedly imposed eventually come to believe such images themselves.

Rather than culture, Kim emphasizes the role of racism in impeding the verbal development of Asian American students. She coined the catchy phrase "Yellow English" to describe the verbal characteristics of Asian Americans. She argues that European Americans have always perceived Asians in America as perpetual foreigners—people incapable of assimilating into Anglo-American society. Since the ability to speak and write English supposedly signifies that foreigners are finally conforming to Anglo-American cultural norms, Asian immigrants and even their American-born children, as perpetual foreigners, are not expected to speak and write English properly. Kim points out that European Americans often exclaim, "You speak such good English!" when they encounter Asian Americans who do, forgetting that English is the native tongue of a considerable number of Asian-looking people in the United States. The fact that "Yellow English" of the "Confucius say" variety has long been used as a comic device in American belles-lettres, onstage, and in the electronic media has further led Asian Americans to become very self-conscious about expressing themselves. In short, according to Kim, if Asian Americans are repeatedly told that mastery of the English language is *not* a skill they are expected to possess, then they will tend to believe that the only English they can speak is "Yellow English."

The analyses offered by Watanabe and Kim were both based on their observations of the Asian American students they had taught in the late 1960s and 1970s, native-English-speakers whose problems did not stem from a lack of knowledge of the English language per se. So much has changed in recent years, however, that I decided it was time to reexamine their hypotheses.

The Classroom as a Research Laboratory

In using my classroom as a laboratory there were ethical issues that I had to address. The students should be told why I was doing what I intended to do. So, I wrote an article for *Asian American Report,* a publication of the Asian American Studies Program mailed to all Asian-surnamed undergraduates at the beginning of each quarter, in which I discussed the design and purpose of my course. At preenrollment, interested students had a chance to ask questions, though few did. During the first class meeting, I explained that I had two concerns: 1) to get the students in the class to help me find a more effective and rapid way to teach oral and written verbal skills to Asian-ancestry students, and 2) to teach them skills that would be transferable to other situations requiring verbal facility.

To appeal to the pragmatic proclivity of today's students, I told them that my analysis of official campus statistics revealed that few Asian-ancestry students major in the humanities and social sciences. It was unlikely that members of the class would be called upon in the future to write literary criticism—one of the skills usually inculcated in reading and composition courses. With the short ten weeks we had, I said, I was less concerned about exposing them to "great books" than teaching them analytical skills. I told the class that even though standard composition handbooks often divide essays into descriptive, narrative, argumentative, and expository types, I personally believe that good writing requires the selective use of all four prose styles. The trick is to learn when to use which essay form. It is important, I said, that they learn to write by strategy rather than by formula. My aim was to help them learn to write clearly; later on, after they had sufficient practice, they could worry about style.

During the first two lectures I presented a simplified version of communication theory because I thought it was important that students understand the social nature of communication. I pointed out that there is a distinction between speech and writing. Oral verbal exchange is a more social act than reading. In both instances a sender encodes the message he or she wishes to send, but in oral exchange the receiver must decode not only words but also body language. In reading, however, the author with whom the reader interacts is not physically present.

Before we proceeded any further I tried to assess the students' encoding versus decoding proficiency. Since most students are required to decode others' messages (taking notes in lectures or trying to understand assigned readings) more frequently than they are required to encode their own messages (writing papers and exams, giving oral presentations, or participating in discussions), I decided to evaluate their decoding proficiency first. I asked them to hand in the notes they had taken during my first lecture and was pleased to see that most of them took reasonably accurate notes. Next, I asked them to write a synopsis of the first reading. Only a few students could do so in the fifteen minutes I allotted them. Those who managed to do so were asked to read their pieces aloud to the class. We discussed why certain ways of summarizing particular paragraphs were more effective than others. Those students who wished to could hand in a written summary of the next reading for my review. I was glad to see that most students who made the effort to write summaries did so reasonably well, but no one used his or her own words. They relied, instead, on words and phrases copied verbatim from the text. When I chastised them for not using their own words, they told me that since the information in the article was new to them they did not know how to express the ideas in words of their choosing. It appeared that Watanabe was right: Asian-ancestry students do not like to take risks.

Perhaps a better way to put it is, my students were verbally timid because they had not grown up with a tradition of verbal "play."

A number of students also brought in their readers to show me how they had highlighted a difficult social science article I had assigned, which was badly written and full of obfuscating jargon. I was quite surprised that most of them could pick out the main ideas even in that piece of writing, which I had purposely included in order to demonstrate that it is possible to "wade through" even very "dense" material. I was relieved to discover that students in this class at least could read and take notes. One possible reason that they were better at this than the freshmen in my introductory history course was that the ones in the composition course had already fulfilled their Subject A requirement, whereas many in the introductory class had not yet done so.

My T.A.s and I decided classtime could most profitably be spent in improving the students' oral and written *encoding* proficiency. For that reason we gave them relatively light readings but many more writing assignments than comparable composition courses require. In addition, we thought it important to teach oral and written skills simultaneously. We observed the students' speech behavior in class and in private conversations. As expected, students spoke more freely in the conversations held in my office with the door closed. I purposely did not keep drop-in office hours that quarter; rather, each week I passed out a sign-up sheet for students to set up times to see me individually. I thought they would take such conversations more seriously if each of them had my full attention for thirty or forty minutes at a stretch. During these conversations I corrected mispronunciations, grammatical errors, and poor word usage. Being alone with me, few seemed embarrassed by this process. I spent over twenty hours a week in office hours that quarter just to cater to the students in this one class. (Students enrolled in the other course I was teaching that quarter, unfortunately, received far less attention.)

In addition, one of my T.A.s devised a way to make students more aware of the impact of their speech. In weekly group tutorials each student had to make a five-minute oral presentation, either on a topic related to the course or on some other subject of the student's choosing. These presentations were (audio) taped and played back to the group. The entire group, including the presenter, would then comment on the effectiveness of the presentation. This approach was so efficacious that I asked my other T.A. to use it in her tutorial group also. In several tutorials that I sat in on, a number of students did not permit a playback of their presentations, but those who did impressed me greatly with the insightful comments they made about their own performance. In general, these sessions confirmed my observation that most Asian-ancestry students today no longer fit the old stereotype of being painfully quiet and shy. At least they are not quiet and shy when they are in a classroom setting in which they feel comfortable.

In contrast to their fairly good speaking ability, few students could write effectively. After I read the first two sets of in-class essays I was appalled at the immensity of the task before us; about a third of the class wrote at a fifth- or sixth-grade level despite the fact they had already all fulfilled their Subject A requirement. Moreover, at least eight students had severe ESL problems. But since I have had no training in teaching English-as-a-Second-Language, and with only eight weeks left in the quarter, I decided I should emphasize analytical skills and tutor those individuals who made the worst grammatical and spelling errors on the side as best I could on an as-needed basis.

As we worked to improve simultaneously the oral and written proficiency of the class, I thought it important that the students realize there are differences between spoken and written texts. In oral communication, I said, the participants frequently rely on meta-linguistic cues such as gestures and a speaker's tone of voice to pick up the meaning of others' utterances. In written texts, however, such cues are absent, so a writer's words must carry the full burden of the message being conveyed. Because written texts are autonomous, I explained, writing can be a rather lonely act, especially if one has no idea who the readers will be. For that reason, beginning writers (and even experienced ones) often feel insecure, for there is no immediate feedback from listeners or readers. To overcome this dilemma, I told the class they must learn to separate the self as writer and the self as reader. I explained that after they write something they must switch roles and become critical readers of their own products. As they read, they must learn to edit their own work—a process that requires not only critical judgment but also the ability to separate one's ego from the product.

Even as I emphasized how they must learn not to allow criticism (whether it be from others or themselves) to shatter their egos, I was careful not to assault their egos too much. Although it was obvious to me that at least half of the students should never have passed Subject A, I refrained from telling them outright how poor their "English" was. Instead, I pointed out there is a difference between ordinary, everyday English and the kind of English required for academic discourse. The latter is something *all* students—regardless of their ethnic origins or place of birth—must learn when they enter college. Academic discourse is more logical, tightly organized, formal, and therefore far more demanding as a medium of communication than is colloquial English. Thus, they should not develop an inferiority complex about their poor "English" just because they, like all other students, must learn a different *kind* of English. Moreover, I emphasized that most professional writers often rewrite their pieces many times. The students should not assume that the T.A.s and I thought they were "stupid" if we asked them to edit or revise their papers. I felt such reassurances were necessary because over the years I have heard countless complaints from students enrolled in ESL classes that the teachers in those classes treated them like children and made them feel dumb. Because of such a perception, learning English had been neither challenging nor fun for them.

We stressed the importance of developing self-reliance because, as I told them, they would probably not receive any further help with their prose after they finished the course. Therefore, it was imperative they learn to help themselves. Having taught thousands of Asian-ancestry students, I knew how much they appreciate structured situations, so I devised a mechanical way to force the students in this class to look carefully at what they had written. I printed up "editing sheets" which the students were to use to analyze each sentence in their take-home essays. Initially, they had to identify only the subject and verb in the main clause of each sentence and make sure they agreed. Then, I asked them to indicate which sentence in each paragraph was the topic sentence. Later in the quarter I designed a more complex editing sheet that required the students to state the development pattern used in each paragraph, based on Frederick Crews' tripartite scheme of direct, pivotal, and suspended patterns. Students also had to decide what level of generality each sentence was at. That is to say, was the sentence a general statement, a specific statement, or an illustrative detail? By the end of the quarter most students could make their subjects and verbs agree, identify topic sentences, and indicate each paragraph's development pattern. However, most of them could not specify the level of generality of the sentences they had written.

I gave my students a lot of practice in writing. In the course of ten weeks, each individual produced at least sixteen pieces of writing: eight in-class essays of approximately three hundred words each, all of which were corrected by me or the T.A.s but only six of which were given a grade; five take-home essays of four to five typed, double-spaced pages, all of which were graded, with three to be revised and graded again; an in-class midterm, a three-hour final exam, and a fifteen-page paper, which could be written individually or collectively. If a group paper was chosen, its length was prorated according to the number of students in the group, with each individual producing about ten pages of text. The students discussed and voted on how much weight to give each piece of writing in computing the course grade. They apportioned the weight intelligently and fairly.

In addition, the T.A.s asked each student to keep a journal. He or she had to write nonstop for ten minutes five times a week on any topic he or she chose. We explained to the class that while the sixteen pieces of "formal" writing were meant to train them to write in an organized, logically consistent, controlled, and reflexive manner, the journal entries, as exercises in "free writing," were meant to "get their juices flowing" so they could learn to produce words on paper effortlessly. I found time to read only a few of the journals and was surprised how frequently the students expressed anxiety about how they were doing in school. There is no question that Asian-ancestry students are heavily burdened by the pressure to perform academically.

Needless to say, the T.A.s and I graded papers around the clock. The two T.A.s graded five of the eight in-class essays, two of the take-home essays, the midterm, the final exam, and half of the term papers. I myself graded three sets of in-class essays, three take-home essays, and half the term papers. I also spot-checked some of the work graded by the T.A.s to make sure they used more or less the same standards. We inspired the students to work hard by working very, very hard ourselves. Whenever students gave excuses for not having done an assignment I had no qualms telling them they should be ashamed of themselves. In how many other classes, I asked, does the professor spend so much time with each student?

We gave a lot of high grades in that class because, even though many students still could not write "clean" English by the end of the quarter, they had improved remarkably. They had not only written more essays than students in equivalent composition courses but they had also done original research for their term papers. Even though they continued to make grammatical errors, most had learned to think more clearly and could, consequently, write more coherently.

What got the class to stop complaining about the amount of work I was giving them was a pep talk I gave them about power. We had been discussing their career aspirations and discovered that everyone wanted a job where he or she would have some control over his or her working conditions. Several students said plainly they wanted to be "boss." So I told them that in the United States, where social relations are far more fluid than in Asia, an individual's ability to handle himself or herself easily in social settings is an important ingredient in leadership. "Who's going to take orders from you," I asked, "if you can't even express yourself clearly?" If they want power, I continued, they must be able to command other people's respect, and the ability to speak and write well is an important means to that end. I believe that little pep talk had a huge impact; from that point on I heard no more complaints, and assignments were all turned in on time.

Having seen the great discrepancy between my students' decoding and encoding abilities, I began to understand how such students manage to get through school. They can graduate from high school and college and accumulate laudable academic records because they are good at *absorbing* information. In courses where grades depend on tests that require the recall and manipulation of information in relatively structured ways, they can do quite well. In contrast, they encounter great difficulty in tests and assignments that require answers couched in their own words. Aware of this weakness, they avoid taking courses that call upon them to write essays using words they must *produce* independently in a format of their own design. But because they are bright—imagine the obstacles they have had to overcome to succeed as well as they do—once they have been "shown the ropes," as I and my T.A.s tried to do in this class, they can write easily enough. The real secret is to offer classes that teach them basic verbal skills without insulting their intelligence. I tried to resolve this contradiction by assigning them challenging essay topics requiring analytical acumen while teaching them basic skills "on the side." Unfortunately, the method we used was so labor-intensive that I doubt few other faculty would want to duplicate it.

Research Questions

In terms of substantive content, the course focused on three topics: 1) the nature of oral and written communication; 2) how cultural background, racial discrimination, socioeconomic status, gender, and an insufficient knowledge of American society and culture may affect the language behavior of immigrant or minority students; and 3) how the history of their language acquisition and the nature of their schooling may affect their English proficiency. Discussing such topics in class, I hoped to draw the students into active participation in helping us understand their language behavior. From a research perspective, I explored seven factors that impinged on the language development of Asian-ancestry undergraduates:

1. how culturally imposed behavior may constrain verbal expression, as hypothesized by Colin Watanabe;
2. how racial discrimination may inhibit the desire to master English, as suggested by Elaine Kim;
3. how a lack of knowledge of American middle-class values and norms may make a student insecure about interacting verbally with others;
4. how that same lack of knowledge may affect a student's ability to write about certain topics that presume, whether explicitly or implicitly, such knowledge;

5. how sexism may affect one's speech patterns, as argued by Robin Lakoff;
6. how acquiring English in a haphazard way may fail to provide foreign-born students with the skills to master "standard" English; and
7. how inadequate elementary and secondary schooling may deny students sufficient instruction and practice in writing.

I shall discuss the first five factors together as environmental constraints on verbal facility and the last two in the section on language acquisition and schooling.

The Environmental Contexts of Verbal Development

To examine the relative impacts of cultural background and racism on my students' verbal development I asked them to write short in-class essays on these topics. Unexpectedly, only seven of them thought the communication pattern in their families was authoritarian and uni-directional. These students admitted they were indeed shy and afraid to speak up in public because of the way they had been brought up. The rest of the class, however, was adamant that the socialization pattern in their homes had little to do with their verbal development. They said Watanabe's hypothesis might have been true in the past but not any more. The class was indeed lively, considering that it met at eight o'clock in the morning. Many more students than we had expected spoke up. Six loquacious ones had to be told from time to time to keep quiet so others might have a chance to say something. Another ten students talked quite frequently, though they did not try to dominate conversations as their more aggressive peers did. While a ratio of sixteen out of thirty-four students may not sound impressive to instructors who have never taught large numbers of Asian-ancestry students, the amount of oral participation in this class was unusual compared to other courses I have taught.

In reacting to Kim's thesis, the students thought racism no longer affects the self-esteem of minority children as adversely as it had in the past. Only a handful of students admitted they had experienced any form of discrimination. At least that was their subjective perception. A Filipino American student whose father was in the U.S. Navy and who had lived in many different places reported that she had encountered severe prejudice only in the South. Most students told me that "California is different" because the number of Asians and Spanish-speakers in this state is so large. They claimed they had never encountered the racist caricatures of "Yellow English" that Elaine Kim had written about. In short, in the experiences of these students, racism and Asian cultural constraints are no longer as salient as they used to be.

But just because these students do not feel discriminated against in their everyday lives does not mean they feel comfortable socially among European Americans, African Americans, or Mexican Americans. The social distance between them and non-Asians is manifested in two ways. First, most of them find it difficult to talk to white authority figures. Three students, who did a survey of the attitude of foreign-born Asian students towards European Americans, found that of all the white people they and their fellow students encounter, they feel most positive about their professors. Even so, they hesitate to talk to these professors even when they have a chance to do so. One student wrote, "I am able to talk to Professor Chan about many things I would never talk to a White professor about." It is apparent that while most of my students like and respect their European American professors and T.A.s they do not feel close to them. They are much less alienated from professors and T.A.s who *look* like themselves.

Interviews conducted by another group of students revealed a second way in which Asian-ancestry students hesitate to interact with non-Asians. The researchers discovered that 40 to 60 percent of the "close friends" of the American-born and 80 percent of the "close friends" of the foreign-born were fellow Asians. The large number of Asians in the San Francisco Bay Area in general, and on the Berkeley campus in particular, apparently enables these students to live more or less in ethnic insularity.

I asked the students how they thought "running around" mainly with other Asian Americans may have influenced their English proficiency. Most of them could not answer that question because they had never experienced any other pattern of social interaction. Only two students thought there may be a connection between the kind of friends they had and the rate at which they became fluent in the English language. A Vietnamese student told the class that when his family first arrived in the United States they were placed in Portland, Maine, by the agency that resettled them. Since there were no other foreign-born students in his junior high school at all, he was compelled to learn English very quickly. Indeed, he spoke a more colloquial and idiomatic English than any other Vietnamese student I have known. Another student who came from Taiwan five years ago said that his spoken English improved most rapidly during the year he had two European American roommates. Now that he lives in a dorm with many other Asian-ancestry students, with whom he socializes exclusively, his English has stopped improving.

Four students who investigated the relationship between English proficiency and social networks observed astutely that Asian-ancestry students have no accurate idea about how good or poor their English may be because they compare themselves only to their peers. They tend to evaluate their own proficiency far more positively than the scores on standardized tests or writ-ten assignments would seem to indicate because almost everyone they know uses a teen-age slang. In that light, they do not think their oral English is bad at all. Almost everyone thought, however, that his or her written English was poor. They could not tell me why they felt that way except to say they have real difficulty thinking of things to write about. Several told me they could never write more than a few sentences in the forty minutes I gave them for their in-class writing exercises because they had learned in their Subject A course that they must begin essays with attention-getting sentences, but they couldn't think of any.

We next examined whether a student's socioeconomic status had any ef-fect on his or her verbal proficiency. A number of writers have argued that scores on standardized tests reflect the test-takers' class background more than their intellectual ability. Unfortunately, since only four of the thirty-four students in my class had parents who held menial jobs, it was difficult to come to any definitive conclusions. There was no discernible correlation between the socioeconomic status of these four individuals and the quality of their written work. As a matter of fact, two of them were among the best students in the class, while the other two received a B and a D- , respectively, in the course. The influence of class background was more observable in these students' oral behavior, however. Three of them were painfully shy. When they did speak, their voices were hardly audible. It was as if they thought that coming from poor families, it was not their "place" to speak in public.

As a starting point for our discussion of the possible effects of gender on language behavior, students read *Language and Woman's Place* by Robin La-koff. While most students understood her thesis, they felt it did not apply to them. In addition, the T.A.s and I observed no noticeable difference between the verbal facility of the male and female students. One Vietnamese female student who was reticent in public told me she said little because she had been brought up to be polite, especially to her teachers, but she felt it had nothing to do with her sex. Rather, she explained, *all* Vietnamese youth are supposed to be polite. A number of the women students said emphatically that their parents were very "liberal" and had not constrained their behavior in any way when they were children. Indeed, the class had more talkative female than male students.

Of the environmental factors we discussed, the one the students thought had the most important impact on their language proficiency was their lack of familiarity with American society. Both American-born and foreign-born students said they had experienced difficulty in their Subject A classes because they knew little or nothing about the topics they were supposed to write about. One American-born student who grew up in Oakland's Chinatown said he had failed the Subject A exam because he simply had nothing to say about the value of spending time in the wilderness—the topic of the exam. He said with considerable annoyance, "I grew up in Oakland; I've never gone camping in my life. I don't know what the wilderness is like—how can I write about it?"

The real problem for these students, I observed, was not so much a lack of knowledge about American society per se as a general ignorance about the larger social and political world we live in. Worse, not too many of them seem particularly interested in learning more. It disturbed me profoundly that some of my students possessed little "culture" of any sort, be it Asian or Western. One of the books we read in the course was Maxine Hong Kingston's *Woman Warrior.* I thought her depiction of cultural conflicts would be compellingly interesting to the class. To my surprise, while some students did enjoy the book, others said they could not identity with the narrator or the problems she faced. They told me they were not familiar with the Chinese or Chinese American culture depicted in the book. Such statements came not only from the American-born but from students born in Taiwan and Hong Kong as well. At the same time, they claimed not to know much about Anglo-American culture. In exasperation, I asked them what culture they identified with. "We're modern," one student responded without hesitation. In other words, "high culture," be it literature, art, or philosophy, means little to them. Neither the Greco-Roman-Judaic tradition nor any Asian tradition entices them or arouses their curiosity.

The perspicacity of the statement "we're modern" was brought home to me in several ways. One student referred to the Fa Mulan legend, as it was retold in *Woman Warrior,* as a "science fiction fantasy." And, in response to a final exam question that asked them to produce an imaginary panel discussion to reflect the views of several authors they had read, some students sketched a television talk show scenario, whereas what I had in mind was a panel discussion at a public forum or scholarly conference. Like their non-Asian peers, these students live in the world of computers, television, and videotapes. Those are the things they are most familiar with and can, therefore, write about most easily. Some of the best papers I received analyzed movies and television shows. The class also wrote good essays on higher education—a topic of considerable interest to them. In contrast, no one had anything to say about "Black English"—the topic of an article I assigned. I had hoped to use this article to stimulate them to think about whether there is such a thing as "Asian English." Most of the students did not think there is. When Asian

Americans do not speak good English, they asserted, it is simply because they don't know how and not because they have created their own argot.

If my observations are accurate, then one of the fundamental challenges facing those of us who believe in the value of a liberal arts education will be to find effective ways to teach traditional humanities courses to our "modern" students. A term paper jointly written by four students corroborated my observation. In their research, the four authors questioned fifty of their peers about why they had chosen the majors they did. Almost across the board, Asian-ancestry students majoring in the sciences or engineering insisted they were doing so *out of interest* and not out of necessity. Science and engineering, they believed, provide the greatest intellectual challenge. In their eyes, science augurs a new age, and they enjoyed being privy to its secrets. They felt insulted when it was suggested that perhaps their poor verbal skills might have caused them to eschew the humanities and social sciences. They insisted that humanities courses had little relevance to their lives. One student made this point graphically; he thought *Madame Bovary,* which he had to read in high school, was a "ridiculous book" because the struggles of the protagonist against the prevailing social mores of her times no longer had any meaning in a world where individuals of any age and of whatever marital status are free to go to bed with whomever they please. He thought the book taught him little and—the ultimate put-down—it was boring, besides.

Language Acquisition and Schooling

As the quarter progressed and I got to know the individual students better, it became increasingly apparent that the quality of the schooling they had received had influenced their language proficiency far more than any of the environmental factors discussed above. In conversations with them I systematically gathered information about their educational history, including:

1. where and when they first learned English;
2. if they were immigrants, how long it took them to begin to comprehend the verbal world around them and what kind of ESL instruction they had received;
3. what they had learned in their high school English classes;
4. how much writing they had done prior to entering Berkeley;
5. how they felt about their verbal versus their math proficiency;
6. how they had fulfilled their Subject A requirement; and
7. what other courses they had taken besides Subject A that required them to write essays.

English was the primary language of social intercourse for only a very small number of the students in my class. Among the twelve American-born, only seven spoke English at home regularly. The other five did not learn English until they were five or six years old—that is, until they began attending public elementary school. They continue to be bilingual. One Chinese American student told me that even though he had been born in Bakersfield, California, he speaks poor English because his immigrant mother's speech patterns have influenced him more than those of anyone else. (She had come from Hong Kong at the age of nineteen.) "Surely," I ventured, "you must have had other speech models." He said they had no influence on him because he never said a word in school and had no playmates. His mother remains the person to whom he is closest—even today, when he is a junior at Berkeley.

Among the foreign-born students who came after they had reached puberty, most had first learned English abroad in junior high schools (called middle school in most Asian countries). Every single person except one said that those English classes had not helped him or her to learn English at all. "Oh, we learned the alphabet and some simple grammar, but nothing more," they claimed. A few said they now realize, in retrospect, that their English teachers did not have a good grasp of the language. When they first arrived in the United States they found it very difficult to understand anything that was said, although they could read a few words. It took one to three years before they began to understand what others around them were talking about. A few insisted they still do not understand fully what others say. Most students in this group had taken ESL courses in high school or college—some for as long as three years. Despite this instruction they still felt that their comprehension was inadequate.

The foreign-born students who arrived before they reached puberty were in much better shape. They learned English in American elementary schools. They began to comprehend spoken English within three months to a year after their entries. The only exception was a student who had come at the age of nine but who still felt completely uncomfortable after nine years' residence in this country. He said the only person he could talk to without feeling self-conscious was his mother, to whom he spoke solely in Cantonese. This group of students also reported having been enrolled in ESL classes either in elementary or junior high school. When I asked them what they had learned in such courses, they told me about the "international days" they had participated in, during which students from different parts of the world brought in clothing and other objects from their countries of origin to show to the other children. As reported by my students, the predominant form of English instruction seemed to have been exercises in self-paced grammar workbooks. Sometimes these exercises were graded, but few of my students remember having received any explanations for why certain answers were erroneous. Students who now speak fluent English told me, "I guess I learned from my friends." Not a single person thought he or she had mastered English through an ESL course.

With the exception of three students, the class had all graduated from American high schools. All of them, therefore, had taken one or more years of high school English, mostly literature courses. Only four students had ever had any instruction in expository writing. Two of them were among the better writers in the class, but since they were both American-born it is difficult to say whether they wrote fluidly because they were native speakers of English or because they had received pertinent training.

High school English classes made little impression on my students. Few of them could remember the titles of books they had read. Most could think of only five or six titles, with *The Scarlet Letter* being named more often than any other book. Shakespeare's plays as well as *The Iliad, The Odyssey,* and a number of works by American playwrights were the most easily recalled items. A number of students could not recall any titles at all. They said things like, "It was a book with a blue cover."

If my students' experiences can be considered representative, then it is apparent that few students these days receive any practice in writing before they enter college. Only three recalled writing anything longer than two or three pages in high school. (In contrast, I had to write twenty-five-page papers in my English, history, and social studies courses at a Long Island City high school in the late 1950s.) Two of the longer papers my students wrote were science reports done at highly competitive Lowell High School in San Francisco; the third was a social studies paper written in a suburban high school. The most common form of high school written assignment was the book report, but when queried what they had written in these reports most replied, "Oh, we had to say whether or not we liked the book and what the story was about." But since they did not have to explain *why* they liked or disliked a certain book, they failed to learn to analyze or criticize other people's writings. Students who had previously attended college elsewhere fared no better. Papers written at community colleges or even four-year institutions averaged five pages. None was a research paper.

When I asked the class what their Subject A or equivalent course had taught them about writing, almost everyone said they had learned they should begin essays with a captivating sentence and that essays are supposed to contain an introduction, a body, and a conclusion. But did they write essays like that when they first appeared in my class? Alas, no.

The first three in-class essays the students produced caused me considerable distress. They had been asked to write four or five paragraphs in forty minutes, but more than half the students could produce at most two paragraphs in the allotted time. A few managed to write only three or four sentences. Only one student, who had the best vocabulary in the class, wrote copiously. This student, who had come from Taiwan at the age of three, was completely bilingual and was the most verbally aggressive individual in the class. Unfortunately, she suffered from psychological stress in the middle of the quarter (partly due to pressure from her mother, who insisted she major in engineering—a subject she had no interest in whatsoever) and had to withdraw from school.

Given the students' initial performance, my T.A.s and I were ecstatic that our students had learned to write four or five cogent paragraphs in twenty minutes by the end of the quarter. In their evaluation of the course a large percentage of students reported that the in-class writing exercises we gave them were the most helpful thing we had done all quarter. Having learned to write under pressure, they said they would no longer "freeze" at the thought of having to answer essay questions during in-class exams.

Some students told me that most Asian-ancestry students they knew avoided courses with in-class essay exams at all costs, but that they feared take-home papers less because they could ask friends to correct their errors before submitting the papers. One student, the quality of whose in-class writing differed markedly from her take-home essays, confessed that her boyfriend, an European American graduate student in English, helped her write her take-home essays. When I reprimanded her for cheating, she replied defiantly, "Wouldn't American students attending college in foreign countries also ask native-speakers to help them?" She felt she had done no wrong.

There was a marked contrast between how the students felt about their verbal ability versus their math proficiency. Every single one of them thought they were good in math. One student said, "I actually hate math, but I'm still good in it." When I tried to probe why or how they came to feel so positive about math, most did not know. Some said they had simply *always* been good at it. A number mentioned how their parents, relatives, or older siblings had stressed they should try to excel in math. I wondered if we were witnessing a self-fulfilling prophesy. Was it possible that Asian immigrant children, who existed "in a fog" verbally, so to speak, for one to three years after their arrival in the United States, instinctively found a way to remain sane in school by excelling in a subject they could comprehend?

The students really liked science also. "Science is so neat!" sums up how several of them felt. Few had the same joyous interest in language-dependent subjects. In particular, students with severe ESL problems experienced great agony. In my first conversation with a student from Taiwan, who had been in this country for about four years, she burst into tears before I could say anything. "It's terrible, terrible!" she sobbed uncontrollably. "These last few years have been the most terrible in my life!"

In these conversations I discovered that an individual's attitude towards language seems to make a great difference in his or her mastery of it. A student from Taiwan, who had been in the United States for less than six years, spoke fluently without any accent even though she made more spelling mistakes than anyone else. When I commented on her fluency, she said, "I guess I'm good in languages. You know, I had studied French for only one semester when I decided to take the French Achievement Test on my College Boards. My French teacher tried to discourage me from taking that test, but I took the exam, anyway, and I got 650 on it." She was obviously very proud of her achievement, as well she should have been. The only other student with positive feelings about his language skills was the most extraordinary student in the class. His family had emigrated from Korea almost four years earlier and had first gone to Brazil. Although he had never heard Portuguese in his life, much less studied it, he made friends with a number of Japanese Brazilian students who helped him to learn Portuguese in less than three months. His family lived in Brazil for almost two years before coming to the United States. He took his College Board exams only seven months after his arrival yet managed to score above 600 in the English Achievement Test—only one of two students out of the thirty-four in my class to have done so. While he continued to make errors in the use of prepositions and articles, he wrote thoughtful, analytical, and well-organized papers. He told me he liked languages a lot and was taking a course in Japanese that quarter. Furthermore, he hoped to study Chinese in the future. Despite such interest he had no intention of becoming a linguist. Instead, he wished to go into international business but was majoring in engineering. "Why?" I asked. "Because engineering courses are very rigorous," he responded. "I want to train my mind and develop intellectual discipline." His statement was yet another manifestation of the respect that Asian-ancestry students have for science and engineering.

Given the many ways students at Berkeley may use to fulfill the Subject A and English 1A-B requirements, a system of self-selection seems to have developed. Those who fear they may not pass the Subject A exam or course at Berkeley try to fulfill the requirement by other means. That students were attempting to do so became apparent when I correlated their initial writing competence with the manner in which they had fulfilled their Subject A requirement. Only six of the thirty-four had been exempted from Subject A. Two had received scores of over 600 in their English Achievement Test, while four had passed the Subject A exam. Of the remainder, six took the Subject A course, three the ESL-Subject A course, eight the Asian American Studies Subject A-equivalent course, one an ESL course at another UC campus, and six took courses elsewhere.

I assessed their initial writing proficiency by averaging their grades on the first three in-class essays. Of the nine students whose performance was abysmal, four had taken the Asian American Studies course, three the ESL–Subject A course at Berkeley, one the ESL course at another UC campus, and one a course at a community college. Among six others whose work was barely passing, two had taken the Subject A course at Berkeley, one the Asian American Studies–Subject A equivalent course, and three an equivalent course at community colleges. All fifteen of the students were foreign-born. It was American-born students, for the most part, who dared to take the Subject A course at Berkeley. Those students who had fulfilled their Subject A requirement at a community college all told me, "I did that because I knew it would be easier." A few claimed their advisors had suggested they take an equivalent course in summer school elsewhere. I observed wryly, "So you cheated yourself." It was obvious, however, that many students view the Subject A and English 1A-B requirements as obstacles to be overcome, not as valuable venues where they might learn an essential skill.

As a member of the faculty in Asian American Studies, I was appalled at how poorly the students who had taken our equivalent course were doing in my class. As chairperson of our department's Curriculum Committee, I began to investigate what was going on, but my efforts met with strenuous objections. After a great struggle we did manage to replace the part-time instructors teaching that course with a new, full-time faculty member who had been trained both in English literature and in Teaching-English-as-a-Second-Language.

It also became apparent that whatever skills students may have acquired in their composition courses were seldom reinforced. Not a single student in my class had taken any courses other than Subject A or its equivalent that required them to write essays. Only two students were enrolled in any course at all with essay exams that quarter.

At the risk of over-simplification, in terms of their writing patterns the students in my class fell roughly into three categories. First were the American-born native speakers of English. Predication errors, comma splices, and imprecise word usage were their most frequent errors. Several of them had a bad habit of writing long strings of run-on sentences. Although each of their sentences read smoothly enough, the cumulative effect sounded "shallow" because the writers tended to spew out sentences without organizing their thoughts. This group made the least improvement in the class, perhaps because they started near the top in terms of initial proficiency. Only one student among them improved his writing significantly, and that was because he was highly motivated.

Next were the genuine ESL students, who could be further divided into three subgroups. There were those who made numerous grammatical errors but knew the rules. When the rules were pointed out to them, they quickly learned to clean up their own grammar. Others did not know the rules at all and should never have been let through the Subject A sieve. I was not able to help these students much because what they really needed was a pre-Subject A course—something I could not provide without dragging the level of my course down to such a low level that the rest of the class would be shortchanged.

The third subgroup consisted of three students I could not handle at all. One, a Filipino American who had been in the United States since the age of five, had no motivation whatsoever to learn. He cut more than half the lectures, did not hand in assignments, and probably cheated on his term paper. He failed the course. A second had come from Taiwan less than two years earlier, was in his late twenties, had passed the Subject A course at another UC campus, but did not write even one error-free sentence during the entire eight weeks he remained in my course. Since he was a graduating senior majoring in architecture, he repeatedly begged me to pass him because failing the course meant he would have to remain in school another year while paying out-of-state tuition. I told him there was no way he could pass, given his performance. Feeling sorry for him, I contacted the dean of his college, who referred me to his academic advisor. It turned out that he received straight A's in the courses in his major and had, inexplicably, received C-minuses in courses he had taken at Berkeley to fulfill his breadth requirements. Given his otherwise excellent academic record, his advisor allowed him to withdraw from my class after the deadline for doing so, with the proviso that he take an equivalent course at a community college the following summer.

The third problem student was one of the most stubborn individuals I have ever taught. She had come from Korea three years earlier, attended a community college for two years, and transferred to Berkeley as a junior majoring in sociology. She was quite bright and tried to write extremely complex essays, refusing to believe that her English was too poor to carry the weight of her ideas. She rejected all suggestions I made, walked out of tutoring sessions, and told me I was wasting her time. Toward the end of the quarter she tried to hustle me into passing her by saying, "I am an immigrant and English is very hard for me. Since you are an immigrant also, you should understand and pass me." Failing to persuade me, she became very angry. She was certainly not the stereotypical meek and shy Asian woman. I did not pass her but informed her she could contest her grade, should she wish to do so, by going to the campus ombudsperson. The difficulties that these three students had with English were obviously only a small part of more complicated problems they were experiencing. I learned long ago not to blame myself for failing to help students in such a state.

The most unpredictable and fascinating students were the ones who had lived in the United States for six to fifteen years. While they made many grammatical and spelling errors, redundancy and imprecise word usage were the most notable characteristics in their writing. Their essays were similar to those described by teachers of basic writing in New York City's public universities, where "open admissions" students, whom one instructor called "residually oral," write essays that "echo the patterns of oral discourse more than they imitate the conventions of literary discourse." According to faculty members who have taught such students, their writing is redundant, employs more concrete than abstract words, contains generalizations that are opinionated and subjective, and is committed in tone. Their essays consist of additive paragraphs where details are piled one on top of another with little coherence. In comparison, persons growing up in a literate, rather than oral, tradition are supposed to be able to produce prose using more abstract words and concepts and can control the way in which they display their knowledge.

About half of my students wrote essays with "residually oral" patterns. Considering how most of them had learned English, it is not surprising that their prose should resemble that of other students who had not grown up in English-literate environments. Those who entered the United States before they reached puberty had learned English almost entirely by ear, more often in the playground than in the classroom. Even their spelling showed the oral origins of their English acquisition. For example, the student who spoke English fluently but made innumerable spelling errors misspelled "difficult" as "diffical." Since few of them read anything for enjoyment, they had little chance to see how words are spelled or what fluent English is like.

When I first realized that the manner in which they had learned English might be the cause of their difficulties, I began to stress, over and over again, that written English—especially English for academic discourse—is not the same as colloquial speech. Some time ago a colleague who teaches technical writing to engineering students appalled me when she said she tells her foreign-born students the best way to write well is to read aloud their essays to themselves in order to see if they "sound right." But how can students who have no model of what proper English *sounds* like surmise whether they are *writing* good prose? What sounds right to these students may, in fact, be poor writing. What sounds right all depends on who is doing the listening.

I also emphasized that written discourse requires a more formal, varied, and complex vocabulary. I pointed out, however, that "big words" are not automatically better. Rather, apt words are preferable to big words. I warned my students against sounding pompous. Since we did not have enough time in class to do any vocabulary-building exercises, and since they had told me they hated to memorize vocabulary lists, I made a self-conscious attempt to lecture in a more formal way than I normally do, incorporating many words in my lectures that I hoped they would learn. I would stop at the end of a sentence containing a word I wished them to learn and ask if anyone knew what it meant. After doing this for a while, I was pleased that students began to stop me in mid-sentence to ask what certain words meant. To give an indication of how elementary their vocabulary was, not a single student knew the meaning of "exacerbate," "pragmatic," or "lucid." Two words the class especially enjoyed learning were "misogynous" and "obfuscating," probably because they are fun to say. Perhaps my greatest accomplishment in teaching that class was getting some students to realize that language-learning can be fun.

What my experience taught me was that while some students indeed come with poor verbal skills, they *can* be helped. Those who wish to help them, however, must understand them sufficiently well to create a learning environment in which the students' strengths can be tapped to overcome their lack of English proficiency. In short, students and teachers need to be partners in an exciting educational adventure.

11 On the Ethnic Studies Requirement: Pedagogical Implications [1989]

This essay is a nostalgic reflection on the "good old days"—good despite all the road blocks we faced because those were the days when we were full of naive optimism and thought we could really change the world. Toward the end of the article, I exhorted my students and colleagues to carry on bravely in the new world aborning.

This chapter, reprinted from Amerasia Journal *15, no. 1 (1989): 267–280, by permission of the journal and the Regents of the University of California, was originally intended to be the first of two articles. I never wrote the second one, in which I had planned to chronicle events at other UC campuses, because I was too busy building the Asian American Studies Program at UC Santa Barbara to write up what I had learned from the face-to-face and telephone interviews I had done. I regret I was not able to discuss the public as well as behind-the-scenes events on those campuses based on what dozens of students, faculty members, and administrators—people who had been intimately involved with the issue—told me.*

My inability to complete the second article on this topic reflects the dilemmas experienced by many colleagues of my generation. "So much to be done, so little time" aptly describes our predicament. In my case, as my physical condition deteriorated I had no choice but to forget about plans to conduct research on or write about many topics. Furthermore, to lessen the psychological stress I felt because of not being able to work fifteen or sixteen hours a day, seven days a week, as I had done from the 1970s to the early 1990s in order to accomplish everything I felt needed to be done, I started giving away some of the notes I had taken as well as research material I had collected over the years. (Nonetheless, I still have a voluminous archive at home.) Having always aspired to finish whatever projects I started, giving away or even throwing away my notes and research data on certain topics reduced my self-imposed guilt of not being able to complete various undertakings. Once the notes are gone, I no longer have to write them up into publishable articles or books.

* * *

Stanford University made national headlines when its faculty debated whether to change the core list of books that first-year students are required to read in its Western Culture Program in response to faculty and student criticisms that works by nonwhites and by women were not included in the "canon." Likewise, the University of California at Berkeley received widespread media coverage when its faculty postponed voting on a proposal to add an "American cultures" course to the university's list of graduation requirements. The actions garnered so much publicity because these two institutions rank among the world's leading research universities. But they are by no means the only campuses where such debates are taking place. As more and more institutions of higher learning in the United States begin to grapple with various aspects of ethnic diversity in the coming years it is important to understand why current efforts at enlarging the curriculum have generated such heated exchanges between supporters and opponents of the proposed reforms.

On the face of it, the very reasonable request that universities require their graduates to learn something about nonwhite peoples and cultures in the United States should not have aroused the intense emotions that it did. The fact that such efforts have been so controversial indicates that something far larger than curriculum reform is at stake. What is being challenged, I think, is the very structure of power within the university—the debate over whether to add one little course being only a sign of a more encompassing struggle.

A similar challenge had been mounted in the 1960s and 1970s when student and faculty activists demonstrated militantly to demand that Ethnic Studies programs be established. Some were indeed set up, but though quite a number have survived, few have expanded in the last twenty years. The campaign to get a campuswide Ethnic Studies requirement passed at various colleges across the nation marks a new stage in the growth of its component fields. This development is encountering stiff resistance in some places because no one can predict how the final outcome will affect existing power relations in American higher education. Like their predecessors, today's activists are asking questions about who makes decisions, based on what criteria, about curriculum, personnel, and the distribution of resources and to whom such decision-makers should be accountable. But beyond these material concerns they are also raising issues about who gets to define reality. By so doing they are calling into question the ideological foundations of society in general and of the university in particular. Were this not the case, we would not be witnessing the sound and fury that have so captured public attention in recent months.

In the last three years, students and faculty at four University of California campuses—Santa Cruz, Riverside, Santa Barbara, and Berkeley—have pushed for the establishment of some kind of Ethnic Studies requirement. While such a requirement is already in force at Santa Cruz and Riverside, the final votes will not be taken at Santa Barbara and Berkeley until the spring of 1989.[1] [In this essay] I shall reflect on how the classroom dynamics in the Ethnic Studies courses I have taught that fulfill a campuswide requirement differ from the situation in classes that do not fulfill one. By analyzing my own reactions to the changes, I hope to clarify some of the commonly held but not always explicitly articulated premises upon which Ethnic Studies—as both an academic enterprise and a political project—have been built.

I began teaching Asian American Studies at Sonoma State University in 1971. Subsequently, I spent ten years on the Asian American Studies faculty at UC Berkeley. At both institutions Asian American students composed at least 97 percent of the enrollment in my classes. (This represents a greater "ethnic concentration" than is found in most Afro-American, Chicano/Latino, or Native American Studies courses, according to colleagues teaching in those areas.) Quite frankly, I rather liked having such an ethnic enclave. My students, however, have reacted to the heavy clustering of Asian Americans in different ways. Many feel more comfortable in these Asian American Studies classes than they do in other classes. After an initial reluctance, they often learn to talk freely in discussions. Some who have grown up in primarily white neighborhoods or who have purposely avoided contact with fellow Asian Americans, in contrast, tend to feel very uneasy when they are first surrounded by people who look like themselves. Yet others experience a virtual catharsis when given the chance to come to terms with who they are. The latter often become strongly committed to the Asian American movement. As is true of other teachers, I have been liked by some of my students and disliked by others. But regardless of how they evaluated my teaching, I always felt that teaching primarily Asian American students was a privilege. The rooms in which we held our classes became, however temporarily, *our* spaces; the lecture hours became *our* time. I did not realize how much this privilege meant to me until I lost it.

At UC Santa Cruz, to which I moved in 1984, the ethnic composition and the atmosphere in my classes did not differ greatly from those at Berkeley.

But after the Santa Cruz Academic Senate approved an Ethnic or Third World Studies requirement in February 1985—a requirement that went into effect in the fall of 1986—things changed in subtle but important ways. I taught the introductory Asian American history course twice that first year. These two classes—though the same course—turned out to be vastly different experiences for me as a teacher. Even though I assigned the same readings and gave more or less the same lectures (my lectures are never *quite* the same from quarter to quarter because I do not read from notes), the overall ambience of the class changed. The shift was probably perceptible to no one but myself, but it troubled me sufficiently to make me wonder what the difference augured.

The first time around there were forty-six students in the class. Thirty-five were Asian American, two were black, two Chicano, one Latin American, and six white. I had no teaching assistants so we had no scheduled discussion sections. But the class was still small enough for spontaneous discussions to occur. At first, almost everybody was shy and I had to pull words out of many individuals. But by the third week or so the ice had broken and several talkative students began to say more and more. In time, the class became so eager to talk that I had to set up discussion sections outside lecture hours so that we could get through the lecture materials.

In these conversations the most important discovery we made was that not only do non-Asians hold biased images of Asian Americans—something we have always known and felt angry about—but that Asian Americans *also* have inaccurate perceptions of white, black, Latino, and other Americans. Moreover, we found that among that group of students, at least, television programs seemed to be the primary source of such stereotypes. A very touching exchange took place one afternoon when several Asian American students talked about how their parents did not love them. Unlike white parents in certain television shows they had watched, who hug, kiss, and say nice things to their children, they said, theirs never embraced them. As tears began to glisten in some of their eyes, one of the white students said very gently, "You know, in real life not all white parents express their affection the way you think they do ... many of our parents are divorced, some of our moms and dads fight a lot and seldom spend time with us ... my mom had to work when I was very young so she was never home waiting with a jar of cookies when I came home from school ... one of the reasons I took this class is that I have always envied Asian Americans who have such close-knit families." The Asian American students who had felt so sorry for themselves just a moment earlier looked up, startled. Other students then told about their childhoods, many of which were not happy. Although the discussion took time away from the lecture I had planned to give that day, I did not stop the students from talking because the factual information they missed hearing from me seemed less important than the common bond they were discovering amongst themselves.

As the quarter progressed I encouraged members of the class to relate the Asian American material to larger issues, particularly their own relationships to the world around them. Like other people, I pointed out, Asian Americans are connected to others through history and a complex web of social interactions in which are embedded unequal power relationships. While some of us accept our lot, others do not. But before we can transform what we do not like, I cautioned, we need to understand clearly how the present situation evolved, why some conditions are so difficult to change, and what the personal and social costs of political action may be. By getting the students to think along these lines I hoped that even if I did not succeed in goading them to do anything significant to change their lives—much less the world—I could at least help them understand how individual psychology is linked to history and sociology so that those who felt wounded by life's cruelties no longer suffered alone.

That class was very satisfying to teach. With Asian American students in the majority, it provided a haven in which those who were verbally reticent could slowly learn to express themselves. At the same time, having a small number of students from a variety of ethnic backgrounds made a more probing exchange of views possible. The following quarter, however, more than a hundred students crowded into a room designed to hold forty. As I looked out over the sea of faces—most of them white—my mind began tying itself into knots: "I have no T.A.s, no readers . . . we can't have this kind of class without discussions . . . the students *must* have an opportunity to talk about and 'process' the emotionally charged issues we'll be dealing with . . . I cannot possibly lead five discussion sections a week and write more than a hundred narrative evaluations[2] without any help . . . certainly not when I am holding two administrative positions! . . . I *must* do something to reduce the class size."

My virtual panic had nothing to do with a fear of crowds. I not only do not mind teaching large classes, I actually *enjoy* teaching them. However, when I taught very large classes at Berkeley, I always had T.A.s to work with. Even though the graduate assistants I hired there often had no training in Asian American Studies per se, they learned quickly and were indispensable to the success of the courses. At Santa Cruz, in contrast, no provision had been made for dealing with the sudden rise in the enrollment in courses fulfilling the new requirement; moreover, even if funds were available, few graduate students were to be had since the campus had only a few Ph.D. programs outside the natural sciences.

"There is no way I can accommodate so many students in this class," I began.

"You can't kick us out!" they exclaimed, before I could finish my sentence. "We *have* to get into a class that fulfills the Ethnic Studies requirement."

"But there are lots of other classes that do," I replied.

"That's not true! There are only five this quarter!"

"The fire marshal won't let you sit all over the aisles."

"Then get a bigger classroom!" they demanded.

"I've already tried; there aren't any available at this hour. You know, there's going to be *lots,* and I mean *lots,* of reading in this course—are you *sure* you want to take this class?"

"We have to! We have no choice."

Well, neither really did I. Having worked so hard get an Ethnic Studies requirement established, was I not morally obligated to take all the students who desired to enroll, with or without T.A.s?

We eventually found a larger classroom in an evening time-slot. That worked out well since I had a grant that quarter to rent a lot of films. Though only four hours were scheduled for the lectures, the class actually met for six hours a week. I was able to show the films after the lectures without reserving another room for them since there was no other class scheduled in that room after mine. Furthermore, since I felt that it was mandatory that we have some discussions, I arranged voluntary discussion sections in the afternoons. I divided the class into four groups, each of which was to meet every other week. There being no T.A.s, I had to lead all the sections myself. This was a heavy burden because I was also administering a college with a long history of antagonistic relations to the university of which it was a component part. What helped me get through the quarter was that the class had an upbeat atmosphere. Attendance was surprisingly good (even though it rained a lot that winter, and dark, wet nights in the redwoods of Santa Cruz can be scary), morale was high, and the students frequently told me how much they were enjoying the course.

But one aspect of the class really bothered me. In the discussion sections, the white students chatted amiably enough, but regardless of how hard I tried, very few Asian American students were willing to say anything. Although many T.A.s who had worked with me at Berkeley had often wrung their hands over Asian American students who would not talk, I have seldom encountered this problem myself. Somehow I had always managed to get at least a few of the students to say something. But in this instance, being numerically overwhelmed, the Asian American students felt vulnerable; they could not very well spill their guts in public.

My colleague Wendy Ng, who has also taught at Santa Cruz, has tried heroically to carry on discussions *during lecture hours* in a class with over a hundred students—something I never found the courage to do. Despite her success she was troubled greatly by the anger that Asian American students felt over the way white students dominated the discussions. My students didn't seem particularly angry, but their silence nevertheless spoke volumes. Behind closed doors in my office I tried to find out why, unlike the group I had the quarter before, these did not open their mouths.

"Surely it can't be so hard to talk to or in front of white classmates . . . don't you have any non-Asian friends?" I asked.

"Yes, but those are our *friends*."

"Some of the students in this class *could* become your friends."

"It's not the same."

Indeed, it was not. Although I received superb teaching evaluations that quarter—from Asian and non-Asian students alike—I could not help feeling an immense and inconsolable sense of loss. The circle of trust within which my Asian American students and I had ensconced ourselves in bygone years was no more.

* * *

That I should feel disconsolate requires explanation, for I am not normally a sentimental person. Why, then, in this case, in spite of the overwhelmingly positive response to my course, did I feel such nostalgia for the way things used to be? To get to the root of my vexation I asked myself anew several old questions. First, for whose benefit are we offering Ethnic Studies courses? Second, what do we actually hope to accomplish in our classes? Third, what undergirds the authority of the faculty teaching such courses? With respect to each question, how does the answer change when our courses become part of a general education requirement? In thinking about these issues, much can be learned about race relations in today's American universities.

At first glance the answer to the question, Whom should our courses benefit? seems simple enough. Since students of color were the primary motive force behind the establishment of the pioneer Ethnic Studies programs, the courses should of course benefit them. But even a cursory look at the faces in our classrooms immediately reveals that "students of color" or "minority students" or "Asian American students" are not monolithic terms. Our students come from different national origins and socioeconomic classes. They were born in places near and far. They have been in the United States for varying lengths of time—fifth-generation Chinese Americans mingle with recently arrived refugees from Vietnam. Those who are immigrants came to this country at different ages, which means they encountered mainstream American culture at different stages in their sociopsychological developments. They have also grown up in contrasting environments. Some are the children of well-off professionals and business executives; others come from families so poor that they have to send part of their financial aid checks home to help support their parents, grandparents, or siblings. Just because we use the handy label "Asian American" to refer to them collectively, it does not mean they have similar interests or that we should expect our lectures and assigned readings to touch them equally.

On the other hand, heterogeneity does not imply a lack of commonality. I have learned through my teaching that what makes "Asian American" a defensible and meaningful *analytical category* is not so much that we or our ancestors all came from somewhere in Asia, but rather, virtually all individuals of Asian ancestry in the United States know what it feels like to be a member of a minority group. I say this despite the fact that some students of Asian ancestry deny vehemently that they have ever encountered racism or discrimination of any kind. But such denial is often a protective device, a defense mechanism. When placed in a situation—such as an Asian American Studies class—where it is socially *acceptable* to discuss how Asian Americans and other minorities have been treated, the memories of such individuals seem all of a sudden to be triggered. They begin to recall little incidents or disquieting feelings they have long forgotten or repressed—experiences that reveal they *have*, after all, encountered racial and cultural subordination. Whether or not we wish to acknowledge it, we discover that in the end it is our status as members of *American-made* minority groups that binds us.

Asian American students respond well to Asian American Studies because in our courses we do dissect the experiences that trouble them. We do so by imparting information about historical and sociological phenomena and by analyzing and interpreting their meanings. It is this cognitive component that differentiates our courses from what goes on in counseling groups. We attempt to link personal experiences to changing social, cultural, economic, and political *structures,* while therapists focus more on *individuals* and their relationships to people closest and most significant to them.

Because I consider efforts to help Asian American students "locate" themselves in society to be so important, I felt as though the rug had been pulled out from under me when my classroom became populated largely by white students. I reacted this way not because I am a "reverse racist" but because I am conscious of the fact that my effectiveness as a teacher of Asian American

Studies depends on my ability to keep my finger on the pulse of a majority of my students. I am tuned in to how most Asian American students think and feel, but I do not think the same "fit" exists between me and my non-Asian American students.

"Fit" matters because for me what kind of students are in my class and how they respond to the materials I present affect how I teach. I believe that in every course there is a "text" and a "subtext." The text is what is in our syllabuses, lectures, and readings—the body of knowledge to be transmitted. But since students are not mere receptacles, the manner in which they absorb and react to what we present becomes a subtext. Thus, even though we may dish out the same text year after year, the subtext changes every time we encounter a new group of students. Teachers who care about *how* students learn take note of such changes and react to them, whether consciously or subconsciously. I, for example, prefer to lecture without reading from notes because it allows me to sweep my eyes across the room, calibrating the amount of details I should present as well as how I should frame particular issues, depending on what my "antenna" is picking up.

When the composition of my class changed from being largely Asian Americans to predominantly white, I told the students my purpose would remain the same—to help them understand what life has been like for Asian Americans through successive historical periods. But at the same time, I realized that instead of *articulating* the experience of the group—on its behalf as I had always done—I now had to, instead, *translate* that experience into terms that non-Asian Americans could comprehend.

Articulation is important when some of our students have not yet found words to describe certain facets of their lives. For them, language has not yet become a tool for making the world intelligible, not because their English is inadequate or they lack intelligence but because in their families and at school some aspects of reality have never been talked about or are not permitted to be talked about. By helping them to express inchoate feelings and to explore suppressed ideas, I provide them with cognitive maps—in the form of a vocabulary and a set of explanations—that enable them to make better sense of their world. To the extent that my analysis reflects and resonates with their own experiences, I validate their existence and offer them a means to get a handle on whatever has vexed them. "Facts" thus become vehicles for self-discovery and empowerment as they realize that being different is not the same as being deviant or inferior.

Having a large number of non-Asian students in my class complicates matters enormously because even though I can still articulate the Asian American experience, when I do so now I risk making my Asian American students feel self-consciously naked—as though they are in a fish bowl for everyone to stare at and possibly to make fun of. As Asian American playwright Philip Kan Gotanda has put it, being a minority person is a real burden because it forces one to constantly "monitor" one's environment. Gotanda tells of an almost magical moment when, after residing in Japan for some years, a period long enough for him to have become fluent in spoken Japanese and to have picked up all the proper body language, all of a sudden he felt he could finally become anonymous and consequently free.[3] For the same reason, I think many Asian American students prefer not to talk in classes where they are not in the majority because they hope silence will spare them ridicule: "If I don't say anything, maybe *they* won't notice that I'm different." But having a teacher express what they themselves might have said is no less disconcerting when it is done in a room full of "strangers." Thus, the very same process of self-delineation—which can be so empowering in an in-group setting—can cause profound discomfort when it occurs in a mixed milieu.

My dilemma is that I feel obligated to cover the same ground even though I know doing so might embarrass the Asian American students and make their white peers uneasy. I believe that if I eschew talking about the more sensitive issues I cheat both my Asian American and my non–Asian American students of the insights they should gain by taking courses such as mine. The challenge then becomes how one can pay equal attention to both subgroups. The solution I found was to translate rather than articulate. A translator must ensure that *both* sets of communicators understand the messages being conveyed. In this instance, even though we are all speaking English, I still play the role of translator because I am explicating a reality known by one subgroup to the other subgroup whose members may not be privy to its secrets. However, translation is not a perfect solution. When I could no longer focus exclusively on Asian American students and their needs, the lucidity born of intimacy was lost.

My sense of loss is tied to my understanding of the different perspectives that can be used to study minority groups. I can think of at least four. The oldest approach—an attitude that permeates the scholarly literature published before the 1960s—treats minority groups as deviant or deficient. According to proponents of this view, to become "normal," members of minority groups must assimilate into the majority culture and discard the "dysfunctional" minority ones. The second perspective focuses on the "contributions" of various ethnic groups. It is a celebratory stance couched in terms of multicultural enrichment, but it seldom probes the causes of inequality. The third viewpoint defines minority groups as victims. Its theorists seek to understand how forces of exploitation and oppression are built into the fabric of society.

The fourth angle of vision sees members of minority groups as agents of history—people who think and feel and make decisions even when their lives are severely circumscribed by conditions beyond their control.

I identify most strongly with the fourth perspective. For that reason, getting quiet Asian American students to talk in class is very important to me because I believe self-expression is one means through which individuals can *externalize* their experiences. Unlike the internalization that occurs when new members of a society—be they children or immigrants—are socialized into the values and norms of the community they have to learn to call home, externalization involves an opposite social process; it allows subjective experiences to acquire *communal* meaning and become a vocalized, hence tangible, element in the culture that the new members enter. Instead of being passive recipients of the host culture, new members who have a voice can play an active role in shaping that culture. Speech provides a means through which many hitherto quiet Asian American students can learn to become agents of history. But they can acquire such agency only when they overcome a double repression: Asian traditions that train the young (especially the female) to be quiet, submissive, and obedient *and* American racism that threatens members of minority groups with harm unless they "stay in their place." Staying in their place means keeping silent. Conversely, breaking silence is an act of rebellion—a declaration that a public self now exists.

I believe that those who control decision-making in the university have opposed the growth of Ethnic Studies courses precisely because they contain such an element of self-discovery and empowerment for students. If all that Ethnic Studies courses try to do is to impart information *about* the history and "exotic" cultural practices of nonwhite groups, they would not be threatening at all. After all, cultural pluralism in and of itself is innocuous and even colorful; it only becomes ominous when it is used as the ideological justification for changing existing arrangements of privilege and power. On the level of scholarship, those academic gatekeepers who determine what kind of work is "legitimate" sometimes dismiss the writings of feminist scholars or minority scholars as "too shrill," "too angry," or "too bitter" precisely because our sharp words puncture the sheath that envelops the mostly male and mostly white world of academic discourse—discourse that pretends it has the sole right to define normalcy, universality, what is human.

Ideally, for Ethnic Studies courses that enroll a large number of nonminority students to succeed in their purpose, they must, first, help students of color arrive at the same conceptual clarity about the history, contemporary manifestations, and meaning of racial inequality that all Ethnic Studies courses aim to achieve. Second, they must help white students come to terms with the fact that they may unwittingly be what Kenneth Clark has called "accessories to profound injustice."[4] Third, they must provide all students with an arena in which to explore a new vision—a world where interdependent groups share a common destiny. The end we seek is mutual empathy. But we can only hope to reach this goal if we do not assume an accusatory stance. The importance of not "guilt tripping" white students was taught me by a student who had acquired a reputation for disrupting the lectures of minority faculty whenever they talked about racism. This student, however, was very well behaved in my class. One day I decided to ask him what had caused him to change his attitude.

"It's not my attitude," he explained. "I got angry in the other classes because every time the professors lectured about racism, I felt they were accusing me *personally* of being racist. But you're very analytical—you try to explain why racism exists and how it has affected Asian Americans—so I don't feel like you are attacking *me* directly."

This observation alerted me to another dilemma. By creating analytical "distance" I avoid alienating white students, but by soft-pedaling racism I rob my Asian American students of an important forum in which to express their confusion, hurt, and anger. In the short space of ten weeks—or even fifteen or twenty weeks—it does not seem possible to meet the needs of white and Asian American students simultaneously. There simply is not enough time to work through all the thoughts and feelings that the course material elicits. A more daunting difficulty is that even if faculty may want to help students overcome the interracial tensions that are so deeply rooted in American society, most of us are not up to the task. Which one of us can claim to be completely free of racism, sexism, homophobia, and class and religious prejudice?

Therefore, to avoid disappointment, bitterness, and cynicism, we must be modest in our goals. We should recognize that courses that fulfill an Ethnic Studies requirement cannot eradicate racism. All we can hope to do, if we are good teachers, is to get our students to listen to us and to one another, to learn a few unpleasant truths, and to gain the insight that people who do not look like ourselves nevertheless face similar dilemmas common to the human condition. Even this will not be easy to accomplish; students who have to take a course because it is required often resent doing so.

Faced with a captive, possibly restive, audience, we may wonder if our authority as professors under such circumstances may have become more tenuous. Could the "threshold of convincibility"—the amount of evidence needed to convince our audience that this or that assertion is indeed true—

now be higher?[5] I worried about such a possibility when I puzzled over why far fewer students challenged all the things I said than I had expected.

It was then that I realized that several of the films I had shown contained scenes of white, male scholars discussing the discrimination Asian immigrants had faced (and continue to face). Not only that, but these colleagues also asserted that such discrimination was clearly racist. In Stephen Okazaki's *Unfinished Business,* for example, Peter Irons and Roger Daniels expound on the racism that led to the incarceration of Japanese Americans during World War II. In Spencer Nakasako's film on Vietnamese refugee fishermen, *Monterey's Boat People,* Sandy Lydon comments on the earlier discriminatory legislation against Chinese and Japanese immigrant fishermen. In *Dollar a Day, Ten Cents a Dance,* a film about Filipino farmworkers by Mark Schwartz and Geoffrey Dunn, Howard DeWitt talks about the racism manifest in the anti-Filipino riot that took place in Watsonville, California, in the early 1930s. Although I had lectured about the same events and their meaning, I could not help but suspect that having Irons, Daniels, Lydon, and DeWitt—who *look and talk* like the white male authority figures with whom all students are familiar—validate my analysis made it easier for my students to accept what they heard. It does not flatter my ego, of course, to think that white male colleagues may have enhanced my credibility; on the other hand, since I want above all else to penetrate the wall of resistance that some students may have unconsciously erected to block out information about the dark, unpleasant "underside of American history," I do not mind using all the means at my disposal.

* * *

As we enter a new stage in our struggle for academic legitimacy and more widespread influence, our central task is to convince colleagues and nonminority students that we, too, are educators—educators competent to teach not only students of color but also *all* students. Such a claim has to be made because during the last two decades we have justified the existence of Ethnic Studies programs primarily by arguing that we meet the special, unmet needs of students of color. Critics of such programs, meanwhile, have charged ad nauseum that the manner in which we have sought to meet those needs has been "nonacademic," too "political," and therefore unacceptable. But we must point out to them that what we are trying to do is but a variant of what the defenders of a liberal education argue it should do.

Faculty who believe in the importance of a liberal education try to provide an overview of the structure of knowledge and how scholars have divided it into different branches, each dealing with some segment of human experience or natural phenomena. They teach students how to think critically about the information they receive by examining the underlying values that influence the way such information is packaged. They encourage those coming of age in these times of flux to understand the constantly changing world in which we live and our relationship to it. They urge students to use the knowledge they gain to improve the quality of human life.

Faculty teaching Ethnic Studies, skeptics need to realize, can play a crucial role in a liberal education even though our contributions have so far not yet been recognized, much less rewarded. Our specialty is to make sense of the historical and contemporary experiences of nonwhite peoples in the United States. We broaden the university's offerings first by unearthing (through research and analysis) and then by imparting (through teaching) information not found in the regular curriculum. When we show students how to think critically, we often do so by suggesting competing perspectives on the world—points of view that have sometimes been suppressed because they challenge the status quo way of looking at things. While our stance may threaten colleagues who are insecure about their own standings in the academy, it can, and should, stimulate others to formulate dazzling new theories or promote collaborative efforts that lead to breakthroughs in the state of knowledge about certain phenomena. Hence, our presence within the university should be treated as an exciting addition and not as an inconvenient political necessity. Finally, when we give students some of the tools they need to enable them to make the world better, future generations benefit. If those of us who have taught Ethnic Studies for many years did not believe all this to be true, we certainly would not have devoted the best years of our lives to developing the field.

Notes

1. The University of California, one of the largest public university systems in the world, consists of nine campuses located at Berkeley, Davis, Irvine, Los Angeles, Riverside, San Diego, San Francisco, Santa Barbara, and Santa Cruz. With the exception of the San Francisco campus, which is a medical school, all the other campuses are comprehensive research universities offering the B.A., B.Sc., M.A., Ph.D., and a variety of professional degrees in a wide range of subjects.

2. The University of California, Santa Cruz, does not have grades. Rather, instructors must write a "narrative evaluation"—ranging from a few sentences to more than a page (single-spaced)—describing and assessing the work each student has done during the quarter. This is a time-consuming task that not all faculty enjoy doing.

3. Philip Kan Gotanda, "Visions of an Asian American Artist," National Asian American Telecommunications Association workshop, San Francisco, December 3, 1988.

4. Kenneth Clark, *Dark Ghetto* (New York: Harper and Row, 1965), 75.

5. I borrow this term from Carol Nagy Jacklin, "Feminist Research and Psychology," in *The Impact of Feminist Research in the Academy,* ed. Christie Farnham (Bloomington: Indiana University Press, 1988), 99.

12 Why an Ethnic Studies Requirement? [1989, 1995]

This chapter combines two short articles that were published in newsletters sent out by the University of California, Santa Barbara. The first was written in 1989 and appeared in L & S at UC Santa Barbara: A Newsletter for Parents of College of Letters and Science Students 13 *(Fall 1989); the second was published in* 93106, *the campus newsletter, on April 17, 1995, 5–6. Because the intended audiences of the two newsletters differ from the faculty and students who read* Amerasia Journal, *my tone in these official university publications is more inclusive. "We" refers to everyone, not just people of color.*

My choice of terms reflects the preferences of students. I began to use the term Euro-American *(or* European American*) after talking in depth with many white students about what they preferred to be called. Many said they did not want to be called* white. *"Is that why so many of you try to get suntans?" I asked in jest. "Sure!" they replied. More surprising is that some also did not want to be called* Caucasian, *but no one was able to tell me why. When I suggested "European American" as a parallel term to* Asian American, African American, Latino American, *and* Native American, *they liked the idea even though it sounded novel at first. I explained that the newer terms refer to the geographic origins of members of these groups rather than to their racial, national, or ethnic origins. Some students asked, "Why can't we all be just Americans?" "Because," I replied, "people in this country still tend to judge people according to the color of their skins or other bodily features." That, I added, is precisely why we have an ethnic studies requirement: All of us will learn to see one another as members of a common human race even as we continue to possess distinctive features, live according to different values, and behave in diverse ways in daily life.*

I do not like the fact that, at UCSB, the requirement is called the "ethnicity requirement" rather than the "ethnic studies requirement." To me, "ethnicity" smacks of essentialism, whereas "ethnic studies" refers to a field of academic inquiry. That is why, in these UCSB publications, I continued to use the term ethnic studies requirement *instead of* ethnicity requirement *(as almost everyone on the UCSB campus calls it).*

* * *

Five University of California campuses, including UCSB, now require their entering students to take a course in Ethnic Studies as part of their general education program. At UCSB, Letters and Science students must take a course that "focuses on the history and the cultural, intellectual, and social experience[s] of racial minorities and/or other ethnic groups in the United States."

Getting the "ethnicity requirement" passed by the Academic Senate was a difficult task. Opponents of the requirement usually cited bureaucratic reasons for their stance; they argued that there are already too many requirements. If an ethnicity requirement is approved, they asked, what additional ones, such as gender studies, will be demanded next?

Groups supporting the requirement, meanwhile, gave diverse reasons for wanting one. Students of color—the phrase that many minority students now use to describe themselves—believe that requiring all students to take such a course will reduce the amount of racism they encounter. Euro-American (white) students who supported the requirement wanted to become better prepared to live and work in an increasingly multiethnic American society. Liberal faculty felt that the university has a responsibility for promoting cultural diversity. Administrators and staff hoped that by increasing interracial "literacy," fewer unpleasant and potentially violent racial incidents would occur.

No ten-week course can eradicate racism, for racism is based not just on prejudice and ignorance but also on the desire of presently privileged groups to retain their power. But having such a requirement can at least help students become more aware of how other people think, feel, and live.

I believe that for courses that fulfill an Ethnic Studies requirement to succeed, they must achieve three goals. First, the courses must be sufficiently analytical to enable students to understand how and why racial inequality developed in the United States and elsewhere in the world. Such insight is necessary before we can begin to change the social, economic, political, and cultural structures that uphold such inequality.

Second, the faculty and teaching assistants staffing such courses must help both students of color and Euro-American students to deal with the resentment each group feels. Students of color are often angry about the discrimination many of them have experienced, while Euro-American students resent being made to feel guilty about a situation for which they do not believe they should be held responsible. Honest and sometimes painful dialogue must therefore be a built-in component of these courses.

Third, the required courses must provide an arena in which students of all ethnic backgrounds can explore a new vision—a world in which interdependent groups share a common destiny. That is, while we begin such courses by explaining differences we must end them by stressing what all human beings have in common and how we, as members of the same society, must join hands to improve the lives of everyone.

A tall order indeed. One solace, fortunately, is that the measure of our success lies not so much in how fully we achieve all three goals but in how hard we try to move closer to them.

* * *

In a brief essay I wrote five years ago for a Letters and Science newsletter I articulated three goals for courses fulfilling the Ethnic Studies requirement. How successful have we been in meeting those goals?

Since more than two-thirds of the courses in my department, Asian American Studies, fulfill the Ethnic Studies requirement, we have collected a lot of anonymous comments from students in the last five years—enough to give us an idea of how our courses have been received. It is quite easy to separate the comments evaluating a faculty member's classroom performance—his or her ability to deliver lectures clearly in a well-organized manner, to convey his or her enthusiasm for the subject matter and for teaching, and so forth—from those that reflect students' reactions to the "ethnicity requirement" per se.

Student evaluations of our courses have been gratifyingly positive. Though we do not ask students to state their ethnic origins on the questionnaires, internal evidence from their written comments show that both Asian and non-Asian students appreciate what they have learned. They write such statements as, "Thank you for opening my eyes," and "This course really helped me to come to terms with my heritage," or ask such questions as, "Why weren't we taught these things in high school?"

The negative reactions, though smaller in number, are also revealing. Students resent being "forced" to take such courses and to listen to what they decry as "political correctness." In one class, a student stated that the course was "absolutely the worst" he or she had ever taken at UCSB because it "allowed minorities to complain." Another student in the same class, however, wrote a long personal note to the instructor, urging her not to feel hurt by the negative comments. "You should know he's a supporter of Newt [Gingrich]," the second student said of the first. Other student critics ask, "Why must we always divide people into ethnic groups?" and "Why can't we interact with each other simply as individuals?"

Overall, I think courses fulfilling the Ethnic Studies requirement have been more successful in introducing information and perspectives not usually found in the traditional disciplines than in promoting the "honest and sometimes painful dialogue" that I argued five years ago "must be a built-in component of these courses." In my own classes it has been difficult to incorporate the desired dialogue for two reasons. First, it has taken a real intellectual juggling act just to squeeze the most basic, essential information into a ten-week quarter. Second, the enrollment in many of our classes is so large (hundreds of students) that it is virtually impossible for meaningful dialogue to occur during lectures.

Another major hurdle to effective dialogue is that many T.A.s and faculty have not been trained to guide discussions of emotionally charged topics in a way that students feel "safe" enough to express themselves freely. Uncertain about whether or not their views will be heard with respect, some prefer to remain silent. Faculty and T.A.s, meanwhile, fearful of potentially explosive confrontations, often gloss over or even deliberately steer discussions away from controversial issues.

Though faculty and T.A.s need more practice in mediating volatile conversations, we must learn to do so in a *pedagogical* manner. The settings in which we work are classrooms and not encounter groups or confidential counseling sessions. Our task, as scholars and teachers, is to analyze a wide range of issues and problems—including those with no obvious solutions. We cannot and should not provide simplistic answers to complex issues, even when we know that some students and other members of the campus community may yearn to hear such answers. The more we can encourage others to recognize that paradoxes, contradictions, and ambiguities are inherent in the human condition, the better teachers we will be.

Relations among ethnic/racial groups, between men and women, straights and gays/lesbians, rich and poor, young and old, immigrants and American-born, are among the most complicated issues facing Americans today. Creating conditions under which these relationships can be discussed with civility and in mutual respect—not just in those courses that fulfill the "ethnicity requirement" but in other courses as well as outside the classroom—is one of the greatest challenges we face as educators.

13 Are You Ready for the Twenty-first Century? [1991]

Every year UC Santa Barbara graduates more than four thousand seniors. Because of the large numbers, five different graduation ceremonies are scheduled. I was asked to deliver the commencement address for one of the two ceremonies for social science majors in the College of Letters and Science on June 16, 1991. It was one of those wonderfully balmy Santa Barbara days, and everyone was in a good mood. When I characterized UC Santa Barbara students as "truly nice people," they clapped, whistled, whooped, and waved their arms in the air.

This speech reflects how I had learned by then to talk to racially and ethnically mixed audiences, male and female, young and old. Thus, even though it has nothing to do with Asian American studies or Asian American students, I include it in this volume because it shows how much I had to tailor my rhetoric according to what audience I was addressing on which occasion. To avoid any "unpleasant" occurrences, the students, faculty, staff members, and administrators who serve on the "graduation committee" within the College of Letters and Science every year go to great lengths to make sure nothing "controversial" will be said. Although I do not approve of such prior censorship, I went along with the vetting process because I agreed that graduation ceremonies should be warm, memorable occasions. I had no intention of using barbed words that might cause anyone pain, but it was a challenge finding ways to make certain points without arousing anyone's ire.

A touching thing happened after the ceremony. As I was getting off the platform, several graduates, male and female, rushed up to me and said, "Thank you for including us." When I looked puzzled, they told me they were gay and lesbian. One woman was apparently so overcome with emotion that she hugged me. Then I saw a man rolling his wheelchair laboriously across the lawn. "Thank

you for saying I'm not a freak," he said. "Well, neither am I!" I responded. The
fleeting exchanges brought home to me how deeply individuals yearn to be
included as "normal" beings in society.

* * *

In ancient Greek mythology, there was a god named Janus who had two
faces that looked in opposite directions. I have always thought that if there
were a patron saint for commencement day, that saint should be Janus, for
commencement, more than any other event, provides us with an occasion
to look both backward and forward—backward to see where we've come
from, to assess what we've learned, to measure and take pleasure in what
we've achieved, and to find strength to overcome our failures; forward to
new challenges, responsibilities, and uncertainties. In short, commencement
is a day for both joyous celebration and sober reflection.

It is in this mood of celebration and reflection that I ask, "Are you ready
for the twenty-first century?" Certainly, if the education you've received at
UCSB has been as good as I think it is, then you should be at least partially
ready for the next century. On the other hand, as large-scale changes occur
in many parts of the world with frightening rapidity, only those who are
brashly over-confident can say, "Of course we're ready."

Being ready for the twenty-first century doesn't mean we can accurately
predict what the world will be like ten years from now or that we have the
answers and solutions to pressing problems. What it does mean is that we
have developed the self-confidence to live with flux and cope with ambiguity. It means we are psychologically and socially flexible enough to try out
different ways of relating to people, of doing things, whenever necessary.

The ability to live with flux and ambiguity will help us remain sane. The
next few decades, I predict, will be difficult ones for Americans. For one thing,
the relatively simple, bipolar world we've known since the end of the Second
World War is fast disappearing. Instead of two superpowers confronting each
other, the world is becoming a multipolar one. The rise of Japan and other
nations in Asia, the emergence of a united Europe, the resurgence of Africa
and Latin America, and the drawing in of Australia and the island nations
of the Pacific Ocean to the community of nations means that Americans can
no longer see world affairs in black and white terms—a world in which we,
the good guys, are battling the communist bloc, the bad guys. Moreover, the
euphoria generated by our victory in the Persian Gulf War notwithstanding, might may no longer always make right. International relations have
become frustratingly complex. National boundaries are becoming increasingly blurred, even as long-suppressed ethnic and religious identities and

separatist agendas within nation-states reassert themselves. Like it or not, we are entering an era full of promises as well as dangers.

If the United States is to retain its leadership in such a world, I believe we Americans—especially individuals of your generation, who will assume leadership positions in the twenty-first century—must learn to function as partners, I repeat, *partners,* with people in other nations rather than as the number-one, dominant force in international affairs. Our goal cannot simply be to win wars, however just and glorious. Our goal cannot be to control and use the largest share of the planet's natural resources, however that may satisfy our desire to consume, in order to fulfill one version of the American Dream. Rather, we must learn to accept our growing interdependence with others for the sake of global survival. The communications revolution we have witnessed in the last few decades means no nation can function in isolation any longer. What happens in other parts of the world invariably affects us, if not today then a few months or a few years hence.

Interdependence is an increasingly visible aspect not only of international relations but of domestic affairs as well. If our country is to remain stable and relatively free of violence, Americans of European ancestry must learn to share political power, economic rewards, and social prestige with members of other ethnic and racial groups. Men must learn to interact with women as equals and vice versa. Those who are straight must learn to accept gays and lesbians. The able-bodied must learn to stop seeing those with physical handicaps as freaks. The rich must learn not to despise the poor. The powerful must learn to change their habit of oppressing the powerless.

I am not advocating that we do all this because we are good liberals or because it is politically correct. Rather, I believe our willingness to accept diversity and our ability to nurture and tap the talents of individuals from as many different backgrounds and walks of life as possible is the key to our collective survival. As problems become more difficult to solve, we need more brains to think about how to solve them. As some of us age, grow tired, and run out of steam, we need new blood and energy to keep the social engine of our nation running.

Often, it is feared that a large influx of people who look different from what "Americans" are supposed to look like will tear asunder our social fabric. But surely America's core values are strong enough to tolerate the introduction of other ideas. Surely the American economy is strong enough to welcome investments from Japan and other nations. Surely American democracy is strong enough to become ever more inclusive.

Instead of fearing foreign influence or the participation of those who have historically been denied any role in our public life, we should welcome newcomers who can and do make significant contributions to the vitality of our nation. I believe it is possible to develop some basic common goals, even as we express divergent opinions. It is possible to build a national community in which many different voices can be heard without eroding fundamental American ideals—ideals that proclaim that people can live in equality and with social justice. Unfortunately, in years gone by we had been rather narrow in who we included among "the people." For our own sake, and for the sake of future generations, we need to broaden our definition of "the people" so that all those who contribute to the well-being of American society can enjoy the fruits of their labor. People must feel they have a real stake in American society if they are to be loyal Americans.

Those of us who have received our higher education at one of the University of California campuses are fortunate indeed, for, regardless of what we've majored in, as students and professors in a world-class research university, whether or not we realize it, we've been exposed to different perspectives, different methods for acquiring knowledge and finding truth. We have intermingled with people from many ethnic groups, from various class backgrounds, from dozens of foreign countries. Even though we may not have always socialized with them, we have at least sat in some of the same classrooms, listened to some of the same lectures, taken tests given by some of the same professors, participated in some of the same discussions led by some of the same T.A.s, partied in some of the same hangouts, conspired to carry out some of the same pranks, danced to some of the same music.

In the process, I hope you've learned a crucial lesson—that individuals can disagree with one another without eroding the friendship and love they share. Marriages that last are ones in which the partners can disagree—indeed, fight—while continuing to love each other. Friendships that remain warm are ones in which individuals continue to trust one another as they argue, do things in opposite ways, or at times even betray one another.

You are also lucky because, as UCSB graduates, you are part of a worldwide community. Since its founding in 1868, the University of California has awarded more than a million degrees. Today, the nine campuses in the UC system hand out more than thirty-seven thousand degrees every year. So, all of you are part of a very large, very vibrant, very productive, very dispersed family. No matter where in the world you may go, you are likely to find another UC graduate there. In short, you never need feel lonely, for you have friends and potential friends everywhere.

Neither will you be completely stymied by problems that will inevitably crop up, for you have received the kind of education that stresses not so much the memorization of "facts" as the ability to ask questions and find answers—especially the ability to evaluate the validity of those questions and answers. Nothing pleases me more as a faculty member than when students tell me that they leave my classes with more questions than when they entered.

Knowing how to ask questions is important because, so far as I'm concerned, skepticism and the courage to challenge authority are among the best safeguards against authoritarianism. Curiosity is a wonderful antidote to apathy. A continual search for new knowledge and new ways of knowing is a good preventive for the atrophy of the mind. The willingness to listen to others, to accept them for who they are, to contribute to their well-being and happiness, are effective cures for cynicism. I believe human beings need meaning in their lives as much as, if not more than, physical comfort to be happy. In my experience, serving others and sharing our riches with them are some of the surest ways to find meaning in life.

I must tell you that fundamentally I am a pessimist, for I believe that people are capable of both good and evil and that, more often than not, evil triumphs. But I've discovered that one way to overcome despair, to not cry too much over what has been called the human condition, is to act as though one were an optimist, to live as though one thinks relations among individuals, among groups, among nations, can be, will be, improved. Those who know me well know that I am a very busy person. I keep busy, doing what I believe in, fighting the good fight, not because I think I shall win but because doing so prevents me from being self-indulgent, from wasting time feeling sorry for myself when things don't go right. If there ever comes a time in your life when you get inconsolably depressed, recall my prescription for getting over the blues: Do something for somebody else. Try it. I assure you, it works.

I've been privileged to be a member of the UC faculty for almost twenty years. During that time I've taught at four different campuses of the University of California and done research at a fifth. Over these two decades I have tried to pinpoint the most salient characteristics of the students at each of these campuses. In my view, what shines out about UCSB students is their sunny disposition, their good-natured approach to life, their refusal to get uptight. UCSB students are truly nice people. Perhaps the fact that the campus has its own beach and our skies are always bright has something to do with it. The ability to be of good cheer, no matter what hurdles are placed in your path, no matter how unjustly you've been treated, will stand you in good stead in your lives ahead.

More than ten years ago, when I was driving all over California doing research, every time I approached Santa Barbara I noticed the special quality of the light in this region—this narrow strip of land, boxed in as it is between the mountains and the sea. I think there is an unusual, perhaps even eerie, luminescence here that exists in few other places. Those of you who are artists will know what I mean, while those who don't have the same practiced eye may think I'm getting a bit too mystical. In any case, eventually I came to UCSB to teach because I am enchanted by this light that illuminates not only our natural but also our social environment.

As you graduate today from the Santa Barbara campus of the world's greatest public university system I salute you for the hard work that has enabled you to make it through school. I applaud you for overcoming the hardships you have encountered. I congratulate you for your many achievements. I wish you a busy, productive, happy, healthy, and meaningful life. But most of all, I hope the special light that bathes our beautiful campus and its environs will follow you wherever you may go. Finally, do not be afraid. The future is yours.

14 My Teaching Philosophy [1998]

When I was nominated for a distinguished teaching award in 1998 I was required to submit a statement on my teaching philosophy. This was the first time I had been asked to pinpoint and explain what I try to do in the classroom. The Distinguished Teaching Award Committee at UC Santa Barbara strictly limits the length of the statement, so I had to put in a nutshell the guiding principles I have followed during my career. I had won a similar teaching award at UC Berkeley in 1978, but in that instance I did not have to write anything. For that reason, I never consciously articulated a "teaching philosophy" until I was required to do so in 1998.

Looking back, however, I have been very consistent in my beliefs and practices. I have implicitly followed a teaching philosophy even though I was not conscious of doing so. I have aged and my students have changed, but some things remain if not eternal verities then at least useful ideas that function as mirrors in which to see and judge ourselves.

* * *

I believe there are certain common elements that characterize effective teaching, regardless of the discipline and field, class size, or the level of the courses that faculty members teach. These include mastery of the subject matter, the ability to communicate clearly and engagingly, and a concern for the well-being of students in and out of the classroom. However, having spent my entire career teaching Asian American Studies and comparative Ethnic Studies, there have been additional challenges I have faced. Given the fact that the subject matter I deal with—American race relations and the multifaceted impacts of racism and other forms of oppression on various subordinated groups—is so troubling, I have had to learn to strike a balance between intellectual honesty and sensitivity. If the analysis I present is to make an impact, it must be nuanced and nonaccusatory. My job is to help students of color understand the larger forces impinging (often negatively) upon their lives while simultaneously giving white students a positive learning experience. Over the years, students of many ethnic backgrounds have thanked me for "opening" their eyes in a manner that did not make them feel like they were mere victims or guilty perpetrators.

The notion of "tough love" lies at the heart of my teaching philosophy. I expect *all* my students—regardless of their ethnic origins, race, class, gender, sexual orientation, handicap, or age—to perform as well as they are capable of. While I will go out of my way to support students who truly make an effort I am not particularly patient with those who are lazy or self-indulgent. The practice of tough love means that I refuse to acquiesce to pleas—whether from students, their parents, or others—to give better grades in order to "help" particular students get into medical school, law school, or some other graduate program. Neither have I pandered to subtle pressures to evaluate nonwhite or female faculty colleagues more leniently when I serve on review committees. My stance has made me unpopular in some quarters, but I have never deviated from it because I think when one gives in to such pressures one becomes complicit in perpetuating a profound form of racism or sexism—the belief that people of color or women should be judged less rigorously because less can be expected of them. I call this the "racism/sexism/classism of low expectations." Such behavior signals that members of minority groups are innately inferior and therefore cannot be expected to perform as well as members of the majority group.

In my attempt to be an effective teacher I have varied my teaching methods according to the kind of classes I teach. In large lecture courses I plan well-timed and clearly structured lectures because I believe the logical progression of ideas matters in large lecture halls even more than they do in smaller classrooms. Since the large lecture courses I teach fulfill various General Education requirements, I work hard at finding ways to talk to students at many different levels of academic preparation and political sophistication—students who are sitting side by side in the same classroom. I strive to explain difficult concepts to lower-division students without insulting the intelligence of upper-division students, although I don't always succeed. In smaller classes, where far more opportunities exist for give and take, I encourage students to express themselves and to explore various ideas as fully as possible. I do not think that smaller classes automatically promote good teaching while larger ones impede meaningful pedagogy. It is possible to excel in both settings if a teacher is attentive to his or her audience and respects students' common sense. In graduate courses or seminars, my main goal is to train potential college faculty to become not only knowledgeable about their field as it presently exists but also to enable them to teach with confidence, do their own research with ease, evaluate the work of others in a collegial manner, and know how to keep up with the burgeoning scholarly writings without feeling overwhelmed.

In my opinion, being a productive researcher is a key ingredient in effective teaching because a continually active researcher is more insightful about how knowledge is constructed, validated, challenged, and modified over time. Moreover, he or she has more opportunities to draw students into research projects, as I recently did with four undergraduates in writing the book *Hmong Means Free: Life in Laos and America* and with a graduate student in my forthcoming book *Not Just Victims: Conversations with Cambodian Community Leaders in the United States*. Teaching and research are mutually beneficial. A faculty who can teach well will also write well because effective communication undergirds both activities.

PART 3

Empowering Ourselves

Although I have never thought of myself as a feminist, I have read a lot of feminist writings. One concept introduced by feminist scholars and activists that makes a lot of sense to me is the claim that "the personal is political." The essays in this section illustrate how the reverse is also true. The political is personal; or, to put a twist to it, "the academic is political" and "the political can be academic."

Having been trained as a social scientist, I was inclined early on to analyze the structural factors affecting economic, political, social, or cultural phenomena. The two prevailing conceptual frameworks I studied in graduate school were structural-functional theory and modernization theory, both of which are now completely outdated and have been forcefully debunked. While teaching Asian American studies, however, I began to see, close up, through conversations with hundreds of students who shared their unhappy as well as happy experiences with me, that large structures affect individuals in unique ways.

At this point I reread the writings of Karl Marx and Mao Zedong, which I had studied earlier but for a different purpose, in order to remind myself that although structures do constrain individual lives, people are not, and need not be, automatons reacting only to external stimuli. People can and do make history. That is, the structures within which we carry on our daily lives are *human* creations. For that reason, human beings can change them. From the writings of Erik Erikson, I learned to look for clues on how biography intersects history. Meanwhile, Frantz Fanon's and Albert Memmi's dissection of colonialism and its impact on individual consciousness alerted me to the deep and enduring psychological consequences of oppression.

I searched for ways to put these insights into practice. Some time in the mid-1980s I transformed myself into a historian when I discovered that historians—particularly social historians—value the concept of agency. It occurred to me that if I learned to write as a historian (even though I had never taken a history course, either in college or in graduate school) rather than as a number-crunching social scientist I could better convey the agency of Asian Americans as they struggled, and continue to struggle, for survival in a land that did and does not always welcome them. A look at the dates when the essays in this volume were written will reveal the gradual transformation in my writing style, from that of a positivist, "objective" social scientist to that of a hermeneutical, humanistic historian. I have retained, however, some of the intellectual habits I learned in graduate school, including that of counting things (a practice a narrative historian once told me makes for inelegant prose), because counting and making lists, especially in oral presentations, can help audiences keep track of the points one wishes to make.

I became a historian for aesthetic, philosophical, and political reasons—aesthetic, because historians value lucidity; philosophical, because developing a longer view of the human journey on earth would make me less impatient and more accepting of failures and weaknesses; and political, because the relatively jargon-free prose of historians would enable me to communicate more effectively with the readers I hope to influence. The politics of communication I practiced is manifested in the textbooks I wrote (*Asian Americans: An Interpretive History* and *Asian Californians*, both published in 1991) or coedited (*Peoples of Color in the American West*, coedited with Douglas H. Daniels, Mario T. Garcia, and Terry P. Wilson [1994] and *Major Problems in California History: Documents and Essays*, coedited with Spencer C. Olin [1997]).

Even when I discuss scholarly research, I keep the potential "dual use" of my writing in mind. That is to say, I try simultaneously to address the concerns of specialists and to ensure that students and the general reading public can easily understand what I write. *Hmong Means Free: Life in Laos and America* (1994), *Not Just Victims: Conversations with Cambodian Community Leaders in the United States* (2003), and *Survivors: Cambodian Refugees in the United States* (2004) are all "dual use" books intended for multiple audiences because very few books and articles about the refugees, immigrants, expatriates, and transmigrants from Cambodia, Laos, and Vietnam are suitable for classroom use.

I have engaged in politics in another way. Since the beginning of my academic career I have volunteered to serve on campus committees, both within my own department and for the campus at large, in order to worm my way into the university's inner recesses. I tried to fathom its complex structure so I could experiment with ways to change it. I was buoyed by the empowerment that comes with the assertion of agency. But, recognizing that the political is personal, I always reflexively asked myself, "Why am I doing this?" "Is this just an ego trip?" "What will be the consequences of my action?" and "Who will benefit and who will be harmed by the changes I seek to make?" I recognized early on that the power structure in college and university campuses is not always obvious to the naked eye and that it, and the actors within it, are mutually constitutive. Power is not monopolized by some abstract entity called "the administration" but, rather, is constantly being contested among administrators, faculty, staff, and students.

My understanding of how a research university is structured, how it functions, and how faculty must behave within it if they hope to make changes is presented in chapters 15 and 16. Chapter 17 describes how I went about trying to transform the university. In chapter 18 I identify what I see as the key challenges facing Asian American studies in the twenty-first century and meditate on what the future may hold for the field. I wrote chapters 17 and 18 specifically for this book.

15   Asian Americans and the Structure of
Power in American Universities [1989]

A shorter version of this essay appeared under the title "Beyond Affirmation Action: Empowering Asian American Faculty" in Change: The Magazine of Higher Learning *(Nov.–Dec. 1989): 48–51. The essay was based on a keynote address I had given at the second national conference convened by Asian Pacific Americans for Higher Education (APAHE) in Los Angeles at the beginning of 1989. Throughout my talk, I used the pronoun* we *to address other Asian Americans. In two published versions, however, I used "they" to refer to Asian Americans until almost the end, when I reverted to "we" in order to signify that I was shifting my gaze from a general audience to a specific one: "We, Asian Americans, must do this or that." The second published version, which discusses several specific events in addition to the general analysis of the university's power structure, was coauthored with Ling-chi Wang, "Racism and the Model Minority: Asian Americans in Higher Education," which appeared in* The Racial Crisis in American Higher Education, *edited by Philip G. Altbach and Kofy Lomotey (Albany: State University of New York Press, 1991), 41–67.*

One prediction I made in my talk has indeed come true. The first two Asian Americans to become chancellors in the University of California system were engineers. Chang-lin Tien, a Chinese American mechanical engineer, became the first Asian American to be named chancellor at a major research university (UC Berkeley) after serving as vice chancellor for research at UC Berkeley and as executive vice chancellor at UC Irvine. Henry Yang, also an engineer, was selected as UC Santa Barbara's chancellor after a long stint as dean of the School of Engineering at Purdue University. Chancellor Yang is today the longest-serving chancellor on the nine University of California campuses.

The academic landscape has changed considerably since I gave my talk in

1989. More and more Asian American scholars are serving as administrators at one level or another or chair important campuswide committees on college and university campuses. In this chapter, I have reinserted some sentences that the editor of Change *deleted due to space limitation.*

* * *

"Word has got around," the dean said, "that you're a tough broad."

Without thinking, I turned around so that my back faced the man. "Hey," I said, pointing at a certain part of my anatomy, "take a look at this—would you say that 'broad' is an accurate description of my physique?"

He guffawed. After he finished laughing, I gave him a conspiratorial look and said in a hushed tone, "Shh. . . . If you go around calling women colleagues 'broads' you might acquire a bad reputation, you know."

The fact that I responded to his sexism with humor made this administrative colleague decide that I was "all right." Several months later, however, he and I had a strong disagreement over a faculty appointment. In the midst of our drawn-out public feud, he told me, "I'm really hurt by your opposition—I thought we were friends."

"Oh, we're friends all right, but this is a *policy* matter, and I *never* capitulate with regard to policy matters. . . . Besides, didn't you once tell me I was a tough broad?"

He didn't laugh this time. But three and a half years later, when I left that university, he wrote me a note to tell me that even though we had our differences, he would miss me.

This little story illustrates a central dilemma that minority and women faculty or administrators such as myself constantly face: often without any time for reflection or analysis, we must make instantaneous decisions about which battles to fight.

In the above instance, I had instinctively dealt with sexism "softly" because there was a larger issue at stake. As the first Asian American woman to become a provost on a University of California campus, I had to show I could be a "good colleague"—a woman who could get along with "the boys." I knew that my ability to do so held the key to my effectiveness within the university's structure of power.

Getting along with the boys does not mean that one must accept racist or sexist remarks; I never let such insults pass unnoticed. Usually I try to deal with them with quick repartees—at least when I have the presence of mind to control my rage. For a fiery-tempered person like me, this is not easy.

One way I've found to curb my anger is always to keep in mind the structure of power in American higher education and to act in accordance with my understanding of it. In this essay, I offer my analysis of the American university from an Asian American perspective—how Asian Americans fit into it, what forms of power we possess or do not possess, and how we may acquire more power and exercise it more effectively. In short, I look beyond affirmative action to the use of our numerical presence to bring qualitative changes in the institutions we serve.

The American university serves more functions than do its counterparts elsewhere in the world, which has led scholars to advance complex models for understanding its organization. Robert Wolff, for instance, thinks of the university in four ways: as a sanctuary for scholarship, as a training camp for the professions, as a social service station to educate the masses, and as an assembly line for socializing "establishment men." Others have argued that the university is best understood as a vast bureaucracy or see it as an arena within which society's political conflicts are adjudicated.

In my experience, no single model explains adequately the structure of the American university. It is simultaneously a social system within which a community of scholars, a bureaucracy, and a political arena coexist. Furthermore, within the community of scholars, the imperatives of teaching, research, and service often pull in different directions. Time management is a skill that faculty members, especially those teaching at major research universities, must master because the amount of time they put into each of the above activities depends not so much on external guidelines as on individual predilections.

Teaching, or the transmission of knowledge, is an open-ended enterprise; the amount of time one spends in preparing lectures, grading papers, and interacting with students can vary greatly. Research that leads to the discovery of new knowledge requires not only creativity but also entrepreneurship, as a great deal of research cannot be done without adequate funding and the ability to organize effective research teams, all of which take effort. University, professional, and public service likewise use up differential amounts of time, depending on how much in demand a faculty member may be and how he or she responds to requests for his or her expertise. Thus, the way we spend our time is elastic.

Within such a multifaceted and elastic system, power takes different forms. Organizational charts of colleges and universities reveal only a small part of the picture, as the boxes and lines on such drawings depict only the formal power structure. There is also an informal power structure which, in my opinion, is far more difficult for outsiders to fathom or for newcomers to breach. Though political scientists draw a distinction between power and influence, in reality these two cannot be easily separated. Both interact, in turn, with a third phenomenon—legitimacy. Individuals who hold formal positions of authority but lose legitimacy in the eyes of those they govern no longer have much influence.

Within the academy, six kinds of power can be discerned. I call them collegial, reputational, administrative, bureaucratic, personal, and agitational power. Asian Americans in higher education today possess these diverse forms of power to different degrees.

Collegial power is exercised by faculty members—primarily senior faculty—through their control of the curriculum, the hiring and advancement of fellow faculty, and the definition of what constitutes legitimate scholarship. Confidential peer reviews, the exclusion of junior and part-time faculty members from certain kinds of decision-making, and academic reputation undergird the power of the senior faculty. Whenever outside forces impinge on their authority they can invoke the sanctity of academic freedom to protect their entrenched positions.

Graduate students and junior faculty members are supposed to absorb through an informal apprenticeship system the standards by which colleagues assess and reward each other's work and make other decisions. But since the values and norms of the academic subculture are seldom explicitly taught, only by close observation of faculty behavior can one learn them.

Asian Americans, other minorities, and women find it very difficult to penetrate the "old boys' network" because it often hinges on personal friendship and influence-trading. Acceptance into the inner circles is very selective; those who won't rock the boat are the most likely to be allowed entry. Members of inner circles want individuals who will perpetuate a system, not change or destroy it. Minority and women faculty who do not exhibit "correct" behavior—a subtle mix of assertiveness and deference—or worse, who do not seem to accept certain aspects of academic culture, are simply not welcome.

For this reason, even though a notable number of Asian American scientists and engineers have achieved international recognition for their work and thus possess *reputational* power, seldom has it been translated into other forms of power, notably collegial power. Whatever their reputation, one seldom sees on-campus Asian Americans heading major committees or a faculty senate; they are all but invisible on the boards of disciplinary societies or the national organizations that shape educational policy.

In contrast to collegial and reputational power, *administrative* power, which comes from occupying formal positions of authority within the university structure, is highly visible. But what many Asian Americans seem not to understand is that administrative power is often more circumscribed than meets the eye. Academic administrators in the United States must be collegial rather than authoritarian toward their faculty and staff colleagues. Just as important, they have to balance multiple and conflicting demands on the limited resources they control.

In major research universities such as the various University of California campuses, where "shared governance" exists, administrators interact routinely with a fairly stable corps of senior faculty members who participate in committee work and perform quasi-administrative functions. Such quasi-administrative groups comprise individuals who maintain old boys' networks among themselves—the collegial power brokers. Among other things, they are the people who sit on search committees, where they instinctively tend to favor individuals who may reproduce their own traits and behavior. Sensing this, many Asian Americans hesitate to participate.

Thus, very few Asian Americans have attained high administrative positions in American universities. The handful who have done so tend to become deans of engineering or the natural sciences—fields in which their reputational power is sufficiently great to overcome the barriers in their path. In campus hallways, one hears alleged reasons for the dearth of Asian American administrators. One is that Asian Americans lack "leadership" qualities, American-style. If foreign-born, the Asian candidate is said to be either insufficiently assertive or too rigidly authoritarian. If American-born, the candidate supposedly lacks self-esteem or is too militant.

The real problem, however, is that many whites refuse to accept nonwhite supervisors with the power to hire, review, and fire them. For that reason, racial minority administrators are most often found in the student-services part of the university bureaucracy. They head units such as educational opportunity programs (EOP), student affirmative action programs, student learning centers, and offices overseeing multicultural activities—units in which the majority of the staff are usually people of color. There, the issue of nonwhites supervising whites will not arise to the same degree as elsewhere in the university's bureaucracy. The small number of racial minority administrators in the academic sector of the university tends to hold staff, not line, positions—carrying out decisions made by others rather than exercising independent decision-making power of their own.

The inability of Asian Americans to advance beyond a certain level in the hierarchy—in universities, in corporations, and in government agencies—is now popularly referred to as the "glass ceiling." To counteract this obstacle, psychologists and personnel managers have proposed that Asian Americans undergo "assertiveness training." Such a remedy, in my view, is simplistic. There are situations where being too assertive can backfire; what works for white males won't work for women or people of color.

How assertive one should be is intertwined with *how* one should deal with sexism, racism, and other forms of discrimination. Should one do so frontally? The answer, I propose, always depends on *circumstances* in the particular environments in which we work. We must remember that when a faculty member or administrator of color reacts militantly to every little expression of prejudice there is always a cost. On the one hand, he or she may quickly be "iced out"—that is, kept in the dark about what's going on or even actively prevented from participating in the social interactions that accompany work. On the other hand, "swallowing" insults and injustice without protest can lead to self-denigration or even self-hate. Asian Americans who aspire to high administrative positions better have thick skins and egos that are not easily bruised.

Far less visible than administrative power is the *bureaucratic* power possessed by staff members—professionals who influence the outcome of decisions more than is sometimes realized. They do so by virtue of their role in the day-to-day implementation of decisions, by their intimate knowledge of university rules and regulations, and by the positions they occupy as gatekeepers controlling access to administrators. The sizable number of Asian Americans in this white-collar sector of the university represents a reservoir of untapped power with considerable potential to bring about change in the university. So far, however, not too many Asian American staff members have tried to break out of the docile, hardworking mode into which they have been cast. Before they can do so they must acquire a consciousness of their own political importance.

A fifth form of power—based on the ability of particular individuals to influence other people—is not embedded in the university structure per se. In most American organizations there is usually room for people to charm and manipulate others; these individuals possess *personal* power. Thus, individuals who do not occupy formal positions of authority can nevertheless accomplish a great deal. An important proviso to the exercise of personal power is that it must not be abrasive. At present, in my observation, Asian American women seem better able than Asian American men at exercising personal power. Perhaps this is due to the fact that women of all ethnic origins have always had to rely on covert or indirect means to achieve the ends they seek.

The sixth kind of power is based on the willingness to agitate. By militance and the sheer force of numbers, hitherto powerless and voiceless groups make themselves heard and get their demands taken seriously. Asian American students and faculty members first tasted *agitational* power in the late 1960s when they participated in the Civil Rights and Anti-War movements, but soon—on East and West Coast campuses, at least—they focused increasingly on efforts to establish Asian American and other Ethnic Studies programs.

Within faculty ranks, agitational power has been exercised mainly by a small number of marginalized Asian American faculty members in Ethnic Studies programs or departments. Often their more moderate colleagues in other departments have found their actions embarrassing. But none can deny that their actions have at times served as an effective check on the tendency of administrators and senior faculty members to abuse power through the denial of tenure and merit increases or informal restrictions on Asian American undergraduate admissions.

The social movements of the 1960s and 1970s changed the "mix" of these different forms of power on campuses where student activists had disrupted classes, gone "on strike," held teach-ins, or occupied offices and even entire buildings. Administrative power became more tenuous while collegial, reputational, and personal power remained virtually untouched. In contrast, agitational power became something administrators and the campus police learned to fear even though it erupted only sporadically.

The "political settlements" that ended these campus battles affected various sectors of the university differently. Administrators were forced to deal with racial minorities and women—be they faculty members, students, or staff. A majority of the nonminority faculty continued to function pretty much as they had always done. Even though a number of women and faculty of color were hired in order to appease the students, they were largely housed in Women's Studies or Ethnic Studies programs—locations that minimized their influence. Isolating these individuals was a form of "encystment" to borrow a term coined by an insightful but cynical administrator. The main legacy of those years of upheaval, therefore, is that "affirmative action" affected administrative sectors of the university more than it did the community of scholars.

Campuses quieted down after American involvement in the wars in Vietnam, Laos, and Cambodia ended, after some token Women's Studies and Ethnic Studies programs were established, and after tutorial centers were set up to help "nontraditional students" make it through college. Furthermore, as economic recession hit the country in the late 1970s and early 1980s, students began to worry more about finding jobs and making money than about changing society.

In the mid-1980s, however, a new and subtle development took place on some campuses. A tenuous working relationship emerged between the radical faculty members in Asian American Studies and their hitherto less politically active Asian-ancestry colleagues in other departments. At the University of California, Berkeley, for example, a noticeable decline in the number of Asian American undergraduates admitted in 1984 struck at the very heart of what Asian Americans, regardless of their political persuasions, hold most dear—upward mobility through education. As a result, some Asian-ancestry faculty in the natural sciences, engineering, and other professional schools, who had up to that point eschewed campus politics, began to serve on campus committees, not just administrative ones that deal with "minority affairs" but standing committees of the Academic Senate through which faculty formulate general university policies and govern themselves. In short, a small Asian American faculty presence finally appeared in Berkeley's structure of power, taking up the exercise of collegial power that had until then largely eluded the grasp of most faculty of color.

Whether this development spreads and becomes a long-term trend remains to be seen. I, for one, am not so sure, for along with the emergence of a small Asian American faculty presence has come a new form of disenfranchisement; when nonwhites or women manage to "win" or get ahead on the basis of existing rules then the rules are often changed.

Up to this point the two main ways of perpetuating Euro-American *cultural* dominance in the academy (and society at large) have been racial exclusion and assimilation. But when exclusion on racial grounds became no longer acceptable—and, indeed, illegal—racial minorities and females could no longer be kept out on the basis of their biological or their phenotypic characteristics. So, efforts had to be made to assimilate them (sometimes by providing them with "mentors"). The belief is that individuals who internalize Euro-American male values and norms can be absorbed into the existing social system without undermining it.

However, when assimilated nonwhites or females begin to *out-perform* those who allowed them into the citadels of power in the first place, then means must be found to ensure that they do not "take over." One way is to claim that an entire *group*—even a highly heterogeneous one such as Asian Americans—lacks certain abilities (for example, impeccable English) or personality traits required of leaders (for example, assertiveness) and to ascribe those alleged characteristics to specific individuals.

As we Asian Americans contemplate our future we must realize that far more important than the efforts of a few individuals to rise to the top is the need for large numbers of us to play our parts and to do so in concert with one another so that collectively we can begin to claim our rightful place in American higher education and in society at large. By "rightful place" I do not mean simply being admitted as students or hired as staff and faculty in increasing numbers. What I have in mind, rather, is a more even dispersal of Asian Americans across the various disciplines and our entry into every sector of the university's structure and participation at every level of decision-making. Instead of shouting the 1960s slogan, "Shut It Down!" our goal in the 1980s and 1990s should be "Open It Up!"

To achieve such a goal we must understand clearly the nature of the university and the role that different members of its community play. Thus, more Asian American faculty must be willing to do committee work so that we can make our way into the corridors of collegial power. At the same time, we must continue to distinguish ourselves as scientists and scholars—not so much for the sake of personal glory but in order to use our consequent reputational power to open doors for our peers and future generations. Those of us who do research, write, publish, and give public talks must learn to address different audiences in different ways, for an effective speaker always takes the composition and interests of his or her audience into account.

We must also create a suitable milieu for training our "successors," not only by mentoring them intellectually as is normally expected but also by sharing with them the insights we have gained with regard to functioning in, as well as changing, the universities in which we work.

More Asian American faculty should also apply for administrative positions and be prepared to cope with the stress that these jobs entail. Since effective administrators depend a great deal on good staff support, getting more Asian Americans into key staff positions shores up our common enterprise. Ideally, the administrator-staff working relationship should be treated not as a hierarchical but as a cooperative one. Administrators must encourage staff to partake of career development opportunities; staff should alert administrators to policies or implementation practices that may have adverse cumulative effects on Asian Americans and on other racial minority groups.

Meanwhile, all Asian Americans can learn better interpersonal skills so that we can exercise greater personal power. Finally, agitational power, when used judiciously, is still a very important—indeed, potent—weapon at our disposal. Through this avenue, students and community groups can participate in educational change. Public pressure is something that only inexperienced administrators dare to ignore.

Once we fathom how the cogs of the university fit together and how we can turn the wheels in certain directions, then we shall be able to move beyond the numbers game called affirmative action.

16 Making It in Academia [1995]

By 1995 I was, without doubt, a "senior faculty." That is, I had earned the privilege to give "advice." This chapter originated as a talk I delivered via videotape (I was not well enough to travel at the time) to faculty gathered on the East Coast for a conference on minorities in higher education. I then wrote up my talk and submitted it to the Office of Academic Personnel at UC Santa Barbara, which included it in a brochure that office prepared: Information for New Faculty at UCSB: Teaching, Research, Tenure, and Living in Santa Barbara *(1995).*

My "advice" elicited mixed responses. One young faculty member said sarcastically that my stance was "disgustingly obsequious." Well, maybe. I could not help but wonder how such a brazen, freshly minted Ph.D. would fare in the years to come. My detractors' oppositional attitude notwithstanding, I think my analysis sheds light on why some faculty members run into hurdles as they try to advance up the faculty ladder. One of the most difficult "truths" I have learned to accept is that not all obstacles encountered by women and racial minority faculty members are due to the existence of various "isms." In academia as elsewhere, etiquette does help to lubricate interpersonal relations, and those who flout etiquette usually encounter problems that are partially of their own making. My career has been premised upon the belief that it is easier to change an institution from within than without. That is why becoming a respected member of the university community is one of the most effective ways to ensure that one's viewpoint is heard and, better yet, gets acted upon.

* * *

Getting ahead in academia can be very difficult for women faculty or faculty of color. I want to distill some of the lessons I have learned over a quarter century of teaching and pass them on to you because I'd like to see more and more of us become a part of the professorate in the United States.

First, the university is a social system. It isn't just made up of classrooms, laboratories, research centers, or even faculty members, students, staff, and administrators. Rather, different groups of university employees have well-defined but not always obvious relationships to one other. As a social system the university can function smoothly only if its members follow certain rules. I am always astonished that despite the fact that we live in a highly bureaucratized society, many young faculty members do not seem to realize that the university itself is a bureaucracy. They resent having to fill out forms or meeting deadlines, but no matter how much you dislike such red tape, it is very important that you not try to buck the system in that respect. Even though some of the procedures may be unreasonable or even discriminatory, it is best for junior faculty members to save their energy for activities other than defying the bureaucratic system. If you do so too frequently, you will be left out in the cold. For example, the grants you apply for may not be sent out for extramural review if you do not give campus reviewers enough time to evaluate your proposals, or you may not get your classes scheduled at the hours you want because you missed telling the departmental secretary in time what your preferences are.

The fact that the university is a social system also means that people need to follow certain etiquette in interacting with one another. There are many subtle forms of deference that you have to pay to those who are above you in the academic hierarchy. Senior faculty don't simply have different titles or make higher salaries; they have the right to make decisions that affect your career advancement. No matter how democratic university faculty members try to be, there are still subtle forms of deference new faculty members must learn. One is to respect the time of senior faculty members by deferring to the time slot *they* prefer for appointments and showing up punctually for them. Another involves who goes to whose office to talk things over. Whenever I seek help or advice from someone more senior than I am, I make a point of going to that person's office. *Where* you end up having a conversation does matter; the younger and more junior you are, the more walking you have to do. This is something very few people think about, but it is an important marker of status. Much as you may dislike a hierarchical system, you are more likely to accomplish your goals if you understand that there are unspoken signs that can be used to show respect to individuals from whom you will someday ask favors.

Another group of persons whose support and cooperation you will need if you are to achieve your goals are members of the staff. It is staff who set up appointments, process paperwork, and implement policies and decisions. Unfortunately, some faculty members, especially those who grew up in societies in which upper- or middle-class people have servants, do not treat staff members with consideration. These thoughtless faculty often do not take care of things until the last minute, and then they disrupt the schedule of everyone else in an office by demanding that other people stop doing whatever they are doing in order to serve them. When such faculty members are reminded that there are other tasks that also require attention, they not only aren't apologetic but also become abrasive. As a majority of the staff continues to be female and a majority of faculty male, this lack of consideration is often a form of sexism.

Second, throughout your career you will be dependent on peer review. Your work, whether in the form of articles, books, grant proposals, or fellowship applications, will be reviewed and evaluated by your colleagues, not only on your own campus but also elsewhere in the country. Whether you get a merit increase, tenure, a fellowship, or a grant depends not only on how good your work is but also on what kind of letters of recommendation you can marshal. What a lot of junior faculty members don't seem to understand is that you cannot call somebody up at the last minute and say, "Will you write me a letter? I need it by tomorrow." To give someone such short notice is extremely rude. Unfortunately, in my experience, some women or faculty of color seem to have a tendency to make such last-minute requests, especially to colleagues of their own gender or ethnic/racial background. If you want support you must plan your schedule better. You have to give people from whom you'd like letters enough time to write good ones. Good letters are not simply vacuously positive; they must evaluate your work *in detail.* Doing so requires careful reflection and takes a lot of time.

Moreover, you really have to spread out whom you ask. You cannot keep imposing on the same two, three, or four persons time after time. Instead, you should cultivate a group of at least six to eight colleagues whom you can call on when you need letters of recommendation. It is also your responsibility to keep colleagues on whom you depend for this service informed of what you're doing. So, instead of waiting until the last minute, you need to send your pool of referees your publications routinely as they appear in print. As is the case with staff members, it is wise to be considerate of your faculty colleagues.

Third, the scholarly community, by definition, is made up of people who are constantly asked to pass judgment over the quality of the work that other people produce. We do this from the first time we serve as a Teaching Assistant in an undergraduate course—that is what giving grades is all about. When faculty members work with graduate students on their papers and dissertations, we likewise have to pass judgment. The most useful evaluations are those that point out *both* the strengths and weaknesses in somebody's work. It is even more important to learn to see the strengths and weaknesses in our own work.

Some of us, however, have a hard time coping with criticism. We get terribly sensitive and think that every criticism is an insult. We read racism, sexism, homophobia, etc. into any assessment that is not completely positive. But criticism is one of the most crucial things we must learn to deal with because, without it, it is very difficult for us to see what is good, or problematic, or poor about what we do. I've observed two opposite reactions to criticism: acting as though our self-esteem has been completely crushed or getting extremely angry. Neither reaction is useful. When someone criticizes a particular idea or even a whole article or book of ours, it does *not* mean that individual is passing negative judgment over our persons as a whole—that is, our entire being.

Fourth, we have to learn to choose which battles to fight because, as faculty of color or women faculty, we may think that every little expression of racism or sexism should be challenged or rebutted. But I have learned one cannot be militant all the time. Faculty who are militant all the time get a reputation for being "difficult." It's unpleasant to carry on a conversation with certain people because they react hastily to all kinds of little remarks they consider offensive.

The point is not that we should not fight battles but rather, by choosing which battles to fight, we are making decisions about which issues we *most* want to do battle over. Do we wish to win a series of small battles over personal affronts, or do we want in the long run to be an effective advocate for such larger issues as affirmative action or multicultural education? When a colleague says something that sounds sexist or racist, the choice that we, as women faculty or faculty of color, must make is this: Do we want to accuse these persons of sexism or racism, or are we more interested in persuading the rest of our colleagues to vote on the issue(s) at hand as we'd like to see them vote?

Fifth, to make it in academia, *you* must take the initiative to get to know others, especially those who will be in a position to judge you. You cannot wait for others to approach you. When I was a junior faculty member, one method I used to strike up a conversation with a senior faculty was to ask that person for advice—even when I didn't really need it. Doing so accomplishes two goals: a) the person from whom you seek advice, being human, feels flattered—you thus put that person in a good mood, and b) you may be winning over somebody who may be a potential enemy.

Finally, and most important of all, none of the above tips on how to behave would do you any good unless you get your work done. Faculty are expected to carry out a variety of responsibilities but seldom are they told explicitly how to use their time. How much time should one spend in preparing lectures? in grading papers? in advising students or doing things with them outside the classroom? in doing research? in writing articles and books for publication? in serving on committees—in one's own department, school, college, and professional association? How many graduate students or post-doctoral fellows should one assume responsibility for? There are seldom exact guidelines because professors are professionals—people who are supposed to be able to exercise considerable autonomy over our working conditions. But in reality no one has complete freedom to spend his or her time entirely as he or she pleases.

Thus, one of the first things that a new faculty member should do is to ask the department chair, dean, or senior colleagues what the expectations for advancement are. If you don't get a clear answer from one person, ask others. There *are* criteria for advancement, even when they are not explicitly stated. Those criteria are invoked whenever you are reviewed for a merit increase, tenure, a fellowship, or some other kind of award. The *range* and combination of accomplishments expected are quite broad and diverse. What is expected depends a great deal on the nature of the institution where you teach. Prestigious research universities put far more emphasis on publications and what awards and honors you win than do institutions where the primary task is teaching and where the teaching load, consequently, is much heavier. You must adapt your behavior to the campus where you work. Becoming acquainted with the "yardsticks" by which your performance will be measured will not only ensure your success but will also help you guard against discrimination.

No doubt there will be people who think my stance is too accommodationist. But I am not arguing that we should avoid confrontation in all instances. Indeed, there are many oppressive situations to which we should never acquiesce, just as there are many individuals with power over us against whom we should struggle. What I suggest, rather, is a thoughtful approach that counsels us to be *selective* in our resistance against injury and insult. We must always think and act *strategically.* Being smart enough to gain the freedom ultimately to function within the university increasingly on *our* terms is quite different from being co-opted. The bottom line is this: How are we going to change the system if we are banished from it as a result of our failure to understand how it works, and how can we help mold it according to our own vision?

17 On Subversion and the Art of Resistance [2001]

In this chapter, I reflect on the past, not because I think that past contains lessons applicable to the conditions facing faculty members who teach Asian American studies at the beginning of the twenty-first century but because the struggles to develop Asian American studies are an integral part of Asian American history. In my view, the historical importance of Asian American studies lies in the fact that it did not emerge simply as a new area of intellectual inquiry on university campuses but was, rather, a part of the broader social movements of the 1960s and 1970s. Compared to other people of color in the United States, relatively few Asian Americans participated in the civil rights, anti–Vietnam War, and feminist movements of that era. Young (and a few older) Asian Americans fought tenaciously, however, to establish Asian American studies, which became an arena in which we battled for a more egalitarian and just future for Asians in America.

Unlike some social movements that thrived in the 1960s and 1970s but disappeared from the national scene in later years, most Asian American studies programs set up between 1969 and the mid-1970s have survived. There then ensued an interregnum of about one and a half decades during which almost no new programs were launched or new faculty hired.

During those lean years, the Asian American studies story centered around how a radical project sited on university campuses struggled incessantly to ensure its survival while trying hard not to be co-opted by the academic establishment. In the late 1980s and early 1990s, as a result of a second wave of student activism, new programs appeared at colleges and universities around the country, and numerous faculty positions became available. Asian American studies' new lease on life, however, brought its own set of challenges, some of which I shall discuss in the final chapter.

* * *

During the years that stretched from the late 1960s to the late 1980s, our most notable achievement, I think, was the fact that we managed to *prevent* negative outcomes in many instances. That is, we managed to prevent efforts by some campus administrators and faculty review committees to close down our programs, to deny tenure to some Asian American studies scholar-activists, and to place de facto quotas on the number of Asian American applicants who would be admitted to prestigious universities, both private and public. We succeeded because, of the six forms of power within American universities that I identified [chapter 15], we knew how to use our agitational power. Agitational power can manifest itself either as open militance or as a sub rosa, and therefore subversive, form of political pressure.

While I was still a student, I, like other participants in the social movements of the 1960s and 1970s, relied on overt militance to make our point. But after I became a faculty member I transformed myself into a "friendly subversive"—friendly because I thought of the university as a key institution that should be preserved, given its crucial role as one of the few channels of upward mobility and empowerment open to people of color and to women, and subversive because the methods I used to try and change that institution were not always apparent. I exerted enormous pressure on individuals who controlled the university but I usually did so behind the scenes.

I first experimented with a subversive approach when I served on the Committee on Courses of Instruction on the Berkeley campus, during which I had to work both sides of the fence, so to speak. On the one hand, in my capacity as chair of the Asian American Studies Curriculum Committee, I tried to persuade my colleagues, many of whom at that time were part-time lecturers, that it would *not* be "counterrevolutionary" to revise our courses in order to increase the probability that they would receive permanent approval, thereby saving us the irksome task of having to submit petitions year after year in order for our courses to be taught. An anomalous situation existed in those days. Campus reviewing agencies had approved our proposal for a major in Asian American studies without checking to see how many of our courses were permanently approved. (In fact, only one year-long course was.)

Such an anomaly could exist because decision-making in some universities is so compartmentalized, often with the left hand not knowing what the right hand is doing. I argued that getting permanent approval for our courses would not be an act of capitulation because we would still control the *contents* of what we taught. All we had to do was to adopt the general *form* that review committees expected all instructors to follow: meeting a requisite number of hours and assigning a certain amount of reading per week, adopting the prevailing T.A.-student ratio, and assigning papers and giving midterm and final examinations. Following such prescribed "standards" would not prevent us from choosing what topics to teach or how to frame particular issues. Should anyone try to veto the subject matter we covered in our courses, we could protest such interference in the name of academic freedom.

On the other hand, I also tried to change the negative view that members of the Academic Senate's Committee on Courses of Instruction had of ethnic studies. Because I wanted my fellow committee members to perceive me as a responsible and sensible "campus citizen," I did my share of the work on that committee as conscientiously as I knew how. I did my work so well that by the second year I served on that committee, even though I was only an assistant professor (in fact, I was the only assistant professor on that committee comprised largely of white-haired old men), no one objected when the committee's chairperson appointed me to head the subcommittee that reviewed course-approval requests from all "non-L & S" departments and programs.

The College of Letters and Science (L & S) was the largest unit on campus, so the number of requests from its constituent departments exceeded the number of requests from all the other teaching units on campus combined. To make the workload manageable, one subcommittee scrutinized courses in L & S, while a second passed judgment over courses from "non-L & S" units. The "non-L & S" subcommittee reviewed petitions from all the professional schools, including Business Administration, Education, Engineering, Environmental Design, Journalism, Library and Informational Science, Natural Resources, Nutritional Science, Optometry, Public Health, Public Policy, and Social Welfare, as well as the ethnic studies programs, which, at that time, were not under any college rubric. Thus, in theory, I had the power to approve or disapprove the courses submitted by my own program as well as those from the other component units of the ethnic studies department. But I was too smart to take advantage of that fact.

To avoid any appearance of a conflict of interest, and confident that our revised syllabi would pass muster, I recused myself and asked the other subcommittee member to review the course proposals from my department. After a careful examination, he told the full committee that he was "surprised" by how good our syllabi looked—surprised, I suppose, because he had not expected anything so well planned from a bunch of "minority" faculty. Instead of calling attention to the racism inherent in that perception, the only thing I said was that granting permanent approval to our courses would rectify an anomaly. I pointed out that while the campus had an Asian American studies major, only one of the courses required for that major had permanent approval. What were students to do, I asked, if certain courses could not be taught during a particular year because the Committee on Courses denied approval for that year? My fellow committee members were astonished; they asked how such an aberrant situation could have arisen. I said I didn't know, which was the truth because the major had been established before I joined the Berkeley faculty. "Yes, yes," the committee members all chimed in, "we can't allow such a situation to continue to exist."

I was pleased that I had managed to change the perceptions and behavior of people on both sides of the aisle, talking in political terms to one group and in bureaucratic terms to the other. I never told anyone what I had done until years later because I did not want anyone to be upset with me for engaging in such political and bureaucratic maneuvers. But based on that experience I began to toy with the notion that acts of resistance are sometimes more an art than a science.

I continued to apply my subversive method in the 1980s when the Berkeley administration tried to curb the number of Asian American applicants it would admit. In response, my Asian American studies colleagues, under the astute leadership of Ling-chi Wang, launched a multipronged campaign to oppose any such move. Although I was no longer on the Berkeley faculty by then, having moved to UC Santa Cruz in 1984, I nevertheless monitored events on the Berkeley campus closely, not only because I cared about the issue but also because I felt betrayed.

One of the mechanisms that campus decision-makers proposed to use to limit the number of Asian American admittees was to take a score of 400 on the SAT verbal test as a cut-off point. Unfortunately, it was I who had first hypothesized that a verbal score below 400 may help to identify students who would need special help with their English and other verbal skills [chapter 8]. My analysis was intended to persuade campus decision-makers that such students were good students who *should* be admitted because all they needed was a little intensive language instruction. I was flabbergasted when I learned that the 400–point score I had highlighted was to be used for an opposite end—to keep such students out.

So, I called up a high-ranking Berkeley administrator and asked, "Do you know about *Yick Wo v. Hopkins?*" "What's that?" he asked. "Oh, it's a case involving a Chinese laundryman that went all the way to the U.S. Supreme

Court." "What does a laundryman have to do with Asian American students at Berkeley?" he asked with annoyance. "Plenty!" I then explained that the situation at Berkeley bore a distinct similarity to the 1886 *Yick Wo* case in which the U.S. Supreme Court ruled that when a statute that seems neutral on its face is applied in such a way as to affect a certain class of persons more negatively than others, then the law's *effect(s)* can be said to be discriminatory. "It is a legal principle that has stood the test of time," I said. "If you don't believe me, you can talk to the chancellor [a lawyer by training] or the faculty in the law school or the lawyers in the Office of the General Counsel of the Regents."

I do not know whether what I said had an effect on the decision-making process with regard to this issue, but I suspect it did, first, because the proposed below 400 cut-off point was never implemented as a mechanism for weeding out Asian immigrant students, and, second, because the administrator I talked to had a lot of political savvy. I did not try to find out explicitly whether the potential use of the *Yick Wo* doctrine in a possible lawsuit might have entered into consideration because over the years I abided by an unspoken bargain I struck with administrators. I would refrain from harassing them in public if they would "do the right thing" behind the scenes. To me, the retraction or nullification of a potentially harmful policy is far more important than getting an apology or mea culpa in public. There is no need to proclaim "We won!" when we know we did.

A third example of how I and my student allies practiced the art of resistance occurred at UC Santa Cruz. When I was interviewed for a job on that campus, students told me about their desire for an ethnic studies graduation requirement. I pledged to support their efforts should I join the faculty there. Soon after I arrived, I met with several students who were leading the campaign. They told me they were planning a large demonstration. I suggested that two other tactics might also prove useful. I proposed that they form teams of two or three students each to visit as many faculty as possible and as soon as possible. I explained that demonstrations mostly affect administrators, but that changes in the curriculum or in graduation requirements are in the province of the faculty. Since all ladder-rank faculty members in the UC system are members of the Academic Senate on their campuses, it is the *faculty* not the administrators who would determine whether the proposed ethnic studies requirement would be approved. That meant the activists involved in the campaign must ensure that as many faculty as possible understood why so many students wanted such a requirement. I urged the students to make sure the teams would be racially/ethnically mixed. In particular, at least one European American student must be in each team, I said, because if the faculty perceived the ethnic studies requirement simply as a "special pleading" on the part of students of color, they might not pass it. The students reacted skeptically to my suggestion. Apparently, they preferred the emotional satisfaction of participating in a large demonstration to the low-key political work of visiting and talking to individual faculty members.

I further suggested that instead of, or in addition to, a demonstration they gather as many signatures as possible on a petition.

"How many would be enough?" they asked.

"I'd say at least two thousand."

"But that's *a lot* of signatures! There are fewer than eight thousand students at Santa Cruz. Do you know how hard it is on this dispersed campus to get people together?"

"Well, those are my suggestions only. All of you will have to decide what tactic or tactics you wish to follow."

As it turned out, the students used both approaches. Several dozen of them formed teams and quietly visited one faculty member after another. They also organized a demonstration. On the day that the ethnic studies requirement was to be debated in the Academic Senate, a crowd of students gathered to chant slogans outside the room where the meeting was to take place while dozens of others stood like silent sentries around the periphery of that room. As the meeting began, several students walked to the front and presented a thick pile of petitions to the chair of the Academic Senate. It is hard to say in retrospect whether the students' acts influenced the faculty's vote, but UC Santa Cruz *did* become the first UC campus to approve such a requirement, and that was what mattered.

A fourth example of the approach that I came to favor occurred at UC Santa Barbara. Even though by the early 1990s the revamped Asian American Studies Program offered dozens of courses every year, students wanted something more; they wanted to be able to major in Asian American studies. Three students—Manhao Chhor, a Sino-Cambodian American; Dede Howard, a Japanese European Amerasian; and Que Dang, a Vietnamese American—began pressuring the faculty to submit a proposal for an Asian American studies major. Manhao was the first student to ask me why we did not have a major in Asian American studies. I told him because it would take time to establish one. He next asked if he could declare an independent major—an option open to students with a grade point average of 3.0 or higher. Unfortunately, he did not qualify because his GPA was then below 3.0. "Sorry, you'll have to get better grades," I said. Two quarters later he returned to see me and said triumphantly, "I've studied really hard the last two quarters and I've raised my GPA to over 3.0. Now you can't stop me!" Accordingly, he made history as the first Asian American studies major at UC Santa Barbara. Dede and Que were the second and third. When the three of them graduated they gave me a photograph of themselves and wrote on the back, "We hope you will always remember us as your first-born." I do.

As more and more students petitioned for an individual major in Asian American studies, the faculty realized we had no choice except to go ahead and design such a major even though our number was still too small to sustain one. I did not like the idea of relying on a large number of temporary lecturers to teach the required courses, but we had no other option. When students asked me what the chances for getting our proposal approved would be, I said, "Maybe 50–50."

"Oh, no!" they proclaimed. "We better hold a demonstration."

"You can't do that yet."

"Why not?"

"Because it's going to polarize the situation. Administrators hate demonstrations. When they think their backs are to the wall, even the ones who aren't hard-liners often become really stubborn. With both sides insisting that everything is non-negotiable, there'll be a stalemate and we'll get nowhere. They may even call the police to arrest you, but you guys sitting in jail won't get us an Asian American studies major on this campus."

"What else can we do?"

"How about gathering signatures for a petition?"

"What good would that do?"

"It'll serve notice to the powers-that-be that such a major has widespread support."

"How many signatures will we need?"

"At least three thousand."

"Why do we need so many?"

"Because three thousand equals approximately 25 percent of the undergraduate enrollment at UCSB this year. That number will make an impression. The message conveyed by such a huge stack of petitions is that we have a lot of potential supporters we can mobilize."

"But there aren't three thousand Asian American students at UCSB!"

"I never said the signatures must all come from Asian American students. In fact, it is crucial that you get as many signatures from students of European, African, Mexican, and other ancestry as possible."

"Why?"

"Because we must not be perceived as an academic ghetto—that's what our detractors call us, you know."

Over the next few months, about half a dozen students eager to major in Asian American studies spent hours and hours spreading out all over campus, petition sheets and pens in hand. They gathered over 2,500 signatures. Que Dang's effort was especially valiant; she single-handedly collected about three-quarters of the total number of signatures. One day she came into my office, soaking wet. "Where have you been?" I asked. She told me that she had stood in the rain outside Campbell Hall—a large auditorium with eight hundred seats that is the campus' largest classroom—in order to waylay as many students as possible as they came out of class. Que and her fellow activists are my heroes!

When the program submitted its B.A. proposal, I put the petitions in an appendix. The petition form had four columns—one for the signer's signature, a second for a legible version of his or her name, the third for his or her major, and the last for his or her class level. The names themselves would make evident that our support was multiethnic, while the range of majors would indicate that students majoring in many different subjects found our courses interesting and meaningful. Did the petitions have an effect? I never asked, but I believe they did. Not only did we get our proposed major approved expeditiously, but UC Santa Barbara also became the first UC campus to establish a full-fledged Asian American studies department a few months after the major came into being. The *threat* of potential student unrest can be as potent as, and perhaps even more potent than, an actual uprising.

The quiet cooperation between me and the student activists enabled us to get what we both desired. With the prospect of student protests hovering in the background, I offered a "moderate" alternative. As I told my student allies, "You and I have different roles to play. Together, we can use a pincer strategy."

"What's that?" they asked.

"It's a relic of World War I tank warfare."

"Tank warfare?"

"Yeah. By closing in on our target from two or more directions, we can encircle it. You form one arm of the pincer and I form the other."

"Cool!" my student friends exclaimed with glee.

"Remember, the more tools we have in our tool kit, and the more skillfully we use them, the more likely we are to succeed."

What little I knew about military strategy came not from the history of warfare among Western nations but from the Chinese classic, *Sanguo Yanyi* [Romance of the Three Kingdoms], a still-popular Chinese historical novel that is chock full of military stratagems, and from the military writings of Mao Zedong, which I had to study in depth while I was writing my Ph.D.

dissertation on Maoist strategy during the Long March. The most important insight I acquired is that in circumstances where the enemy is stronger than we are, we must find the fissures in his or her armor and focus on attacking those rifts.

The principles of guerrilla warfare can be used on American university campuses because those administrators who wish to remain in office for a long, long time or who hope to rise up the administrative ladder do have cracks in their armor. Their ambition makes them act in self-serving ways, which means they *will* back off when under pressure if they perceive the potential outcomes to be detrimental to their career advancement. By figuring out accurately the self-interest of particular individuals, it *is* possible for us to use such knowledge to our own advantage. We, too, can divide and conquer. Several events that occurred in the late 1990s confirmed the veracity of this insight. Unfortunately, I cannot discuss them because they involved confidential personnel matters.

Another lesson Mao Zedong taught me is the importance of observing and analyzing concrete, *local* conditions. Though Mao's legacy is in much dispute—indeed, in disrepute—these days, I, for one, still consider some of his insights to be brilliant. Understanding local conditions and acting according to them means that there can be no single blueprint that will work in every instance. One must act on the basis of what seems possible under *particular* conditions. Whenever faculty members and students at other campuses who were trying to start Asian American studies programs in the 1990s contacted me for suggestions on what to do, I always told them to look around their campuses and to identify who their potential friends and enemies might be. I suggested that they try to figure out the institutional niches those individuals occupied and to predict how they might act. An effective strategy, I said, must be based on a clear understanding of the institutional structure of a particular campus and the strengths and weaknesses of the individuals who control segments of it. That is to say, we must understand the institutions that, in the Foucauldian sense, govern and discipline us.

Despite the pervasive power of such disciplinary institutions, I choose to believe that human beings *can* work to counteract and even change them. In this endeavor, tools are important. But each tool we use must be appropriate for the task at hand. While we may not be able to use the master's tools to dismantle the master's house, we can, at times, use some of those tools to remodel that house.

18 Whither Asian American Studies? [2003]

Beginning in the late 1980s in the wake of a second round of student activism, new Asian American studies programs started appearing at colleges and universities around the country. By the 2000s, a number of old as well as new programs had become autonomous departments that enjoy the right to hire their own faculty, which means they no longer have to secure joint appointments in other departments for appointees. Once again, students who were determined to have Asian American studies by any means necessary were the motive force that enabled the field to grow.

Though administrators and faculty review committees still resisted setting up such programs, their resistance in the 1990s was milder compared to the intransigence that characterized the late 1960s to the late 1980s. By the 1990s, Asian American students had become a demographic force in many universities, so their concerns could not be ignored. Some administrators had also learned hard lessons about the consequences of turning down the students' requests out of hand.

This relatively more hospitable environment, however, does not mean that the field no longer has problems, because it does. In this chapter, I discuss two interrelated challenges that I believe the field must meet now and in years to come if it hopes to remain a distinctive enterprise on American campuses. First, there is still no graduate program anywhere in the country that systematically trains future faculty members to teach Asian American studies, although there are several Ph.D. programs in comparative ethnic studies. The professional pathways that incoming faculty have followed to date have been diverse—indeed, one might say, haphazard. Second, there are many disagreements over how the field should be conceptualized in this age of transnationalism and globalization and what its goals should be. In particular, should its political legacy be erased or discarded?

These issues are hard to deal with because they embody contradictions that revolve around struggles for power and dominance. That is why the answers to "Whither Asian American Studies?" will depend a great deal on how these differences are played out. Although the existence of different viewpoints can lead to creative innovations, the underlying struggles for power can also, sadly, cause the field to self-destruct.

* * *

A superficial look at Asian American studies today indicates that we have made considerable progress. Since the early 1990s, professional associations in various disciplines have included panels on Asian American topics in their annual conferences. Scholars in the field have given talks all over the country. A few senior faculty members have played a power broker's role on campuses other than their own, helping to negotiate political settlements to student unrest. More faculty positions opened up in the 1990s than in the 1970s and 1980s combined. At least half a dozen academic presses now publish book series on Asian Americans. Hundreds of people attend the annual meetings of the Association for Asian American Studies, presenting papers on a wide range of topics, some of which espouse theoretical frameworks that the field's founders could never have imagined. However, even though these developments seem to indicate that the field has finally "arrived," we cannot rest on our laurels. Despite our new visibility and vigor, we continue to exist on contested terrain. And the contestation today is not only between us and the university but also among ourselves.

One urgent problem facing the field is the absence of graduate programs that specifically train future faculty members to teach Asian American studies. To gain some insight into the academic trajectories that the present faculty members in a great variety of institutional settings have followed, I conducted a survey on behalf of the Curriculum Committee of the Department of Asian American Studies at UC Santa Barbara in January 1999. I sent questionnaires to 304 faculty listed in the 1998 directory of the Association for Asian American Studies. Seventy-five responses drifted in over a six-month period. Even though the response rate was low (only 24.6 percent), still, the survey results offer a rough indication of what kind of people compose the Asian American studies professorate and how they got there.

The survey collected five kinds of information: the respondents' academic training and present institutional locations, the relative importance of various factors that entered into their decisions to teach Asian American studies, what activities have been most useful in preparing them to teach Asian American studies, what preparations did they *wish* they had but did not, and what kind of graduate degree program they thought most marketable in today's job market. The respondents included tenured and not-yet-tenured full-time faculty as well as part-time lecturers. Some of the latter had not yet completed their Ph.D.s at the time they responded to the survey.

Among the seventy-five respondents, the largest number, fourteen, are historians. They are followed by twelve sociologists, ten literary scholars, six scholars with Ph.D.s in ethnic studies, and five psychologists. The rest are in American studies, anthropology, art, economics, education, folklore, geography, law, mathematics, music, Pacific Islands studies, philosophy, political science, rhetoric, South Asian studies, and urban planning. This broad array of fields does not mean that all of them offer courses in programs or departments explicitly named Asian American studies. Rather, the individuals who now teach one or more courses on Asian Americans, for one reason or another, developed a sufficient commitment to the field to offer courses with Asian American content regardless of their own educational backgrounds or institutional locations.

Forty-one of the respondents are affiliated with only one program or department. Of these, sixteen teach solely in an ethnic studies or an Asian American studies program or department. Twenty-nine individuals have joint appointments, but only twenty-two in this group have joint appointments in units named "Asian American studies." That means only thirty-eight of the respondents have a formal affiliation with units called ethnic studies or Asian American studies. The rest teach courses that focus on Asian American groups, issues, or topics within the disciplinary units housing them.

The survey asked respondents to indicate the relative importance of various factors that had influenced their decisions to teach Asian American studies. The eleven possible factors were 1) I had taken undergraduate courses in Asian American studies; 2) I had taken graduate courses in or related to Asian American studies; 3) I had written a B.A. honors thesis or an M.A. thesis on an Asian American topic; 4) I had written a Ph.D. dissertation on an Asian American topic; 5) I had read books by or about Asian Americans; 6) my graduate advisor urged me to apply for Asian American studies jobs; 7) I had been active in Asian American issues on campus or in the community; 8) I had worked in one or more Asian American community organizations; 9) the best jobs available when I went on the job market were in Asian American studies; 10) I am an Asian American, so I have a personal interest in the field; and 11) I was responding to student interest and demand for Asian American studies on my campus. For each factor, respondents could check "extremely important," "very important," "fairly important," "somewhat important," "not important at all," or "not applicable."

The five most influential factors were self-directed reading, personal interest, writing a Ph.D. dissertation on an Asian American topic, involvement in Asian American issues, and responding to student interest and demand. Fifty-two percent of the respondents said reading books by and about Asian Americans on their own was "extremely important," while 18.6 percent said it was "very important," giving a combined 70.6 percent. Personal interest was "extremely important" to 38.6 percent and "very important" to 25.3 percent, yielding a combined 64.9 percent. For 38.6 percent of the respondents, writing a Ph.D. dissertation on an Asian American topic was "extremely important," while 10.6 percent said it was "very important," giving a combined 49.2 percent. Active involvement in Asian American issues was "extremely important" to 32 percent and "very important" to 14.6 percent, adding up to a total of 46.6 percent. Responding to student demand was "extremely important" to 21.3 percent and "very important" to 18.6 percent, making a combined score of 39.9 percent.

The factors deemed "somewhat important" and "not important at all" were writing a B.A. or M.A. thesis on an Asian American topic (combined 74.6 percent), taking undergraduate courses in Asian American studies (combined 61.3 percent), being advised by a graduate mentor to apply for jobs in Asian American studies (combined 49.3 percent), and taking graduate courses in Asian American studies (combined 48 percent).

Thus, formal course work in the field, especially at the undergraduate level, had relatively little to do with the respondents' decisions to teach Asian American studies. Very few had taken any undergraduate courses in Asian American studies, and only 29.2 percent had taken one or more graduate course, seminar, or directed reading in the field even though 49.2 had written Ph.D. dissertations on Asian American topics. That is to say, the choice of dissertation topic was not strongly linked to prior undergraduate or graduate course work and ranked only slightly higher than active involvement in Asian American issues. Although the questionnaire did not ask the respondents to indicate what "Asian American issues" they had been involved in, it can be surmised that one important issue was probably the struggle to establish Asian American studies on the campuses where they were located. Based on my own observations over the years, since the field's beginnings it has been individuals who became involved in Asian American studies while they were still in graduate school who eventually became its most dedicated faculty. Even though there are very few graduate courses about Asian Americans taught anywhere, graduate students in many fields with little relationship to

Asian American studies have been exposed to it while they work(ed) as T.A.s (teaching assistants) in large Asian American studies undergraduate courses on campuses with such courses. Finding this experience meaningful, they made up their minds to pursue an academic career teaching Asian American studies.

The most disappointing finding, to me at least, is that even though dozens of colleges and universities now offer undergraduate courses in Asian American studies, very few of the undergraduates who take such courses end up teaching Asian American studies at the college or university level. When I talked to Asian American studies majors at UC Santa Barbara about their career plans, I discovered that relatively few of them aspire to a university career. "Why?" I asked. Their answers ranged from "I'm tired of going to school," "I want to earn money as soon as possible," and "I'd rather go to law school where I'll be done in three years," to "I've seen how hard you and the other faculty work—day, night, and weekends! I'd rather have a job that gives me time to have a life." "Well," I responded, "teaching and research *are* our lives." The usual retort was, "Maybe for you, but not for me!"

Another, and to me more disturbing, reason is that most of the Asian American studies majors who do want to go to graduate school want to major in Asian American studies *only,* but there are few graduate programs they can apply to. At present, those who do not wish to leave California can apply mainly to the M.A. degree program in Asian American studies at either UCLA or San Francisco State University or to the comparative ethnic studies Ph.D. program either at UC Berkeley or UC San Diego. The two institutions that grant ethnic studies Ph.D.s are highly competitive, and undergraduates with only average grade point averages (GPAs) are unlikely to get admitted. Graduate students at campuses such as UC Irvine may choose an "emphasis" in Asian American studies but they cannot yet get a Ph.D. in the field.

At UC Santa Barbara, many Asian American studies majors are very bright, but their cumulative GPAs are not high because they received low grades during their first two years of undergraduate study. In many instances they had initially chosen a science or engineering major, partly as a result of parental advice and/or pressure even though they themselves were not really interested in those subjects and had a difficult time doing well in them. In fact, some of them barely managed to stay in school during their freshmen and sophomore years. Fortunately for them, since UC Santa Barbara has a long list of General Education requirements, and Asian American studies courses fulfill some of those requirements, somewhere along the way these science and engineering students get exposed to Asian American studies. Loving our courses, they change majors and transfer to our department despite the opposition of some parents. "Does that mean you came to Asian American studies as refugees?" I asked wryly. "Yes!" they replied. "We love Asian American studies because it's a home away from home."

At the graduate level, some of the M.A. students aspiring to become college or university professors also strenuously resist the idea of getting Ph.D.s in any of the traditional disciplines. They said emphatically that they would feel alienated in such fields, so they did not even want to give them a try. Much as I understand and appreciate the existential imperatives that fuel such a sense of alienation, at the same time I am bothered by the anti-intellectualism this attitude reflects—that is, they want to study only subject matter that is of personal interest to them, but they do not wish to undergo training in any traditional discipline. The bottom line is, despite all the progress we have made, there is still no well-defined academic *ladder* that leads systematically from one rung up to the next within Asian American studies.

As a result, with the exception of those getting Ph.D.s in comparative ethnic studies at UC Berkeley and UC San Diego, and those getting Ph.D.s in disciplinary departments at UCLA and at other universities, where they manage to find graduate advisors who support their desire to write dissertations on Asian American topics, the Asian American studies professorate is largely self-trained. Thus, even though a significant number of jobs have opened up since the early 1990s, only a small proportion of the job applicants had become Asian American studies "specialists" before they started teaching. Due to the paucity of "already prepared" applicants, during the nine years I served as chairperson of Asian American studies at UC Santa Barbara I had no choice except to hire a number of faculty who had only a passing acquaintance with the scholarly literature (beyond their dissertation topic) in Asian American studies but who promised to learn it as quickly as possible. One historian to whom we had offered a position in the early 1990s and who had already published a well-researched book in Chinese American history resigned before he even made the move to California because he felt completely overwhelmed by a bibliography I sent him of books he might want to start reading during the summer before his move. He realized there was no way he could instantaneously transform himself into a historian of Asian America. As his wife pointed out, he told me apologetically, his life would be a lot more relaxed if he simply continued to teach the history of East Asia, in which he had been trained.

Since the challenge of mastering the ever-burgeoning literature in the field is so daunting and since some new faculty members, when they are first hired, are barely acquainted with the writings on Asian Americans in their own disciplines, much less with Asian American–related publications in other disciplines, the questionnaire asked the respondents to indicate what had helped them the most to prepare for a teaching career in Asian American studies. The eighteen possible factors listed on the questionnaire were 1) undergraduate courses I have taken; 2) graduate courses I have taken; 3) readings I had done on my own before I began teaching full-time; 4) readings I am currently doing on my own; 5) readings suggested by the professors who taught me in graduate school; 6) readings suggested by my current colleagues; 7) readings suggested by nonacademic friends; 8) research I did for my M.A. thesis; 9) research I did for my Ph.D. dissertation; 10) my current research; 11) formal faculty seminars I have attended; 12) informal exchanges with colleagues on my own campus; 13) informal exchanges with colleagues on other campuses; 14) Association for Asian American Studies annual meetings; 15) meetings of other professional organizations; 16) teaching experience while I was a teaching assistant; 17) teaching experience while I was a part-time faculty member; and 18) teaching experience while I was a tenure-track faculty member at another campus before I got my present job.

The critical significance of reading the existing literature is again highlighted in the responses to this set of questions. Fully 65.3 percent of the respondents indicated that the current readings they are doing on their own are "extremely useful" while 22.6 percent said they are "very useful," giving a combined 87.9 percent. As for readings done before teaching began, 61.3 percent deemed them "extremely useful" and 18.6 percent said they were "very useful," yielding a combined score of 79.9 percent. Next in importance is the respondents' current research: 60 percent said it is "extremely useful" and 18.6 percent checked "very useful" (a combined score of 78.6 percent). Readings suggested by colleagues were "extremely useful" to 29.3 percent and "very useful" to 30.6 percent (a combined 59.9 percent).

In comparison, only about a third of the respondents thought their prior teaching experience was useful. Experience as teaching assistants was "extremely useful" or "very useful" to a combined 33.3 percent of the respondents, while their experience as part-time faculty was "extremely useful" or "very useful" to a combined 36 percent. Exchanges with colleagues on other campuses (a combined 64 percent) are considerably more useful than exchanges with colleagues on their own campuses (a combined 49.3 percent)—figures that reflect the fact that with notable exceptions, most universities have only a handful of Asian Americanists and few colleagues in the traditional disciplines know enough about the histories, contemporary lives, and cultural expressions of Asian Americans to engage in meaningful conversations with them. Such person-to-person informal exchanges, however, are nevertheless considered more important than interactions at either the Association for Asian American studies annual meetings (a combined percentage of 40 percent) or those of other professional organizations (a combined percentage of 25.2 percent).

There was room in the questionnaire for respondents to write in the preparation they wish they had received but did not. The largest number, not surprisingly, said they wished they had been able to take courses in Asian American studies, especially at the graduate level, that address both substantive and theoretical issues. In addition, some individuals also wished they had received better training in theories of race and ethnicity; in cultural studies; the writings of Marx, Althusser, Lacan, Foucault, and other theorists; "epistemological and political" issues related to Asian American studies; quantitative research methodologies; how to do interdisciplinary research; and Asian languages. Aside from substantive and theoretical knowledge, some respondents also wished they had known before they started teaching how to cope with "school politics"; to effectively teach students of different class, racial, and ethnic backgrounds all sitting in the same classrooms; to engage in collaborative teaching and research projects; to design courses in uncharted areas; and to combine academic and community work. One person wrote that having a graduate seminar on the professional, academic, and institutional issues that women faculty and faculty of color are likely to face would have been really helpful.

Finally, respondents were asked to rank the perceived marketability of various graduate degrees in light of the current job market. The possible choices were 1) a degree in a traditional discipline; 2) a degree in a traditional discipline but with an emphasis in ethnic studies or Asian American studies; 3) a degree in Asian American studies; 4) a degree in comparative ethnic studies; and 5) a degree in American studies. The answers indicate that the respondents considered a degree in a traditional discipline with an emphasis in ethnic or Asian American studies to be the most marketable in the prevailing job market: 46.7 percent chose "extremely marketable" and 30.7 percent chose "very marketable," giving a combined 77.4 percent. The percentages for a traditional discipline alone were 10.7 and 40 percent, respectively; comparative ethnic studies is thought to be "extremely marketable" by 17.3 and "very marketable" by 25.3 percent. Only 16 and 14.7 percent, respectively, thought a Ph.D. in Asian American studies (alone) would be "extremely marketable" and "very marketable." The scores for American studies were 4 and 28 percent, respectively.

Written comments illustrate the difficulties of finding workable ways to train new generations of Asian Americanists. Many commentators observed that while it may be wonderful to be able to get a Ph.D. in Asian American

studies, a majority of the job openings are in existing disciplinary departments. So, a Ph.D. in Asian American studies is not particularly useful. As
one person put it, "Given that traditional disciplines/departments still hold
the power of hiring, Asian American Ph.D.s need to demonstrate a mastery
of traditional fields. From what I've seen, candidates who can teach not only
Asian American studies but also [courses in the] traditional disciplines appear
to have the broadest appeal to schools, especially small liberal arts colleges." A
second respondent wrote, "I'm not sure if a Ph.D. in Asian American studies
would be productive at this point—up against too much opposition even
from allies of Asian American studies. More effort should be spent *capturing*
talented scholars who are still in 'traditional' disciplines in graduate school
and *converting* them early." A third commentator noted how aspiring Asian
American studies faculty get two conflicting messages:

> One message emerges from the recent development of curricula and programs
> where student and community activism has led to the ultimate establishment of
> courses and instructors. The message points to the need for people who have a
> high level of commitment to program development, teaching, and community
> outreach. The second message, however, is connected to the traditional structure
> of the university since its scientific and corporate transformation over recent
> decades. That message is, "You must research and publish quality scholarship in
> sufficient amounts in order to receive merit increases, promotion, and tenure."
> The [second] message thoroughly conflicts with, and in many ways counters,
> the first.... Any program granting a doctorate in Asian American studies would
> need to be attentive to this dilemma.

Some respondents couched their comments in intellectual rather than
pragmatic terms. One person wrote, "I am opposed to bounded ethnic studies
units . . . [because of] identity politics [and because they] narrow intellectual
and political growth. I would rather have interdisciplinary emphases across
traditional departmental lines." In contrast, another faculty pointed out
that the main advantage of having an Asian American studies program or
department is that in such a setting, works can be presented with an "emphasis on how [particular writings] work as Asian American texts and [how
they] differ in theoretical and/or methodological orientation from traditional
disciplinary approaches. Candidates applying for Asian American studies
positions appear to be increasingly well trained in their disciplines but know
little about Asian American Studies." Yet another respondent cautioned that
"mounting a Ph.D. program in Ethnic and/or Asian American studies is a
daunting task. You need to have faculty who are not only willing but able to
teach across disciplines and to train [incoming graduate] students who may

be untutored/unmentored in the tools, pedagogies, and epistemologies of Asian American Studies. [Training graduate students] also takes a lot away from existing undergraduate teaching."

Though the above findings are only suggestive, it is clear that advocates of Asian American studies must constantly wrestle with the question of whether it would be preferable to pressure disciplinary departments to hire faculty with a teaching and research interest in Asian American studies or for campuses to establish autonomous Asian American studies programs or departments. This is a complex and vexed issue because there are advantages and disadvantages to each of the currently available institutional arrangements.

As I see it, faculty housed in departments in the disciplines in which they had received their graduate training are subjected simultaneously to both less and more pressures than those housed in Asian American or ethnic studies programs or departments. Less, because they can feel secure about their disciplinary grounding and need worry only about acquiring substantive knowledge about Asian Americans within the confines of their own disciplines. They are not compelled to learn and keep up with writing by scholars in disciplines other than their own. At the same time they may also experience more pressure because their departmental colleagues may not respect their specialization in Asian American studies or, worse, may resent the fact that they had been coerced by students and other supporters of the field to hire someone in Asian American studies. In such a situation, Asian Americanists are only grudgingly accepted and may always feel marginal and powerless.

In contrast, faculty who join autonomous Asian American studies programs or departments that can do their own hiring without input from other academic units experience different kinds of pressure. Since these programs or departments are, at least in theory, supposed to be multidisciplinary (or even interdisciplinary) and house faculty trained in a variety of disciplines, there is an implicit obligation to read, learn, and keep up with the pertinent writings related to Asian Americans in more than one discipline. As that body of literature grows, it is becoming well-nigh impossible for anyone to be truly multi- or interdisciplinary. Not surprisingly, as it exists today, Asian American studies is at best multidisciplinary; there has not been much intellectual cross-fertilization despite the fact that its practitioners have invoked interdisciplinarity as a goal for more than three decades. Having tried to be interdisciplinary in my own research and teaching, I know what a lot of effort that takes. I could spend an enormous amount of time acquainting myself with the literature in several disciplines only because I have no children and manage to function on very little sleep.

A second challenge confronting autonomous Asian American studies programs or departments is that not only does each discipline have its own theories and methodologies but different disciplines also measure "productivity" in different ways. A lack of understanding regarding such differences may lead to strong disagreements when departmental colleagues trained in disparate disciplines evaluate one another's work during promotion and tenure reviews. Since there is usually only one historian, or one sociologist, or one psychologist, or one literary scholar in a small Asian American studies program or department, colleagues may, in fact, not be fully qualified to judge the quality of one another's work, which is, in most instances, still grounded in the disciplinary training we received. To get around this problem, the Asian American Studies Department at UC Santa Barbara has often invited one or more senior colleagues from the discipline in which a reviewee was trained to advise us during such reviews. This is, however, at best, a band-aid solution.

A more troubling problem in stand-alone programs or departments is that because Asian American studies faculty often feel so besieged, some expect their colleagues to evaluate their records in glowing terms, regardless of what they have or have not accomplished. Such individuals are easily offended by any kind of criticism, no matter how constructive. The implicit assumption is that, as coethnics, we are not supposed to evaluate one another in the same critical way that non-Asians judge us. The expectation that more senior faculty members should unquestioningly and unconditionally support more junior faculty members makes it difficult for the field to demonstrate that it *does* have "standards" even though they may not be a carbon copy of those that traditional disciplines claim to uphold. For example, a colleague of mine filed a formal grievance against me some years ago when I was department chair because he/she felt I had "discriminated" against him/her by not presenting his/her record in sufficiently laudatory terms. This individual objected to the fact that I had used the word "excellent" to characterize his/her teaching. "Excellent," he/she averred, "is such a banal word."

Two additional factors make it difficult for autonomous Asian American studies programs or departments to function with integrity: a new kind of racism and sexism that some administrators now seem to espouse and a grab-what-you-can attitude that some faculty members seem to exhibit. I first discovered the changing administrative attitude when an administrator told me that I better "go easy" on a new faculty member who had complained that I expected too much of him/her. Administrators at some "liberal" campuses had reason to "go easy" on women faculty and faculty of color in the mid-1990s. The UC Santa Barbara campus in particular lost a major lawsuit filed by a senior Chicano studies faculty who failed to get an offer from the campus—a lawsuit that cost the University of California several million dollars. Moreover, UC Santa Barbara's "faculty affirmative action statistics" did not look very good in those days because many traditional departments still resisted hiring female or nonwhite faculty. Therefore, the three ethnic studies departments at UC Santa Barbara performed a crucial function for the campus: the faculty we hired helped increase the number of "minorities" on the faculty. For that reason, instead of resisting the appointment of "minorities" and scrutinizing their records, as was done in the past, administrators increasingly treated the ones hired within ethnic studies units with kid gloves. They usually cannot treat the "minority" faculty hired by traditional departments in a similarly paternalistic or maternalistic way because the senior faculty members in those departments would object vehemently to "double standards."

Though seemingly supportive, I saw the soft touch as an insidious form of sexism and racism—the sexism/racism of low expectations. The unspoken subtext of the message to me was "Don't be so demanding on your faculty. We shouldn't expect too much from them because . . . well, you know, . . . they come from 'disadvantaged' backgrounds, after all." I pointed out that not all women faculty members or faculty of color are "disadvantaged." No matter. In the administrators' eyes, they are "minorities," and their hiring improved the university's affirmative action statistics. And *that* was what counted during the years when affirmative action was still mandated by university policy.

Such thinking is diametrically opposite to my own. While I have done everything in my power to get competent faculty of color appointed, I also believe that once they join the faculty they should follow the same rules—in terms of work load and promotion criteria—as everybody else. It offends me deeply when we are treated simply as boosters of affirmative action statistics. While some faculty of color may welcome a lowering of the bar, I think it robs us of dignity and self-respect. It would be better that we be rewarded for our performances and not our phenotypical characteristics. Racism can take disparate forms, but all of them, including those that seem "supportive" of women and people of color, are ugly.

Another kind of faculty behavior can also undermine the integrity of Asian American studies. In my own department two faculty members hired at the full-professor level demanded accelerated promotions only a year after their arrival even though they had already "skipped" several steps when they joined our faculty. Full-time faculty in the UC system are called "ladder-rank faculty" because they are reviewed at fixed intervals as they advance up the faculty ranks, and the amount of salary increase between steps is also specified. While exceptions are possible, such exceptions are made only for those individuals whose accomplishments are truly extraordinary or who have competing offers (in writing) from other universities of equal stature. Because UC faculty members normally go up one step at a time each time they are reviewed, I could not in good conscience support demands for out-of-line promotions when the initial appointment levels were *already* much higher than warranted. One person sarcastically branded me a "gatekeeper" for the establishment. How ironic! Had I not worked so hard for so many years to pry open the gates of the university, these individuals probably would not have become UC faculty. Such self-serving behavior is so detrimental because it confirms the suspicions harbored by non–ethnic studies faculty members—that autonomous ethnic studies departments are incapable of acting "objectively" when it comes to faculty appointments, salary increases, or promotions.

I never anticipated these problems because I had been too single-mindedly focused on opening the gates of the university to "unconventional" applicants, but I failed to take into account who might apply for the jobs that became available as a result of the political pressures exerted by students and faculty in Asian American or ethnic studies in the 1990s. In other words, while I developed considerable insight into how universities are structured and how they function, I paid no attention to the larger changes in the world that are impinging upon faculty applicant pools in the United States.

I initially attributed the differences between me and some faculty members we hired to a generation gap. Because the field had remained stagnant in terms of faculty numbers from the mid-1970s to the late 1980s, the notion of "generation gap" seemed pertinent. It would be more accurate, however, to use the plural, "generations," because academic generations do not last very long. In that fifteen-year interval of virtually zero growth, three or four generational cohorts would have been formed had faculty positions been available. But they were not. Thus, on a superficial level one might attribute the differences between me and the new faculty members who entered the field decades after I had done so to a multigeneration gap.

Chalsa Loo, Don Mar, and Michael Omi first analyzed such a gap in three essays they contributed to *Reflections on Shattered Windows* (1988).[1] The titles of those essays reflect the authors' concerns: "The 'Middle-Aging' of Asian American Studies," "It Just Ain't the Sixties No More: The Contemporary Dilemmas of Asian American Studies," and "The Lost Second Generation of Asian American Scholars." In the fifteen years following the publication of those essays it seems that the gap has not only not narrowed but also mutated into new forms. After reflecting deeply upon my own experience, I concluded that if there is indeed a gap it is not one of age, generation, nativity, ethnicity, or class. In my own case, students and I continued to understand and appreciate one another, and my relationship with the two youngest faculty members, who joined the faculty while in their twenties, was friendly. What separated me from the three individuals who became very antagonistic towards me were fundamental differences in our subject positions and ideologies.

Faculty members who joined Asian American studies in the 1990s did so within a context quite different from those that had existed in earlier decades. Because I was quite ill with post-polio syndrome during the years when Asian American studies at UC Santa Barbara grew most rapidly, I did not pay much attention to the world outside of the university's narrow confines. It was not until I helped design a new major in global studies in the late 1990s that I became aware of the immense and multifaceted impacts that globalization is making on faculty applicant pools on American campuses. After the United States liberalized its immigration laws in 1965, mass immigration from Asia resumed after decades of exclusion or semi-exclusion.

Initially, many post-1965 immigrants were family members of individuals already here. By the mid-1970s, however, well-educated professionals from Asia (and other continents) also began making their way to America. Those who come for graduate studies arrive as adults with well-formed personalities, well-defined worldviews, and great personal ambition. As they complete their graduate education, some look for jobs in academia. Since they had not been "minorities" in their natal countries, some of them apparently feel uncomfortable about being placed into a "minority" slot in American society. One convenient way to avoid such a racialized identity is to insist that they are a part of various Asian diasporas and that they have diasporic or transnational identities. That is, they intentionally *dis*identify with the country in which they now live and earn a living. For example, a colleague in another department once snapped at me, "Don't ever call me an Asian American!" Taken aback by the annoyance this person, who had lived in the United States since he/she was a young teenager, expressed, I asked, "What should I call you, then?" "I'm an overseas Chinese" was the curt reply.

Unlike members of the diasporas of old—the classic diaspora being that of the Jews—who nursed a never forgotten yearning for the "home(s)" left behind, members of today's diasporas have little desire to return to their natal countries while they are still in their prime. Some say that when they are ready to retire they may return to their countries of origin—but only if political conditions there are stable, if the economies are prosperous, and if they can enjoy a social standing much higher than what they have managed to achieve in the countries where they currently live and work.

In my opinion, given their contingent attitude, "transnational" is a more accurate adjective than "diasporic" to describe such people. Transnational migrants (or transmigrants) maintain ongoing ties to people and developments in two or more countries without committing themselves, in terms of political allegiance, to any. They seem interested mainly in advancing the fortunes of themselves and their families. Some transmigrants from Asia have little desire to become "Americans" because becoming "Americans" means being incorporated into U.S. society as ethnic or racial "minorities." Even though Asian Americans may be perceived as "a model minority," they are members of a *minority* nonetheless. A "minority" status is not only disadvantageous but also psychologically uncomfortable. Some people resist any kind of deeper identification with American society even after they acquire U.S. citizenship. That is, they obtain U.S. citizenship only because it guarantees their right to remain, among other privileges, but they prefer to possess "hybrid identities"—identities that are constantly in flux and are "deterritorialized."

In light of these world-shaking transformations, ideological differences manifest themselves within Asian American studies in ways that are related only tangentially, if at all, to age, generation, ethnicity, or even nativity. What really divides faculty who teach in the field, I think, are, first, the intensity of one's concern for rapid career advancement and personal aggrandizement versus one's commitment to serving students and communities and engaging in "progressive" politics, and, second, how one perceives the integrationist U.S. civil rights movement and the later separatist Black Power movement and the value judgments one confers on them. Since the Asian American movement did not begin until the heyday of the civil rights movement was over, the Black Power movement had a greater influence on Asian American activists. The ramifications of that fact have not yet been completely explored and explicated.

While it may be possible in a few rare instances for Asian American studies faculty members to advance up the ladder *while* serving students and communities, in most instances the two goals pull in opposite directions. Every activity takes time, and there are only twenty-four hours in a day. As young faculty members form families, they must also spend time with their spouses and children. Given such multiple and conflicting pressures, over the years more and more Asian American studies faculty abandoned the goal of serving "the community." Only a handful of individuals have remained true to that vision. The rest of us, myself included, salve our conscience by saying that our students *are* the communities we serve. Some of us borrow Antonio Gramsci's concepts of "organic intellectuals" and "hegemony" to justify why our efforts are focused largely on what goes on within the academy. Consequently, the contrary pull between teaching and community service is no longer as vexatious as it used to be.

What remains as a powerful divide are differences in how Asian Americanists regard the civil rights and the Black Power movements. The first movement focused on gaining equality for African Americans, while the second aimed truly to empower them. Asian Americans who identified with either or both movements, therefore, at one level or another, supported the myriad forms of struggles that African Americans engaged in as well as our own battles. Many senior faculty in the field (some of whom, including myself, were not even born in the United States) take pride in having participated, however peripherally, in the social movements of the 1960s. There are also many younger scholars, regardless of where they were born, who likewise believe in the necessity of continuing the struggles for justice and equality, not only on campuses but in the world at large. That is to say, while we may have stopped trying to serve "the community" we have not given up "politics."

The above two groups of faculty differ from a third whose members see the social movements of the 1960s and 1970s, including the movement to establish the various branches of ethnic studies, as relics of the past that should be discarded. Possessing no emotive connection to those movements, such individuals do not think the "originary vision" of Asian American studies is worth upholding. They frame the issue as a contrast between doing "research" versus engaging in "politics." What they fail to understand is that the thinking of the older generation of scholars was never so simplistic. We long ago recognized the necessity of engaging in *both* scholarship and political action, as the essays in Part 1 of this book make so clear.

The real contrast, I think, is between faculty who identify with and participate in "minority" issues and those who do not. The latter spent their childhood and formative years in countries—including those formerly colonized by Europeans and that now exist as postcolonial societies—in which they were members of the *majority* population, at least in terms of numbers if not power. After arriving in the United States, they think they can use their middle- or upper-class standing to evade "minority" status. When individuals who did not grow up as minorities teach Asian American studies they have a hard time comprehending why so many American-born or American-reared youth of Asian ancestry have to struggle so hard to develop self-esteem and self-respect; why Asian American studies is more than an academic field of inquiry; and why taking our courses can be a cathartic, life-transforming experience for some of our students.

Despite their aversion to being identified as racial/ethnic minorities, some Asian transmigrant scholars have applied for jobs in Asian American studies because many of the positions available during the 1990s and the 2000s were or are at "prestigious" universities. That is, they were/are "desirable" jobs to status-conscious individuals. Starting their careers at prestigious universities enables ambitious scholars to climb the career ladder as quickly as possible because the teaching load is lighter and research support is more available. Transmigrant scholars have been quite successful in their job searches because their academic credentials are usually good. More important, from the point of view of administrators and senior faculty members in the traditional departments doing the hiring, they offer the added (though unspoken) advantage of being "ethnic" but not "radical."

Ironically, the very name of our field—*Asian* American studies or *ethnic* studies—has put us in a bind. Just because job applicants belong to the same "ethnicity" as the faculty who first developed the field, it cannot be assumed they share the latter's vision. Being coethnics does not guarantee a shared consciousness. Not only do some faculty members who entered the field in the 1990s and thereafter have different worldviews, but a few have expressed considerable impatience with the old-timers. As Philip Q. Yang stated in 2000:

> To be sure, the mission of ethnic studies and the process of establishing and sustaining an ethnic studies program are political. Ethnic studies is a voice for progressive social change, humane treatment of ethnic groups, and improved intergroup relations. Each step forward entails hard-fought political battles. *However, the discipline and curriculum of ethnic studies should not be politicized.* As a discipline, ethnic studies is a systematic study of ethnicity, ethnic groups, and intergroup relations using interdisciplinary, multidisciplinary, and comparative methodologies. It is by no means synonymous with political activism [emphasis added].[2]

There is a contradiction in that passage that its author does not seem to recognize: the "hard-fought political battles" could not have been won without "political activism." "Progressive social change" and more "humane treatment" came about only as a result of political engagement.

Min Zhou, a sociologist and a prolific writer, analyzed the existing tensions this way:

> While the ongoing discussion of goals and methodologies is at once refreshing and evident of the field's continuing vitality, it also testifies to the degree to

which intellectual and organizational tensions are built into the field. On the one hand, the very language of the debate, often filled with jargon and trendy concepts, stands in conflict with the self-professed orientation toward the community and its needs. On the other hand, there is a certain nostalgia among veteran activists, now mainly tenured professors, for the spirit of the 1960s and, to some extent, that yearning for the past ironically threatens to produce a divide between U.S.-born (and/or U.S. raised) scholars and some of their Asian-born counterparts, especially those whose education in the United States was more likely to begin at the college and graduate level, and who may not share the same connection to a history that they never experienced. Moreover, the ideological suppositions of the scholars oriented toward the Movement has the potential to create distance between them and the growing number of Asian American (often Asian-born) scholars who work on Asian American topics, but from the standpoint of the more traditional disciplines.[3]

What caught my eye was her assertion that the "distance" is being created by the "veteran activists." As I see it, that "distance" is *also* being forged by the newcomers' disdain for the allegedly outmoded goals of the earlier generations of Asian Americanists. The gulf, in short, is being mutually constituted.

While I recognize that aging scholars such as myself need to move aside and to relinquish whatever power that we "mainly tenured professors" are seen to possess, the faculty members who entered the field in more recent years should realize that many of them have the jobs they hold today mainly because student activists, who have been consistently vocal and committed, and the first-generation faculty members, who have labored under the most adverse working conditions, collectively have kept the various components of ethnic studies alive. Regardless of whether or not these late-entering cohorts of faculty feel any connection to the "Movement," they owe it a special debt in terms of their personal career advancement. Therefore, however uncomfortable some of them may feel about the political history of Asian American studies, they should not denigrate, much less erase it.

As an increasing number of faculty members who have no use for the political legacy of Asian American studies enters the field we hear more and more talk about why Asian American studies needs to be transformed into something other than what it has been. Should Asian American studies merge with Asian studies? with American studies? with postcolonial studies? with cultural studies? As these questions become increasingly salient in the years to come we must be honest with ourselves and admit that such debates are not simply intellectual discussions; rather, they camouflage thinly disguised struggles for dominance within the Asian American professorate in terms of who gets to set the agenda for the field.

As I see it, the crux of the dilemma isn't theory but practice. I think the transnational, diasporic, globalization, cultural studies, poststructural, postmodernist, or postcolonial studies conceptual frameworks are *all* important as heuristic devices for analyzing key developments in the late twentieth and early twenty-first centuries. The extraordinary heterogeneity of the population of Asian ancestry now living in the United States (note that I am carefully not saying "Asian Americans" here because I do not want to offend those who do not consider themselves to be "Americans") *mandates* that multiple frameworks be used to guide our research. We must help our students as well as ourselves not only to understand the racialized (and still largely "minority") positions in American society to which we continue to be relegated but also to make sense of the ever more complex transnational linkages that now form webs encompassing virtually every aspect of our lives. We must ponder deeply not only what it means to be American citizens but also what it means to be "global citizens." At the same time, we need to realize that the various branches of ethnic studies will lose their critical edge if we forget why they were established and the political nature of the historical moment that gave them birth.

The tug between "scholarship" and "politics" is not unique to Asian American studies. In women's studies, feminist scholars Ellen Carol DuBois and her coauthors made a resounding declaration in 1987 that concisely captures the contradiction: "We believed—we still believe—that the connection to a political movement is the lifeblood of feminist scholarship, not its tragic flaw."[4]

In cultural studies, another multidisciplinary field with a "political" history, Stuart Hall posed the issue this way:

> The enormous explosion of cultural studies in the U.S., its rapid professionalization and institutionalization, is not a moment which any of us who tried to set up a marginalized Centre [for Contemporary Cultural Studies] in a university like Birmingham could, in any simple way, regret. And yet I have to say, in the strongest sense, that it reminds me of the ways in which, in Britain, we are always aware of institutionalization as a moment of profound danger. . . . Why? Well, it would be excessively vulgar to talk about such things as how many jobs there are, how much money there is around, and how much pressure that puts on people to do what they think of as critical political work and intellectual work of a critical kind, while also looking over their shoulders at the promotions stakes and the publication stakes, and so on.[5]

In American studies, another field in ferment, George Lipsitz recalled "the transformative power of public political action" during the 1960s and contrasted that era with today's conditions:

Intellectuals and artists today often live disconnected from active social movements. . . . They work within hierarchical institutions and confront reward
structures that privilege individual distinction over collective social change.
. . . Artistic and intellectual work takes place today in a contradictory context,
and it produces people with a contradictory consciousness. . . . they are . . .
pressured to segregate themselves from aggrieved communities, and to work
within the confines and ideological controls of institutions controlled by the
wealthy and powerful. . . . The contradictory consciousness that pervades the
lives of academic intellectuals, artists, and cultural workers present specific
impediments to progressive politics.[6]

The above statements all resonate with the issues being debated within
Asian American studies at the dawn of the twenty-first century. Furthermore,
the same tensions roil an Asian-ancestry population now demographically
dominated by post-1965 immigrants. Looking at the political landscape outside the academy, Paul Ong and David Lee noted:

Although Asian immigrants are a part of a minority group that has been subjected to past acts of overt racism, they are not strongly aligned with the civil
rights agenda. For many immigrants, Asian American history is not their history, so they have no sense of membership in a historically victimized population. Although Asian immigrants do experience discrimination, many attribute
that discrimination to cultural and linguistic differences rather than race. . . .
As a consequence . . . most Asian immigrants do not readily support minority-
oriented efforts and programs. . . . The emergence of an immigrant majority
can have profound implications for Asian American politics. One impact . . .
is the threat it might pose to progressive activists.[7]

To those of us who still care about "progressive" politics—that is, struggles
for racial equality, socioeconomic justice, and political empowerment—the
historical legacy of Asian American studies must not be pushed aside because
the political-cum-scholarly work that the first generation of Asian American,
African American, Chicano/Latino, and Native American scholars tried to
do still needs to be done. What undergirded the foundations of those fields
was a critique of American society. Today, our critiques must be directed not
only at the American nation-state but also at an entire world dominated by
a form of capitalism that is flexible, dispersed, transnational, and robust.

But even as we supplant the older American-based antiracist critique in order to avoid becoming theoretically and substantively "outdated" we should
keep in mind that while global forces are affecting all strata of the world's
inhabitants, it is the upper stratum that benefits while the middle and lower
strata get mired in ever more destitute forms of poverty. The current world

order is characterized by a growing disparity between the rich and the poor. While many ethnic studies pioneer scholars also came from middle-class backgrounds, at least we (counting myself in this group) identified ideologically and politically with oppressed people, not just in the United States but around the globe. Teaching ethnic studies gave us a way to participate in the fight for equality, justice, and self-empowerment.

Even as a commodified, globalized, but American-dominated popular culture touting consumerism as the answer to all problems increasingly reigns supreme, we cannot allow that trend to camouflage the abject miseries that characterize an ever larger proportion of the world's inhabitants. Just because professionals of various hues are now accepted as members of the middle and even upper classes in the United States and in other "First World" countries or former "metropoles," that acceptance should not blind us to the fact that discrimination based on race, national or ethnic origins, class, gender, sexual orientation, and physical handicaps continues to structure social relations in the countries where many transnational professionals now live.

What I am arguing for is this: while we certainly should add the currently modish schools of thought to our intellectual pantheon, we must also be aware of at least three hidden dangers in using such academically chic theories as normative guides to *action*. First, while the repudiation of "master narratives" is indeed a needed corrective to the underlying assumptions and exclusions of the Enlightenment project, we should recognize that the fragmentation and the often radical relativism that such theories valorize make it more difficult to develop solidarity as we attempt to form coalitions to counter the oppressiveness of the conditions under which the middle and lower strata of the population, including "minorities" of various kinds, still live. Members of the relatively small, multiracial or multiethnic transnational elite can indeed easily travel to, buy homes in, do business with, and find work any place they please, but the privileges they enjoy are out of reach for the downtrodden majority among the world's population. Should scholars in Asian American studies care about such inequality? Some of us think so. That is why even though we may be a fast-disappearing numerical minority within Asian American studies, our drumbeat is still insistently loud. *There's* the rub for impatient colleagues who wish we would disappear into the walls of old folks' homes.

Second, while the extraordinary emphasis on culture, especially culture read textually, as a major arena of contestation is also a needed corrective to the economic determinism that structured the ways in which some of us used to think about the world, I believe we must continue to monitor and analyze economic and political changes that cannot be reduced to culture per se, regardless of how capaciously "culture" may be understood. Cultural politics cannot be the only kind of politics we engage in. The materialist foundations of human life are fundamental sources of oppression; as such they must not only be studied alongside the miseries we experience in the symbolic realm of the imagination but also combatted in whatever limited ways may be possible in the material world.

Third, I do not think it is time yet to throw out every aspect of the Enlightenment project. The students and young scholars who fought for the establishment of the various branches of ethnic studies did so by arguing that their right to a "relevant" education was a form of civil rights—that is, the rights we should all enjoy as citizens and permanent residents of the United States. We could make claims on the university because it is state-supported—supported, that is, by taxpayers such as ourselves and our parents. We could make claims on the United States because we insisted we are Americans, regardless of our skin color. One strategy we used was to turn the rhetoric of a supposedly liberal state upon itself. We were quite aware that during much of the nation's history there was a huge gap between ideology and reality. But by embracing the liberal democratic state's professed norms of inclusiveness we exposed the hypocrisies in the society in which we live. We called upon that society to reform itself so that it can realize its true promise. No one could stop us from *invoking* the rights supposedly guaranteed by the U.S. constitution and by various laws because we claimed those laws apply to us darker-hued Americans as well. Because the American nation-state is a manifestation of the Enlightenment project, an "ethnic studies project" that made its claims based upon the American creed was at once a critique and an affirmation of such Enlightenment values as progress, rationality, freedom, equality, justice, and democracy. Just because so many scholars now scoff at the Enlightenment, its metaphorical babies—the ideals it professed—need not be thrown out with the bath water.

At least, not yet. Because some members of the U.S. power structure still pay lip service to these liberal ideals, scholar-activists in ethnic studies and in other fields have been able to carve out a tiny space—indeed, small *bases* of resistance—from which we offered counter-hegemonic narratives to the prevailing national myths rooted in the Enlightenment vision. For that reason, the moral, legal, and political reasons we used to make our claims are not yet outmoded. So, why the rush to throw out the "minority" paradigm, even though it is indeed embedded in a still-unjust American society, when it has not yet outlived its utility?

To be sure, there are scholars who argue we can also make claims on the basis of "human rights"—a more universal form of rights not rooted in any nation-state. Unfortunately, the institutional structures for enforcing human rights are still in a nascent stage of development. While globalization is indeed eroding the power of nation-states, still, in terms of immigration and civil rights, the American state apparatus remains potent. Just ask the undocumented migrants who risk their lives daily to enter the United States, many of whom are caught, jailed, and deported, or worse, die in the attempt. Therefore, should we, in our rush to keep "up to date" theoretically, kick the "nationalist" moorings from under ourselves, as some transnationally oriented colleagues argue we should do, we will lose a truly useful tool that may yet ensure our continued survival in whatever hard times may lie ahead. And there *will* be hard times as neoconservatives, who have become smart enough to accept "diversity" as an imperative, develop more and more sophisticated methods to seduce some of us into joining their camp while simultaneously doing everything in their power to make the rich richer and the poor poorer.

It is not nostalgia, therefore, but a cold, clear-eyed realism that leads to the following exhortation: Let us not jettison the very tools we have used to get to where we are today.

Notes

1. Gary Y. Okihiro et al., eds., *Reflections on Shattered Windows: Promises and Prospects for Asian American Studies* (Pullman: Washington State University Press, 1988).

2. Philip Q. Yang, *Ethnic Studies: Issues and Approaches* (Albany: SUNY Press, 2000), 276.

3. Min Zhou and James V. Gatewood, eds., *Contemporary Asian America: A Multidisciplinary Reader* (New York: New York University Press, 2000), 7–8.

4. Ellen Carol DuBois et al., *Feminist Scholarship: Kindling in the Groves of Academia* (Urbana: University of Illinois Press, 1987), 8.

5. Stuart Hall, "Cultural Studies and Its Theoretical Legacies," in *Cultural Studies*, ed. and with an introduction by Lawrence Grossberg, Cary Nelson, and Paula Treichler (New York: Routledge, 1992), 85–86.

6. George Lipsitz, *American Studies in a Moment of Danger* (Minneapolis: University of Minnesota Press, 2001), 58, 277–78.

7. Paul M. Ong and David E. Lee, "Changing of the Guard? The Emerging Immigrant Majority in Asian American Politics," in *Asian Americans and Politics: Perspectives, Experiences, Prospects,* ed. Gordan H. Chang (Washington: Woodrow Wilson Center Press and Stanford, Calif.: Stanford University Press, 2001), 165–66.

Epilogue:
Where Biography Intersects History

How did an immigrant kid like me become a professor of Asian American studies? Looking back, I think the forces that propelled me in the direction I eventually followed originated in my childhood. Had my mother had a different personality; had the United States Information Service (USIS, now known as USIA—the United States Information Agency) not had a library in Penang, Malaya (renamed Malaysia after gaining independence from British colonial rule), where my family lived for some years; and had I not attended Swarthmore College and the University of California, Berkeley, I likely would not have found such a calling. I probably would have become a medical doctor or a natural scientist.

Among my childhood memories, one stands out. When I was a little over three, I broke something (I do not remember exactly what the object was) while my nanny was feeding me in the kitchen. Hearing the clatter, my mother came into the kitchen and flew into a rage, not at me but at the "servant" who took care of me. In later years I figured out that I must have broken a rice bowl because Chinese who believe in omens think that breaking a rice bowl, which symbolizes livelihood and prosperity, is a really bad omen. I came to this conclusion because my mother was extremely superstitious despite the fact that she was very well educated. Her beliefs exacted a psychic toll on my younger sister and me as we grew up because she refused to tell us which omens were good and which were bad. She thought that dire things would happen if people named or talked about the bad ones. Consequently, my sister and I have always been on edge around her because we had no way to anticipate what might set her off.

My mother was capable, competitive, status-conscious, strong-willed, charming, vivacious, sociable, beautiful, and energetic. She had a darker side as well. High-strung and intolerant of views contrary to hers, she became very angry when something displeased her or when someone dared to disagree with her. Even though that happened only occasionally, her anger lasted hours, spewing out like molten lava from a volcano. As I grew older I observed that she became angry only at subordinates—people she considered to be "servants"—as well as at my father, whom she dominated, and my sister and me, who were expected to obey her every wish. Thus, long before I studied any sociology and learned the meaning of "social stratification" I saw class privilege at work: my mother scolded my nanny instead of me because the woman was poor and came from a lower class than did my family. Even though such behavior was perfectly normal in terms of the class hierarchy that characterized early-twentieth-century Chinese society, my mother's inability to manage anger left indelible marks on her daughters.

My family left China in 1949, spent a year in Hong Kong, and then moved to Malaya, where my father's side of the family had resided for four generations. There, my parents discussed whether to send me and my sister to a school that taught its classes in English or one that used Chinese as the medium of instruction. My mother, who made all the key decisions in our family, decided that we should go to an English-language school because she planned to send us either to Great Britain or the United States for our college education. She wanted us to master the English language at an early age while our tongues were still supple. She intended to teach us Chinese at home but did so only sporadically. She expected us to learn to read and write Chinese somehow by osmosis, without formal instruction.

Stricken with polio at the age of four, I was not allowed to play with other children lest they knock me down. To amuse myself I became a voracious reader, but I could read only books written in English because my knowledge of Chinese was (and still is) rudimentary. It so happened there was a USIS library in Penang, where we lived. Every week my father drove me to that library, where I checked out seven books at a time because I devoured a book a day. The aim of the USIS library was to promote a positive view of the United States—USIS/USIA being a propaganda arm of U.S. foreign policy—so its shelves were full of books that extolled the wonders of American democracy. Based on what I read, I marveled at the difference between an egalitarian society and a hierarchical one.

A precocious child who had few playmates and read hundreds of books written for adults, I mentally became a grown-up while still in my early teens. Many of the books I read described an alternative model of how societies can be organized and how class prejudice need not structure all of human life. I also loved reading science books because the rational and systematic nature of scientific inquiry and discovery offered a different way of seeing and thinking—different from a world in which omens and superstitions reigned supreme. I had the freedom to develop a different worldview because my mother seldom showed any curiosity about what I read, thought, or wrote; all she cared about was whether I won awards. Because I did, she made no attempt to exercise surveillance over my mind, as she did my body.

My family immigrated to the United States in January 1957. Living and attending high school in the borough of Queens in New York City, I became aware of racial discrimination and injustice. What I observed shattered the rosy image I had of the United States. My dislike of class prejudice easily broadened to include an abhorrence of racial prejudice.

When I entered Swarthmore College in 1959, my disillusion with the yawning gap between American ideals and American realities led me to become a student activist. As soon as we heard that several black youths sat in at the segregated lunch counter at a Woolworth's store in Greensboro, North Carolina, in early 1960, some of my friends formed the Swarthmore Political Action Committee (SPAC). In imitation of and in solidarity with the courageous black youths in the South, SPAC members began sitting in every weekend at the lunch counter in the Woolworth's store in nearby Chester, Pennsylvania, a community with a large number of African American residents. There was only a handful of black students at Swarthmore at the time, so the participation of an Asian American like me enabled our group to be more "integrated" than it otherwise might have been. We became a small part of what came to be called the Northern Student Movement.

During the rest of my college years I participated in numerous civil rights demonstrations and was often the only Asian face in the crowd. Founded by the Society of Friends (Quakers), Swarthmore College supports students who "bear witness" to inhumanity. What we bore witness to and struggled against in the early 1960s was racial inequality. I raised thousands of dollars to bail friends who went on Freedom Rides in the South out of jail, but I did not dare go on a Freedom Ride myself, even though I really wanted to, because the members of my family had not yet become naturalized U.S. citizens. Should I land in jail, I worried, we might all be deported.

I had entered Swarthmore as a pre-med student but ended up majoring in economics and minoring in political science when I realized that racial oppression is undergirded by economic, political, social, and cultural inequality. Believing in the unity of theory and praxis, I wanted what I studied to resonate with my political extracurricular activities. Because I could not go on a Freedom Ride, I volunteered instead to participate in a project sponsored by the American Friends Service Committee to improve housing conditions in Harlem in the summer of 1961. On weekdays I worked as a laboratory assistant in the pharmacology department at Columbia University's College of Physicians and Surgeons. In the evenings and on weekends I helped spruce up dilapidated apartments, spending hour after hour scraping lead-based paint from walls and repainting them with less toxic paint. That summer was the first opportunity I had to work alongside young African Americans in the setting of their everyday lives.

Soon after I came to Berkeley, California, in 1966 for my second round of graduate studies (the first was at the University of Hawaii), I went on a march that began on Market Street in downtown San Francisco and ended in Kezar Stadium—a very strenuous trek for a cripple like me—to protest the American involvement in the War in Vietnam. A lot of "flower children" participated in that march. I was appalled when I saw a naked woman singing and dancing on a flatbed truck that formed part of the procession. I felt that the public image created by people primarily interested in the counterculture movement rather than the civil rights or the antiwar movements diminished the solemnity called for by such an occasion. The "California version" of what constitutes a social movement bothered me so much that I participated only marginally in the antiwar movement while I studied for a Ph.D. degree in political science, specializing in the comparative study of revolutions and minoring in public administration.

Two years later, when students went on "Third World" strikes at San Francisco State University and the University of California, Berkeley, to demand that ethnic studies programs or departments—or even a school—be established, I found a new arena for political activism. After Yuji Ichioka coined the term *Asian Americans,* it caught on rapidly. I loved the concept because it enabled me to take pride in being Asian while claiming my rightful place in America. Better yet, the broad and somewhat amorphous pan-Asian concept freed me from the specificities of the cultural constraints imposed on Chinese females. In 1971, before I finished my dissertation, I got a full-time job at Sonoma State College, teaching Asian American studies, which I had to help "invent," and third world studies, which made use of a part of my graduate education. Discovering how much I enjoyed teaching, I took a year of unpaid leave to complete my dissertation in 1973. My career in Asian American studies began in earnest in 1974 when I joined the Asian American studies faculty at the University of California, Berkeley.

And that's my story.

Selected Bibliography

This bibliography is organized chronologically in four parts, according to year of publication; the fifth part is a listing of other bibliographies. The chronologic order demonstrates how the field of Asian American studies has blossomed since the late 1980s. Only books, special issues of journals, a selected number of government documents about Asian immigrants, and selected autobiographies by Asian Americans are listed. Creative writing, journal articles, and chapters in books have not been included because doing so would take thousands of pages. (There are, however, a few exceptions, such as *America Is in the Heart* by Carlos Bulosan, the genre of which is indeterminate.) Additional citations appear in the annual bibliographies in *Amerasia Journal* and the publications listed under "Bibliographies."

Some of the books listed are virulently racist, but I included them because they reveal a mindset of historical significance. For a clarification of the ideological orientations of specific authors, see *The Columbia Guide to Asian American History* (New York: Columbia University Press, 2001) by Gary Okihiro, who groups authors as "anti-Asianists," "liberals," and "Asian Americanists." For creative writing and literary studies, see King-Kok Cheung and Stan Yogi, *Asian American Literature: An Annotated Bibliography* (New York: Modern Language Association of America, 1988), and *A Resource Guide to Asian American Literature,* edited by Sau-ling C. Wong and Stephen H. Sumida (New York: Modern Language Association of America, 2001).

Books and Special Issues of Periodicals, before 1970

A number of items published after 1970 are included in this section because they were originally M.A. theses and Ph.D. dissertations written years before 1970. R and E Research Associates of San Francisco published them without editorial changes.

Adams, Ansel. *Born Free and Equal: Photographs of the Loyal Japanese-Americans of Manzanar Relocation Center, Inyo County, California.* New York: U.S. Camera, 1944.

Adams, Romanzo. *Interracial Marriage in Hawaii.* New York: Macmillan, 1937.

Ai, Chung Kun. *My Seventy-Nine Years in Hawaii.* Hong Kong: Cosmorama Pictorial, 1960.

Allen, Charles R. *Concentration Camps, U.S.A.* New York: Marzani and Munzell, 1966.

Annals of the Academy of Political and Social Science 34 (Sept. 1909), and 93 (Jan. 1921).

Asiatic Exclusion League. *Proceedings.* San Francisco: Asiatic Exclusion League, 1908–12.

Ave, Mario P. "Charactistics of Filipino Organizations of Los Angeles." M.A. thesis, University of Southern California, 1956. Published in book form: San Francisco: R and E Research Associates, 1974.

Bailey, Thomas A. *Theodore Roosevelt and the Japanese-American Crisis: An Account of the International Complications Arising from the Race Problem on the Pacific Coast.* Stanford: Stanford University Press, 1934.

Bamford, Mary Ellen. *Ti: A Story of San Francisco's Chinatown.* Chicago: David C. Cook, 1899.

Barth, Gunther. *Bitter Strength: A History of the Chinese in the United States, 1850–1870.* Cambridge: Harvard University Press, 1964.

Bell, Reginald. *Public School Education of Second-Generation Japanese in California.* Stanford: Stanford University Press, 1935.

Bloom [Broom], Leonard, and Ruth Riemer. *Removal and Return.* Berkeley: University of California Press, 1949.

Boddy, Manchester E. *Japanese in America.* Los Angeles: the author, 1921.

Bonham, Frank. *Burma Rifles: The Story of a Young Japanese-American Fighting with Merrill's Marauders.* New York: Berkley, 1960.

Bose, Sudhindra. *Mother America: Realities of American Life as Seen by an Indian.* Raopura, India: M. S. Bhatt, 1934.

Bosworth, Allan R. *America's Concentration Camps.* New York: W. W. Norton, 1967.

Bromley, Isaac H. *The Chinese Massacre at Rock Springs.* Boston: Franklin, 1886.

Broom [Bloom], Leonard, and John I. Kitsuse. *The Managed Casualty: The Japanese American Family in World War II.* Berkeley: University of California Press, 1956.

Buaken, Manuel. *I Have Lived with the American People.* Caldwell, Idaho: Caxton, 1948.

Bulosan, Carlos. *America Is in the Heart: A Personal History.* New York: Harcourt, Brace, 1946; repr. Seattle: University of Washington Press, 1973.

Burrows, Edwin G. *Hawaiian Americans: An Account of the Mingling of Japanese, Chinese, Polynesian, and American Cultures.* New Haven: Yale University Press, 1947.

California Department of Industrial Relations, Division of Fair Employment Practices. *Californians of Japanese, Chinese, and Filipino Ancestry.* San Francisco: Division of Labor Statistics and Research, 1965.

California Legislature, Senate, Special Committee on Chinese Immigration. *Chinese Im-*

migration: Its Social, Moral, and Political Effect. Sacramento: California State Printing Office, 1878.

California State Board of Control. *California and the Oriental: Japanese, Chinese and Hindus.* Sacramento: California State Printing Office, 1920.

California State Department of Industrial Relations. *Facts about Filipino Immigration into California.* Special Bulletin no. 3. San Francisco: California State Printing Office, 1930.

Cariaga, Roman. "The Filipinos in Hawaii: A Survey of Their Economic and Social Conditions." M.A. thesis, University of Hawaii, 1936. Published in book form: San Francisco: R and E Research Associates, 1974.

Catapusan, Benicio T. "The Filipino Occupational and Recreational Activities in Los Angeles." M.A. thesis, University of Southern California, 1934. Published in book form: San Francisco: R and E Research Associates, 1975.

———. "The Social Adjustment of Filipinos in the United States." Ph.D. diss., University of Southern California, 1940. Published in book form: San Francisco: R and E Research Associates, 1972.

Cather, Helen V. "The History of San Francisco's Chinatown." M.A. thesis, University of California, Berkeley, 1932. Published in book form: San Francisco: R and E Research Associates, 1974.

Charyn, Jerome. *American Scrapbook.* New York: Viking, 1969.

Chiang, Yee. *The Silent Traveller in Boston.* New York: W. W. Norton, 1959.

———. *The Silent Traveller in New York.* New York: John Day, 1950.

———. *The Silent Traveller in San Francisco.* New York: W. W. Norton, 1964.

Chinn, Thomas W., Him Mark Lai, and Philip P. Choy, eds. *A History of the Chinese in California: A Syllabus.* San Francisco: Chinese Historical Society of America, 1969.

Chiu, Ping. *Chinese Labor in California, 1850–1880: An Economic Study.* Madison: State Historical Society of Wisconsin, 1967.

Civil Rights Digest 9 (Fall 1967).

Coleman, Elizabeth. *Chinatown, U.S.A.* New York: John Day, 1946.

Coloma, Casiano Pagdilao. "A Study of the Filipino Repatriation Movement." M.A. thesis, University of Southern California, 1939. Published in book form: San Francisco: R and E Research Associates, 1974.

Coman, Katherine. *The History of Contract Labor: The Hawaiian Islands.* New York: Macmillan, 1903.

Common Ground 1–10 (Autumn 1940–Autumn 1949).

Commonwealth Club of California. *Transactions,* vol. 24: *Filipino Immigration.* San Francisco: Commonwealth Club of California, 1929.

Conroy, Hilary. *The Japanese Frontier in Hawaii, 1868–1898.* Berkeley: University of California Press, 1953; repr. New York: Arno Press, 1978.

Consulate-General of Japan, comp. *Documented History of Law Cases Affecting Japanese Americans in the United States, 1916–1924.* 2 vols. San Francisco: Consulate-General of Japan, 1925.

Conwell, Russell H. *Why and How: Why the Chinese Emigrate and the Means They Adopt for the Purpose of Reaching America.* Boston: Lee and Shepard, 1871.

Coolidge, Mary Roberts. *Chinese Immigration.* New York: Henry Holt, 1909.

Corpus, Severino F. "An Analysis of the Racial Adjustment Activities and Problems of the Filipino-American Christian Fellowship in Los Angeles." M.A. thesis, University of Southern California, 1938. Published in book form: San Francisco: R and E Research Associates, 1975.

Courtney, William J. "San Francisco Anti-Chinese Ordinances, 1850–1900." Ph.D. diss., University of San Francisco, 1956. Published in book form: San Francisco: R and E Research Associates, 1974.

Cressey, Paul G. *The Taxi Dance Hall: A Sociological Study in Commercialized Recreation and City Life.* Chicago: University of Chicago Press, 1932.

Cross, Ira B. *A History of the Labor Movement in California.* Berkeley: University of California Press, 1935.

Daniels, Roger. *Concentration Camps, U.S.A.: Japanese Americans and World War II.* New York: Henry Holt, 1970.

———. *The Politics of Prejudice: The Anti-Japanese Movement in California and the Struggle for Japanese Exclusion.* Berkeley: University of California Press, 1962.

———, and Harry H. L. Kitano. *American Racism: Exploration of the Nature of Prejudice.* Engelwood Cliffs: Prentice-Hall, 1970.

Das, Rajani K. *Hindustani Workers on the Pacific Coast.* Berlin: Walter de Gruyter, 1923.

Daws, Gavan. *Shoal of Time: A History of the Hawaiian Islands.* Honolulu: University of Hawaii Press, 1968.

DeWitt, Howard A. *Anti-Filipino Movements in California: A History, Bibliography, and Study Guide.* San Francisco: R and E Research Asscociates, 1970.

Dillon, Richard. *The Hatchet Men: The Story of the Tong Wars in San Francisco's Chinatown.* New York: Coward, 1962.

Dobie, Charles C. *San Francisco's Chinatown.* New York: Appleton-Century, 1936.

———. *San Francisco Tales.* New York: Appleton-Century, 1935.

Dorita, Mary. "Filipino Immigration to Hawaii." M.A. thesis, University of Hawaii, 1954. Published in book form: San Francisco: R and E Research Associates, 1975.

Eaton, Allen H. *Beauty behind Barbed Wire: The Arts of the Japanese in Our War Relocation Camps.* New York: Harper and Row, 1952.

Eaves, Lucile. *A History of California Labor Legislation.* Vol. 2, University of California Publications in Economics. Berkeley: University of California Press, 1910.

Edmiston, James. *Home Again.* Garden City: Doubleday, 1955.

Elliot, Albert H., and Guy C. Calden, comps. *The Law Affecting Japanese Residing in the State of California.* San Francisco: privately printed, 1929. Reprinted in *Three Short Works on Japanese Americans,* edited by Roger Daniels. New York: Arno Press, 1979.

Faderman, Lillian, and Barbara Bradshaw, eds. *Speaking for Ourselves: American Ethnic Writing.* Glenview: Scott, Foresman, 1969.

Farwell, Willard B. *The Chinese at Home and Abroad.* San Francisco: A. L. Bancroft, 1885.

Feria, Benny F. *Filipino Son.* Boston: Meador, 1954.

Fisher, Anne M. *Exile of a Race: A History of the Forcible Removal and Imprisonment by the Army of the 115,000 Citizens and Alien Japanese Who Were Living on the West Coast in the Spring of 1942.* Sidney, B.C.: Peninsula, 1965.

Flowers, Montaville. *The Japanese Conquest of American Opinion.* New York: George H. Doran, 1917.

Fong, Stanley L. M. "The Assimilation of Chinese in America: Changes in Orientation and Social Perception." M.A. thesis, San Francisco State College, 1963. Published in book form: San Francisco: R and E Research Associates, 1974.

Fuchs, Lawrence. *Hawaii Pono: A Social History.* New York: Harcourt, Brace, and World, 1961.

Galedo, Lillian, Laurena Cabanero, and Brian Tom. *Roadblocks to Community Building: A Case Study of the Stockton Filipino Community Center Project.* Davis: University of California, Davis, Asian American Studies Program, 1970.

Gibson, Otis. *The Chinese in America.* Cincinnati: Hitchcock and Walden, 1877.

Girdner, Audrie, and Anne Loftis. *The Great Betrayal: The Evacuation of the Japanese-Americans during World War II.* New York: Macmillan, 1969.

Givens, Helen L. "The Korean Community in Los Angeles County." M.A. thesis, University of Southern California, 1939. Published in book form: San Francisco: R and E Research Associates, 1974.

Glick, Carl. *Shake Hands with the Dragon.* New York: Wittlesley House, 1941.

Griggs, Vera. *Chinaman's Chance: The Life Story of Elmer Wok Wai.* New York: Exposition, 1969.

Grozdins, Morton. *Americans Betrayed: Politics and the Japanese Evacuation.* Chicago: University of Chicago Press, 1949.

Gulick, Sidney L. *American Democracy and Asiatic Citizenship.* New York: Charles Scribner and Sons, 1918; repr. New York: Arno Press, 1978.

———. *The American Japanese Problem: A Study of the Racial Relations of the East and the West.* New York: Charles Scribner and Sons, 1914.

———. *American-Japanese Relations, 1916–1920: A Retrospective.* New York: Federal Council of Churches of Christ in America, 1921.

Harada, Margaret. *The Sun Shines on the Immigrant.* New York: Vantage, 1960.

Harvey, Nick, ed. *Ting: The Cauldron, Chinese Art and Identity in San Francisco.* San Francisco: Glide Urban Center, 1970.

Hata, Donald T., Jr. "'Undesirables': Early Immigrants and the Anti-Japanese Movement in San Francisco, 1892–1893." Ph.D. diss., University of Southern California, 1970. Published in book form: New York: Arno Press, 1978.

Hosokawa, Bill. *Nisei: The Quiet Americans.* New York: William Morrow, 1969.

Hoy, William. *The Chinese Six Companies: A Short, General Historical Resume of Its Origin, Function, and Importance in the Life of the California Chinese.* San Francisco: Chinese Consolidated Benevelent Association, 1942.

Hsu, Francis L. K. *Americans and Chinese: Two Ways of Life.* New York: Henry Schulman, 1953.

Hui, Kin. *Reminiscences.* Beijing: San Yu, 1932.

Ichihashi, Yamato, *Japanese Immigration: Its Status in California.* San Francisco: Marshall, 1915.

———. *Japanese in the United States: A Critical Study of the Problems of the Japanese Immigrants and Their Children.* Stanford: Stanford University Press, 1932; repr. New York: Arno Press, 1969.

Inouye, Daniel K., with Lawrence Elliot. *Journey to Washington.* Englewood Cliffs: Prentice-Hall, 1967.

Inui, Kiyo Sue. *The Unsolved Problem of the Pacific: A Survey of International Contacts, Espe-cially in Frontier Communities, with Special Emphasis upon California and an Analytical Study of the Johnson Report to the House of Representatives.* Tokyo: Japan Times, 1925.

Irwin, William H. *Old Chinatown: A Book of Pictures by Arnold Genthe.* New York: Mitchell Kennerly, 1913.

Isaacs, Harold. *Scratches on Our Mind: American Images of China and India.* New York: John Day, 1958; repr. White Plains: M. E. Sharpe, 1980.

Iyenaga, Toyokichi, and Kenosuke Sato. *Japan and the California Problem.* New York: G. P. Putnam's Sons, 1921.

Japanese Agricultural Association. *Japanese Farmers in California.* San Francisco: Japanese Agricultural Association, 1918.

Japanese Association of the Pacific Northwest. *Japanese Immigration: An Exposition of Its Real Status.* Seattle: Japanese Association of the Pacific Northwest, 1907; repr. San Francisco: R and E Research Associates, 1972.

Johnson, Herbert B. *Discrimination against Japanese in California: A Review of the Real Situation.* Berkeley: Courier, 1907.

Johnson, Julia L., comp. *Japanese Exclusion.* New York: H. W. Wilson, 1925.

Kachi, Teruo. "The Treaty of 1911 and the Immigration and Alien Land Law Issue between the United States and Japan, 1911–1913." Ph.D. diss., University of Chicago, 1957. Pub-lished in book form: New York: Arno Press, 1979.

Kang, Younghill. *East Goes West: The Making of an Oriental Yankee.* New York: Scribner's, 1937.

Kanzaki, Kiichi. *California and the Japanese.* San Francisco: Japanese Association of America, 1921.

Kawakami, Kiyoshi Karl. *Asia at the Door: A Study of the Japanese Question in Continental United States, Hawaii and Canada.* New York: Fleming H. Revell, 1914.

———. *The Real Japanese Question.* New York: Macmillan, 1921.

Kehoe, Karon. *City in the Sun.* New York: Dodd, 1946.

Kitano, Harry H. L. *Japanese Americans: The Evolution of a Subculture.* Englewood Cliffs: Prentice-Hall, 1969.

Konvitz, Milton. *The Alien and the Asiatic in American Law.* Ithaca: Cornell University Press, 1946.

Kung, Shien-woo. *Chinese in American Life: Some Aspects of Their History, Status, Problems, and Contributions.* Seattle: University of Washington Press, 1962.

Kuo, Helena Ching Ch'iu. *I've Come a Long Way.* New York: Appleton, 1942.

Kuykendall, Ralph S. *The Hawaiian Kingdom,* vol. 1: *Foundation and Transformation, 1778–1854;* vol. 2: *Twenty Critical Years, 1854–1874;* vol. 3: *The Kalakaua Dynasty, 1974–1893.* Honolulu: University of Hawaii Press, 1938, 1953, 1967.

Lasker, Bruno. *Filipino Immigration to Continental United States and to Hawaii.* Chicago: University of Chicago Press, 1931; repr. New York: Arno Press, 1969.

La Violette, Forrest E. *Americans of Japanese Ancestry: A Study of Assimilation in the American Community.* Toronto: Canadian Institute of International Affairs, 1945.

Lee, Calvin. *Chinatown, U.S.A.* Garden City: Doubleday, 1965.

Lee, C. Y. *The Land of the Golden Mountain.* New York: Meredith Press, 1967.

Lee, Rose Hum. *The Chinese in the United States of America.* Hong Kong: Hong Kong University Press, 1960.

———. "The Growth and Decline of Chinese Communities in the Rocky Mountain Region." Ph.D. diss., University of Chicago, 1947. Published in book form: New York: Arno Press, 1979.

Leighton, Alexander H. *The Governing of Men: General Principles and Recommendations Based on Experience at a Japanese Relocation Camp.* Princeton: Princeton University Press, 1945.

Leong, Gor Yun [Virginia H. Ellison]. *Chinatown Inside Out.* New York: B. Mussey, 1936.

Lin, Yutang. *Chinatown Family.* New York: John Day, 1948.

Lind, Andrew. *Hawaii's People.* Honolulu: University of Hawaii Press, 1955.

Lowe, Pardee. *Father and Glorious Descendant.* Boston: Little, Brown, 1943.

Lui, Garding. *Inside Los Angeles Chinatown.* Los Angeles: N.p., 1948.

Mariano, Honorante. "The Filipino Immigrants in the United States." M.A. thesis, University of Oregon, 1933. Published in book form: San Francisco: R and E Research Associates, 1972.

Martin, Ralph G. *Boy from Nebraska: The Story of Ben Kuroki.* New York: Harper and Row, 1946.

Mather, L. P. *Indian Revolutionary Movement in the United States of America.* New Delhi: S. Chand, 1970.

Matsumoto, Toru. *Beyond Prejudice: A Story of the Church and Japanese Americans.* New York: Friendship, 1946.

McClatchy, V. S. *Japanese Immigration and Colonization: Brief Prepared for Consideration of the State Department.* N.p.: n.p., 1921; repr. San Francisco: R and E Research Associates, 1970.

McKenzie, Roderick D. *Oriental Exclusion.* New York: Institute of Pacific Relations, 1928.

McLeod, Alexander. *Pigtails and Gold Dust.* Caldwell, Idaho: Caxton, 1947.

McWilliams, Carey. *Brothers under the Skin.* Boston: Little, Brown, 1943; rev. ed. 1951; repr. 1964.

———. *Factories in the Field.* Boston: Little, Brown, 1939; repr. Hamden: Archon Books, 1969, and Santa Barbara: Peregrine Books, 1971.

———. *Prejudice: Japanese Americans, Symbol of Racial Intolerance.* Boston: Little, Brown, 1944.

Mears, Eliot G. *Resident Orientals on the American Pacific Coast.* Chicago: University of Chicago Press, 1928.

Michener, James A. *Hawaii.* New York: Random House, 1959.

Miller, Stuart C. *The Unwelcome Immigrant: The American Image of the Chinese, 1785–1882.* Berkeley: University of California Press, 1969.

Millis, Harry A. *The Japanese Problem in the United States.* New York: Macmillan, 1915.

Minke, Pauline. "Chinese in the Mother Lode, 1850–1870." Seminar paper, 1960. Published in book form: San Francisco: R and E Research Associates, 1974.

Miyamoto, Frank S. *Social Solidarity among the Japanese in Seattle.* University of Washington Publications in the Social Sciences 11, no. 2 (1939). Published in book form: Seattle: University of Washington Press, 1984.

Murphy, Thomas D. *Ambassadors in Arms: The Story of Hawaii's 100th Battalion.* Honolulu: University of Hawaii Press, 1954.

Obando, Aquilino B. "A Study of the Problems of Filipino Students in the United States." M.A. thesis, University of Southern California, 1936. Published in book form: R and E Research Associates, 1974.

O'Brien, Robert W. *The College Nisei.* Palo Alto: Pacific, 1949.

Okubo, Mine. *Citizen 13660.* New York: Columbia University Press, 1946; repr. New York: AMS, 1966; paperback ed., Seattle: University of Washington Press, 1983.

Orientals and Their Cultural Adjustment. Fisk University Social Science Source Documents no. 4. Nashville: Fisk University Press, 1946.

Ota, Shelley A. M. *Upon Their Shoulders.* New York: Exposition, 1951.

Otani, Andrew N. *Hope Shines in the White Cloud: An Issei's Story.* Minneapolis: Minnisei, n.d.

The Pacific Review 1 (Dec. 1920).

Pajus, Jean. *The Real Japanese in California.* Berkeley: James J. Gillick, 1937.

Palmer, Albert W. *The Human Side of Hawaii.* Boston: Pilgrim Press, 1924.

———. *Orientals in American Life.* New York: Friendship, 1934.

Park, No-Yong. *Chinaman's Chance: An Autobiography.* Boston: Meador, 1940.

Paul, Rodman W. *The Abrogation of the Gentlemen's Agreement.* Cambridge: Phi Beta Kappa Society, 1936.

Penrose, Eldon R. "California Nativism: Organized Opposition to the Japanese, 1890–1913." M.A. thesis, California State University, Sacramento, 1969. Published in book form: San Francisco: R and E Research Associates, 1973.

Riggs, Fred W. *Pressures on Congress: A Study of the Repeal of Chinese Exclusion.* New York: King's Crown, 1950.

Ritter, Edward, Helen Ritter, and Stanley Spector, eds. *Our Oriental Americans.* San Francisco: McGraw-Hill, 1965.

Sandmeyer, Elmer C. *The Anti-Chinese Movement in California.* Illinois Studies in the Social Sciences 24, no. 3. Urbana: University of Illinois Press, 1939, 1973.

San Francisco Chinese Community Citizens' Survey and Fact Finding Committee. *Report.* San Francisco: H. J. Carle, 1968.

Saniel, J. M., ed. *The Filipino Exclusion Movement, 1927–1935.* Quezon City: University of the Philippines, Institute of Asian Studies, 1967.

Saund, Dalip Singh. *Congressman from India.* New York: E. P. Dutton, 1960.

Scherer, James A. B. *The Japanese Crisis.* New York: Frederick A. Stokes, 1916.

Schrieke, Bertram J. O. *Alien Americans: A Study of Race Relations.* New York: Viking, 1936.

Seward, George F. *Chinese Immigration in Its Social and Economic Aspects.* New York: Charles Scribner and Sons, 1881.

Shepherd, Charles R. *Lim Yik Choy: The Story of a Chinese Orphan.* New York: Fleming H. Revell, 1932.

———. *The Story of Chung Mei, Being the Authentic History of the Chung Mei Home for Chinese Boys Up to Its Fifteenth Anniversary, October 1938.* Philadelphia: Judson, 1938.

———. *The Ways of Ah Sin: A Composite Narrative of Things as They Are.* New York: Fleming H. Revell, 1923.

Shirey, Orville. *Americans: The Story of the 442nd Combat Team.* Washington: Infantry Journal, 1946.

Shridharani, Krishnalal. *My India, My America.* New York: Duell, Sloan and Pearce, 1941.

Smith, Bradford. *Americans from Japan.* Philadelphia: J. B. Lippincott, 1948.

Smith, William C. *Americans in Process: A Study of Our Citizens of Oriental Ancestry.* Ann Arbor: Edwards Brothers, 1937; repr. New York: Arno Press, 1970.

Sone, Monica. *Nisei Daughter.* New York: Atlantic Monthly, 1953; repr. Seattle: University of Washington Press, 1979.

Spicer, Edward H. et al. *Impounded People: Japanese Americans in the Relocation Camps.* Washington: Government Printing Office, 1946; repr. Tucson: University of Arizona Press, 1969.

Steiner, Jesse F. *The Japanese Invasion: A Study in the Psychology of Inter-Racial Contacts.* Chicago: A. C. McClurg, 1917.

Strong, Edward K. *Japanese in California: Based on a Ten Percent Survey of Japanese in California and Documentary Evidence from Many Sources.* Stanford: Stanford University Press, 1933.

———. *The Second-Generation Japanese Problem.* Stanford: Stanford University Press, 1934.

———. *Vocational Aptitude of Second-Generation Japanese in the United States.* Stanford: Stanford University Press, 1933.

Sue, Stanley, and Nathaniel N. Wagner, eds., *Asian Americans: Psychological Perspectives.* Vol. 1. Palo Alto: Science and Behavior, 1973.

Sugimoto, Etsu Inagaki. *A Daughter of the Samurai.* Garden City: Doubleday, 1925; repr. Rutland: Charles E. Tuttle, 1966.

Sui Sin Far. *Mrs. Spring Fragrance.* Chicago: A. C. McClurg, 1912, repr. in *Mrs. Spring Fragrance and Other Writings,* edited by Amy Ling and Annette White-Parks. Urbana: University of Illinois Press, 1995.

Sung, Betty Lee. *Mountain of Gold: The Story of the Chinese in America.* New York: Macmillan, 1967. Published in paperback as *The Story of the Chinese in America.* New York: Macmillan, 1967.

tenBroek, Jacobus, Edward N. Barnhart, and Floyd Matson. *Prejudice, War, and the Constitution.* Berkeley: University of California Press, 1954.

Thomas, Dorothy S. *The Salvage.* Berkeley: University of California Press, 1952.

———, and Richard Nishimoto. *The Spoilage.* Berkeley: University of California Press, 1946.

Tokutomi, Ichiro. *Japanese-American Relations.* New York: Macmillan, 1922.

Tow, J. S. *The Real Chinese in America.* New York: Academy, 1923.

U.S. Congress, House of Representatives. *Exclusion of Immigration from the Philippine Islands.* Washington: Government Printing Office, 1930.

———. *Japanese Exclusion.* House Document no. 600 by John B. Trevor. 68th Cong., 2d sess. Washington: Government Printing Office, 1925.

———, Committee on Immigration and Naturalization. *Hearings to Grant a Quota to*

Eastern Hemisphere Indians and to Make Them Racially Eligible for Naturalization, 79th. Cong., 1st sess. Washington: Government Printing Office, 1945.

————. *Hearings on India-Born Residents of the U.S. Request for Naturalization,* 76th. Cong., 1st sess. Washington: Government Printing Office, 1939.

————. *Hearings on Japanese Immigration,* 66th Cong., 2d sess. Washington: Government Printing Office, 1921.

————. *Hearings on Restriction of Immigration of Hindu Laborers,* 63rd Cong., 2d sess. Washington: Government Printing Office, 1914.

————, Committee of the Judiciary, Subcommittee no. 5. *Hearings on Japanese-American Evacuation Claims,* 83rd Cong., 2d sess. Washington: Government Printing Office, 1954.

————, Senate, Joint Special Committee to Investigate Chinese Immigration. *Hearings on Chinese Immigration,* report no. 689, 44th Cong., 2d sess. Washington: Government Printing Office, 1877.

————, Senate, Committee on Immigration. *Hearings on Japanese Immigration,* 68th Cong., 1st sess. Washington: Government Printing Office, 1924.

————. *Hearings to Permit All Persons from India Residing in the United States to be Naturalized,* 79th. Cong., 1st sess. Washington: Government Printing Office, 1945.

————. *Hearings to Permit the Naturalization of Approximately Three Thousand Natives of India,* 78th. Cong., 2d sess. Washington: Government Printing Office, 1944.

U.S. Department of Labor, Bureau of Labor Statistics. *Chinese Migration, with Special Reference to Labor Conditions.* Bulletin no. 340 by Chen Ta. Washington: Government Printing Office, 1923.

U.S. Department of State. *Report of the Honorable Roland S. Morris on Japanese Immigration and Alleged Discriminatory Legislation against Japanese Residents in the United States.* Washington: Government Printing Office, 1921.

Valk, Margaret A. *Korean-American Children in American Adoptive Homes.* New York: Child Welfare League of America, 1957.

Wakukawa, Ernest K. *A History of the Japanese People in Hawaii.* Honolulu: Toyo Shoin, 1938.

Wallovits, Sonia Emily. "The Filipinos in California." M.A. thesis, University of Southern California, 1966. Published in book form: San Francisco: R and E Research Associates, 1972.

Wells, Mariana K. "Chinese Temples in California." M.A. thesis, University of California, 1962. Published in book form: San Francisco: R and E Research Associates, 1971.

Wentworth, Edna Clark, *Filipino Plantation Workers in Hawaii: A Study of Incomes, Expenditures and Living Standards of Filipino Families on an Hawaiian Sugar Plantation.* San Francisco: Institute of Pacific Relations, 1941.

Wilson, Carol G. *Chinatown Quest: One Hundred Years of Donaldina Cameron House.* Stanford: Stanford University Press, 1931; repr. 1950; rev. ed. San Francisco: California Historical Society and Donaldina Cameron House, 1974.

Wong, Jade Snow. *Fifth Chinese Daughter.* New York: Harper and Row, 1945; repr. Seattle: University of Washington Press, 1989.

Wood, Ellen R. "California and the Chinese: The First Decade." M.A. thesis, University of California, 1961. Published in book form: San Francisco: R and E Research Associates, 1974.

World Peace Foundation. *Japanese Immigration.* Boston: World Peace Foundation, 1924.

Wu, Ting Fang. *America through the Spectacles of an Oriental Diplomat.* New York: Frederick A. Stokes, 1914.

Wynne, Robert E. "Reaction to the Chinese in the Pacific Northwest and British Columbia." Ph.D. diss., University of Washington, 1964. Published in book form: New York: Arno Press, 1978.

Yung Wing. *My Life in China and in America.* New York: Henry Holt, 1909; repr. New York: Arno Press, 1978.

Books and Periodicals, 1971–80

Ai, Li Ling. *Life Is for a Long Time: A Chinese Hawaiian Memoir.* New York: Hastings, 1972.

Asian American Women. Stanford: Asian American Women's Collective, 1976.

Asian Women. Berkeley: University of California, Berkeley, Asian American Studies Program, 1971.

Bailey, Paul. *City in the Sun: The Japanese Concentration Camp at Poston, Arizona.* Los Angeles: Westernlore, 1971.

Barlow, Jeffrey, and Christine Richardson. *China Doctor of John Day.* Portland: Bindford and Mort, 1979.

Blicksilver, Edith, ed. *The Ethnic American Woman: Problems, Protests, Lifestyles.* Dubuque: Kendall/Hunt, 1978.

Bonacich, Edna, and John Modell. *The Economic Basis of Ethnic Solidarity: Small Business in the Japanese American Community.* Berkeley: University of California Press, 1980.

Book, Susan W. *The Chinese in Butte County, California, 1860–1920.* San Francisco: R and E Research Associates, 1976.

Brown, Emily C. *Har Dayal: Hindu Revolutionary and Rationalist.* Tucson: University of Arizona Press, 1975.

Buddhist Churches of America. *Buddhist Churches of America, Seventy-fifth Anniversary.* 2 vols. Chicago: Nobart, 1974.

Bulletin of Concerned Asian Scholars 4, no. 3 (1972).

Bullock, Paul, ed. *Minorities in the Labor Market.* Los Angeles: University of California, Los Angeles, Institute of Industrial Relations, 1978.

Cabezas, Amado Y., and Harold T. Yee. *Discriminatory Employment of Asian Americans: Private Industry in the San Francisco-Oakland SMSA.* San Francisco: ASIAN, Inc., 1977.

California Advisory Committee to the U.S. Commission on Civil Rights. *A Dream Unfulfilled: Korean and Pilipino Health Professionals in California.* Washington: Government Printing Office, 1975.

California History 57 (Spring 1978).

Char, Tin-Yuke. *The Bamboo Path: Life and Writings of a Chinese in Hawaii.* Honolulu: Hawaii Chinese History Center, 1977.

———, ed. *The Sandalwood Mountains: Readings and Stories of the Early Chinese in Hawaii.* Honolulu: University Press of Hawaii, 1975.

Chen, Jack. *The Chinese of America: From the Beginning to the Present.* San Francisco: Harper and Row, 1980.

Chen, Peter W. "Chinese-Americans View Their Mental Health." Ph.D. diss., University of Southern California, 1976. Published in book form: San Francisco: R and E Research Associates, 1977.

Chin, Doug, and Art Chin. *Uphill: The Settlement and Diffusion of the Chinese in Seattle.* Seattle: Shorey Book Store, 1973.

Chinese Historical Society of America, ed. *The Life, Influence, and the Role of the Chinese in the United States, 1776–1960.* San Francisco: Chinese Historical Society of America, 1976.

Chow, Willard T. "The Emergence of an Inner City: The Pivot of Chinese Settlement in the East Bay Region of the San Francisco Bay Area." Ph.D. diss., University of California, Berkeley, 1974. Published in book form: San Francisco: R and E Research Associates, 1977.

Choy, Bong-Youn. *Koreans in America.* Chicago: Nelson-Hall, 1979.

Chuman, Frank. *The Bamboo People: The Law and Japanese-Americans.* Del Mar: Publishers, 1976.

Coffman, Tom. *Catch a Wave: A Case Study of Hawaii's New Politics.* Honolulu: University Press of Hawaii, 1973.

Connor, John W. *Tradition and Change in Three Generations of Japanese Americans.* Chicago: Nelson-Hall, 1977.

Conrat, Maisie, and Richard Conrat. *Executive Order 9066: The Internment of 110,000 Japanese Americans.* Cambridge: M.I.T. Press, 1972; paperback ed., San Francisco: California Historical Society, 1972; repr. Los Angeles: University of California, Los Angeles, Asian American Studies Center, 1992.

Conroy, Hilary, and Scott T. Miyakawa, eds. *East Across the Pacific: Historical and Sociological Studies of Japanese Immigration and Assimilation.* Santa Barbara: ABC-Clio, 1972.

Daniels, Roger. *The Decision to Relocate the Japanese Americans.* Philadelphia: Lippincott, 1975; rev. ed. Malabar, Fla.: R. E. Krieger, 1986.

De Witt, Howard A. *Violence in the Fields: California Farm Labor Unionization during the Great Depression.* Saratoga, Calif.: Century Twenty One, 1980.

Duus, Masayo U. *Tokyo Rose: Orphan of the Pacific.* Translated by Peter Duus. Tokyo: Kodansha International, 1979.

Elsensohn, M. Alfreda. *Idaho Chinese Lore.* Cottonwood: Idaho Corporation of Benedictine Sisters, 1971.

Endo, Russell, Stanley Sue, and Nathanial N. Wagner, eds. *Asian-Americans: Social and Psychological Perspectives.* Vol. 2. Palo Alto: Science and Behavior, 1980.

Espina, Marina F. *Jacinto E. Esmele: Profile of a Successful Filipino in the United States of America.* New Orleans: A. F. Laborde, 1980.

Fisher, Maxine P. *The Indians of New York City: A Study of Immigrants from India.* Columbia, Mo.: South Asia Books, 1980.

Fukei, Budd. *The Japanese American Story.* Minneapolis: Dillon, 1976.

Fukuda, Moritoshi. *Legal Problems of Japanese-Americans: Their Story and Development in the United States.* Tokyo: Keio Tsushin, 1980.

Gallimore, Ronald, Joan W. Boggs, and Cathie Jordan. *Culture, Behavior, and Education: A Study of Hawaiian-Americans.* Beverly Hills: Sage, 1974.

Garret, Jesse A., and Ronald C. Larson, eds. *Camp and Community: Manzanar and the Owens Valley.* Fullerton: California State University, Fullerton, Oral History Project, 1977.

Gee, Emma et al., eds. *Counterpoint: Perspectives on Asian America.* Los Angeles: University of California, Los Angeles, Asian American Studies Center, 1976.

Glick, Clarence E. *Sojourners and Settlers: Chinese Migrants in Hawaii.* Honolulu: University Press of Hawaii, 1980.

Hansen, Arthur A., and Betty E. Mitson. *Voices Long Silent: An Oral Inquiry into the Japanese American Evacuation.* Fullerton: California State University, Fullerton, Oral History Project, 1974.

Hata, Donald T., Jr. *"Undesirables": Early Immigrants and the Anti-Japanese Movement in San Francisco, 1892–1893.* New York: Arno Press, 1978.

Hildebrand, Lorraine Barker. *Straw Hats, Sandals and Steel: The Chinese in Washington State.* Tacoma: Washington State American Revolution Bicentennial Commission, 1977.

Hoexler, Corinne K. *From Canton to California: The Epic of Chinese Immigration.* New York: Four Winds, 1976.

Hom, Gloria S. *Chinese Argonauts: An Anthology of the Chinese Contributions to the Historical Development of Santa Clara County.* Los Altos Hills: Foothill Community College, 1971.

Hosokawa, Bill. *Thirty-five Years in the Frying Pan.* New York: William Morrow, 1978.

Hsu, Francis L. K. *The Challenge of the American Dream: The Chinese in the United States.* Belmont: Wadsworth, 1971.

Hundley, Norris, Jr., ed. *The Asian American: The Historical Experience.* Santa Barbara: ABC-Clio, 1974.

Hune, Shirley. *Pacific Migration to the United States: Trends and Themes in Historical and Sociological Literature.* Washington: Smithsonian Institution Press, 1977.

Hunter, Louise H. *Buddhism in Hawaii: Its Impact on a Yankee Community.* Honolulu: University of Hawaii Press, 1971.

Hurh, Won Moo. *Comparative Study of Korean Immigrants in the United States: A Typological Approach.* San Francisco: R and E Research Associates, 1977.

———, Hei Chu Kim, and Kwang Chung Kim. *Assimilation Patterns of Immigrants in the United States: A Case Study of Korean Immigrants in the Chicago Area.* Washington: University Press of America, 1978.

Ignacio, Lemuel F. *Asian Americans and Pacific Islanders (Is There Such an Ethnic Group?)* San Jose: Pilipino Development Associates, 1976.

Ishigo, Estelle. *Lone Heart Mountain.* Los Angeles: Anderson, Ritchie, and Simon, 1972; repr. as *Heart Mountain High School Class of 1944.* Distributed by the National Japanese American History Museum, Los Angeles, 1989.

Ito, Kazuo. *Issei: A History of Japanese Immigrants in North America.* Translated by Shin-ichiro Nakamura and Jean S. Gerard. Seattle: Executive Committee for Publication of *Issei*, 1973.

Jacobs, Paul, Saul Landau, and Eve Pell, eds. *To Serve the Devil*, vol. 2: *Colonials and Sojourners*. New York: Random House, 1971.

Journal of Social Issues 29 (Spring 1973).

Kachi, Teruko O. *The Treaty of 1911 and the Immigration and Alien Land Law Issue between the United States and Japan, 1911–1913*. New York: Arno Press, 1978.

Kagiwada, George, Joyce Sakai, and Gus Lee, eds. *Proceedings of National Asian American Studies Conference II*. Davis: University of California, Davis, Asian American Studies Program, 1973.

Kaneshiro, Takeo. *Internees: War Relocation Center Memoirs and Diaries*. New York: Vantage, 1976.

Kashima, Tetsuden. *Buddhism in America: The Social Organization of an Ethnic Religious Institution*. Westport: Greenwood Press, 1977.

Kelly, Gail P. *From Vietnam to America: A Chronicle of the Vietnamese Immigration to the United States*. Boulder: Westview Press, 1977.

Kiefer, Christie W. *Changing Cultures, Changing Lives*. San Francisco: Josey-Bass, 1974.

Kikuchi, Charles. *The Kikuchi Diary: Chronicle from an American Concentration Camp*, edited by John Modell. Urbana: University of Illinois Press, 1973, 1993.

Kim, Bok-Lim C. *The Asian Americans: Changing Patterns, Changing Needs*. Montclair: Association of Korean Christian Scholars in North America, 1978.

———. *The Korean-American Child at School and at Home: An Analysis of Interaction and Intervention through Groups*. Administration for Children, Youth, and Families Project Report. Grant no. 90–C-1335 (01). Washington: U.S. Department of Health, Education, and Welfare, 1980.

Kim, Hyung-chan, ed. *The Korean Diaspora: Historical and Sociological Studies of Korean Immigration and Assimilation in North America*. Santa Barbara: ABC-Clio, 1977.

———, and Wayne Patterson, eds. *The Koreans in America, 1882–1974: A Chronology and Fact Book*. Dobbs Ferry: Oceana, 1974.

Kim, Sangho J. "A Study of the Korean Church and Her People in Chicago, Illinois." M.A. thesis, McCormick Theological Seminary, 1975. Published in book form: San Francisco: R and E Research Associates, 1975.

Kim, Warren Y. *Koreans in America*. Seoul: Po Chin Chai, 1971.

Kitagawa, Daisuke. *Issei and Nisei: The Internment Years*. New York: Seabury, 1967.

Koh, Kwang Lim, and Hesung C. Koh, eds. *Koreans and Korean-Americans in the United States: Their Problems and Perspectives*. New Haven: East Rock, 1974.

Kuo, Chia-ling. *Social and Political Change in New York's Chinatown: The Role of Voluntary Associations*. New York: Praeger, 1977.

Kwock, Charles M. *A Hawaiian Chinese Looks at America*. New York: Vintage, 1977.

Kwong, Peter C. *Chinatown, New York: Labor and Politics, 1930–1950*. New York: Monthly Review, 1979.

Lai, Him Mark, Genny Lim, and Judy Yung. *Island: Poetry and History of Chinese Immigrants on Angel Island, 1910–1940*. San Francisco: Hoc Doi Project, 1980; repr. Seattle: University of Washington Press, 1990.

———, and Philip P. Choy. *Outlines: History of the Chinese in America*. San Francisco: Chinese Culture Foundation, 1973.

Laing, Michiko et al., eds. *Issei Christians: Selected Interviews from the Issei Oral History Project.* Sacramento: Issei Oral History Project, 1977.

Lan, Dean. "Prestige with Limitations: Realities of the Chinese-Americans." Ph.D. diss., University of California, Davis, 1975. Published in book form: San Francisco: R and E Research Associates, 1976.

Lee, C. Y. *Days of the Tong Wars.* New York: Ballantine, 1974.

Lee, Don Chang. "Acculturation of Korean Residents in Georgia." M.A. thesis, University of Georgia, 1975. San Francisco: R and E Research Associates, 1975.

Lee, Samuel S. O., ed. *Seventy-fifth Anniversary of Korean Immigration to Hawaii, 1903–1978.* Honolulu: Seventy-fifth Anniversary of Korean Immigration to Hawaii Committee, 1978.

Li, Peter S. "Occupational Mobility and Kinship Assistance: A Study of Chinese Immigants in Chicago." Ph.D. diss., Northwestern University, 1975. Published in book form: San Francisco: R and E Research Associates, 1977.

Light, Ivan H. *Ethnic Enterprise in America: Business and Welfare among Chinese, Japanese, and Blacks.* Berkeley: University of California Press, 1972.

Liu, William T., Maryanne Lamanna, and Alice Murata. *Transition to Nowhere: Vietnamese Refugees in America.* Nashville: Charter House, 1979.

Loewen, James W. *The Mississippi Chinese: Between Black and White.* Cambridge: Harvard University Press, 1971.

Lydon, Edward C. *The Anti-Chinese Movement in the Hawaiian Kingdom, 1852–1886.* San Francisco: R and E Research Associates, 1975.

Lyman, Stanford M. *The Asian in North America.* Santa Barbara: ABC-Clio, 1977.

———. *Chinese Americans.* New York: Random House, 1974.

Martin, Mildred Crowl. *Chinatown's Angry Angel: The Story of Donaldina Cameron.* Palo Alto: Pacific, 1977.

Martinello, Marian L., and William T. Field Jr. *Who Are the Chinese Texans?* San Antonio: University of Texas, San Antonio, Institute of Texan Cultures, 1979.

Maykovich, Minako K. *Japanese American Identity Dilemma.* Tokyo: Waseda University Press, 1972.

McClatchy, Valentine S. *Four Anti-Japanese Pamphlets.* New York: Arno Press, 1978.

McClellan, Robert. *The Heathen Chinese: A Study of American Attitudes toward China, 1890–1905.* Columbus: Ohio State University Press, 1971.

McDermott, John F., Jr., Wen-Shing Tseng, and Thomas W. Maretzki, eds. *People and Cultures of Hawaii: A Psychocultural Profile.* Honolulu: University Press of Hawaii, 1974.

Melendy, Brett H. *Asians in America: Filipinos, Koreans, and East Indians.* Boston: Twayne, 1977.

———. *The Oriental Americans.* Boston: Twayne, 1972.

Mindel, Charles H., and Robert W. Habenstein, eds. *Ethnic Families in America: Patterns and Variations.* New York: Elvesier Scientific, 1976.

Mirikitani, Janice, ed. *Ayumi: The Japanese American Anthology.* San Francisco: Glide, 1976.

Misrow, Jogesh C. "East Indian Immigration on the Pacific Coast." Ph.D. diss., Stanford University, 1915. Published in book form: San Francisco: R and E Associates, 1971.

Modell, John. *The Economics and Politics of Racial Accommodation: The Japanese of Los Angeles, 1900–1942.* Urbana: University of Illinois Press, 1977.

Montero, Darrel. *Japanese Americans: Changing Patterns of Ethnic Affiliation over Three Generations.* Boulder: Westview Press, 1980.

———. *Vietnamese Americans: Patterns of Resettlement and Socioeconomic Adaptation in the United States.* Boulder: Westview Press, 1979.

Morales, Royal F. *Makibaka: The Filipino American Struggle.* Los Angeles: Mountainview, 1974.

Munoz, Alfredo N., *The Filipinos in America.* Los Angeles: Mountainview, 1971.

Myer, Dillon S. *Uprooted Americans: The Japanese Americans and the War Relocation Authority during World War II.* Tucson: University of Arizona Press, 1971.

Navarro, Jovina, ed. *Diwang Pilipino.* Davis: University of California, Davis, Asian American Studies Program, 1974.

———. *Lahing Pilipino: A Pilipino American Anthology.* Davis: University of California, Davis, Mga Kapatid–Pilipino Student Association, 1977.

Nee, Victor G., and Brett de Bary Nee. *Longtime Californ': A Documentary Study of an American Chinatown.* New York: Pantheon, 1972.

Nelson, Douglas W. *Heart Mountain: The History of an American Concentration Camp.* Madison: State Historical Society of Wisconsin, 1976.

Nordyke, Eleanor. *The Peopling of Hawaii.* Honolulu: University of Hawaii Press, 1977.

Oda, James. *Heroic Struggles of Japanese Americans: Partisan Fighters from America's Concentration Camps.* North Hollywood: The author, 1980.

Ogawa, Dennis. *From Japs to Japanese: The Evolution of Japanese-American Stereotypes.* Berkeley: McCutcheon, 1971.

———. *Jan Ken Po: The World of Hawaii's Japanese Americans.* Honolulu: University of Hawaii Press, 1973.

———. *Kodomo no tame ni: For the Sake of the Children: The Japanese American Experience in Hawaii.* Honolulu: University of Hawaii Press, 1978.

Okahata, James H., ed. *A History of Japanese in Hawaii.* Honolulu: United Japanese Society of Hawaii, 1971.

Okimoto, Daniel I. *American in Disguise.* New York: Walker/Weatherhill, 1971.

Pacific Historical Review 43 (Nov. 1974).

Personnel and Guidance Journal 51 (Feb. 1973).

Petersen, William. *Japanese Americans: Oppression and Success.* New York: Random House, 1971.

Quinsaat, Jesse et al., eds. *Letters in Exile: An Introductory Reader on the History of Pilipinos in America.* Los Angeles: University of California, Los Angeles, Asian American Studies Center, 1976.

Saran, Parmatma, and Edwin Eames, eds. *The New Ethnics: Asian Indians in the United States.* New York: Praeger, 1980.

Saxton, Alexander. *The Indispensable Enemy: Labor and the Anti-Chinese Movement in California.* Berkeley: University of California Press, 1971.

Shibutani, Tamotsu. *The Derelicts of Company K.* Berkeley: University of California Press, 1978.

Shim, Steve S. "Korean Immigrant Churches Today in Southern California." Ph.D. diss., School of Theology at Claremont, 1975. Published in book form: San Francisco: R and E Research Associates, 1977.

Shin, Myongsup, and Daniel B. Lee, eds. *Korean Immigrants in Hawaii: A Symposium on*

Their Background History, Acculturation, and Public Policy Issues. Honolulu: Korean Immigrant Welfare Association of Hawaii and University of Hawaii, College of Education, Operation Manong, 1978.

Social Casework 57 (March 1976).

Sue, Stanley, and Nathaniel N. Wagner, eds. *Asian Americans: Psychological Perspectives.* Vol. 1. Palo Alto: Science and Behavior, 1973.

Sung, Betty Lee. *Statistical Profile of the Chinese in the United States: 1970 Census.* New York: Arno Press, 1978.

———. *A Survey of Chinese-American Manpower and Employment.* New York: Praeger, 1976.

Sunoo, Brenda Paik, ed. *Korean American Writings: Selected Material from* Insight: Korean American Bimonthly. New York: Insight, 1975.

Suzuki, Lester E. *Ministry in the Assembly and Relocation Centers of World War II.* Berkeley: Yardbird, 1979.

Tachiki, Amy, Eddie Wong, Franklin Odo, and Buck Wong, eds. *Roots: An Asian American Reader.* Los Angeles: University of California, Los Angeles, Asian American Studies Center, 1971.

Third World Women. San Francisco: Third World Communications, 1972.

Thompson, Richard A. *The Yellow Peril, 1890–1924.* New York: Arno Press, 1978.

Tinker, Hugh. *The Banyan Tree: Overseas Emigrants from India, Pakistan, and Bangladesh.* New York: Oxford University Press, 1977.

Tule Lake Committee, ed. *Kinenhi: Reflections on Tule Lake.* San Francisco: Tule Lake Committee, 1980.

Tung, William L. *The Chinese in America, 1820–1973: A Chronology and Fact Book.* Dobbs Ferry: Oceana, 1974.

Vallangca, Robert V., ed. *Pinoy: The First Wave.* San Francisco: Strawberry Hill, 1977.

Weglyn, Michi. *Years of Infamy: The Untold Story of America's Concentration Camps.* New York: William Morrow, 1976.

———, and Betty E. Mitson, eds. *Valiant Odyssey: Herbert Nicholson In and Out of America's Concentration Camps.* Upland, Calif.: Brunk's, 1978.

Weiss, Melford S. *Valley City: A Chinese Community in America.* Cambridge: Schenkman, 1974.

Wilson, Carol G. *Chinatown Quest: One Hundred Years of Donaldina Cameron House.* Stanford: Stanford University Press, 1931, 1950; rev. ed. San Francisco: California Historical Society and Donaldina Cameron House, 1974.

Wilson, Robert A., and Bill Hosokawa. *East to America: A History of the Japanese in the United States.* New York: William Morrow, 1980.

Wollenberg, Charles M. *All Deliberate Speed: Segregation and Exclusion in California Schools, 1855–1975.* Berkeley: University of California Press, 1976.

Wong, Eugene F. *On Visual Media Racism: Asians in the American Motion Pictures.* New York: Arno Press, 1978.

Wu, Cheng-Tsu. *"Chink!" A Documentary History of Anti-Chinese Prejudice in America.* New York: World, 1972.

Yatsushiro, Toshio. *Politics and Cultural Values: The World War II Japanese Relocation Centers and the United States Government.* New York: Arno Press, 1978.

Yellow Peril. New York: Basement Workshop, 1972.

Yoshida, Jim. *The Two Worlds of Jim Yoshida.* New York: William Morrow, 1972.

Zo, Kil Young. *Chinese Emigration into the United States, 1850–1880.* New York: Arno Press, 1978.

Books, 1981–90

Alcantara, Ruben R. *Sakada: Filipino Adaptation in Hawaii.* Washington: University Press of America, 1981.

Almirol, Edwin B. *Ethnic Identity and Social Negotiation: A Study of a Filipino Community in California.* New York: AMS, 1985.

Anderson, Robert N., with Richard Collier and Rebecca F. Pestano. *Filipinos in Rural Hawaii.* Honolulu: University of Hawaii Press, 1984.

Arkush, R. David, and Leo O. Lee, eds. *Land without Ghosts: Chinese Impressions of America from the Mid-Nineteenth Century to the Present.* Berkeley: University of California Press, 1989.

Asian Women United of California, eds. *Making Waves: An Anthology of Writings by and about Asian American Women.* Boston: Beacon Press, 1989.

Axford, Roger W. *Too Long Silent: Japanese Americans Speak Out.* Lincoln: Media, 1986.

Barringer, Herbert R., and Sun-Nam Cho. *Koreans in the United States: A Fact Book.* Honolulu: University of Hawaii Center for Korean Studies, 1989.

Beechert, Edward D. *Working in Hawaii: A Labor History.* Honolulu: University of Hawaii Press, 1985.

Caplan, Nathan, John K. Whitmore, and Marcella H. Choy. *The Boat People and Achievement in America: A Study of Family Life, Hard Work, and Cultural Values.* Ann Arbor: University of Michigan Press, 1989.

Chan, Sucheng. *This Bittersweet Soil: The Chinese in California Agriculture, 1860–1910.* Berkeley: University of California Press, 1986.

Cheng, Lucie, and Edna Bonacich, eds. *Labor Immigration under Capitalism: Asian Workers in the United States before World War II.* Berkeley: University of California Press, 1984.

Chin, Ko-lin. *Chinese Subculture and Criminality: Non-Traditional Crime Groups in America.* Westport: Greenwood Press, 1990.

Chinn, Thomas W. *Bridging the Pacific: San Francisco Chinatown and Its People.* San Francisco: Chinese Historical Society of America, 1989.

Chu-Chang, Mae. *Asian- and Pacific-American Perspectives in Bilingual Education: Comparative Research.* New York: Columbia University Teachers College Press, 1983.

Cohen, Lucy M. *Chinese in the Post-Civil War South: A People Without a History.* Baton Rouge: Louisiana State University Press, 1984.

Collins, Donald E. *Native American Aliens: Disloyalty and the Renunciation of Citizenship by Japanese Americans during World War II.* Westport: Greenwood Press, 1985.

Commission on Wartime Relocation and Internment of Civilians. *Personal Justice Denied.* Washington: Government Printing Office, 1982.

Conquerwood, Dwight, and Paja Thao. *I Am a Shaman: A Hmong Life Story with Ethnographic Commentary.* Southeast Asian Refugee Studies Occasional Paper no. 8. Translated by Xa Thao. Minneapolis: University of Minnesota Center for Urban and Regional Affairs, Southeast Asian Refugee Studies Project, 1989.

Corbett, P. Scott. *Quiet Passages: The Exchange of Civilians between the United States and Japan during the Second World War.* Kent: Kent State University Press, 1987.

Cordova, Fred. *Filipinos: Forgotten Asian Americans, a Pictorial Essay, 1763–circa 1963.* Seattle: Demonstration Project for Asian Americans, 1983.

Criddle, JoAn D., and Teeda Butt Mam. *To Destroy You Is No Loss: The Odyssey of a Cambodian Family.* New York: Atlantic Monthly Press, 1987.

Crouchett, Lorraine J. *Filipinos in California from the Days of the Galleons to the Present.* El Cerrito: Downey Place, 1982.

Daniels, Roger. *Asian America: Chinese and Japanese in the United States since 1850.* Seattle: University of Washington Press, 1988.

———. *Concentration Camps, North America: Japanese in the United States and Canada during World War II.* Malabar, Fla.: R. E. Krieger, 1981.

———. *The Decision to Relocate the Japanese Americans.* Malabar, Fla.: R. E. Krieger, 1986.

———. *History of Indian Immigration to the United States: An Interpretive Essay.* New York: Asia Society, 1989.

———, ed. *American Concentration Camps: A Documentary History of the Relocation and Incarceration of Japanese Americans, 1941–1945.* 9 vols. New York: Garland, 1989.

———, Sandra C. Taylor, and Harry H. L. Kitano, eds. *Japanese Americans: From Relocation to Redress.* Salt Lake City: University of Utah Press, 1986.

Dasgupta, Sathi S. *On the Trail of an Uncertain Dream: Indian Immigrant Experience in America.* New York: AMS, 1989.

Davis, Daniel S. *Behind Barbed Wire: The Imprisonment of Japanese Americans during World War II.* New York: E. P. Dutton, 1982.

Dower, John. *War without Mercy: Race and Power in the Pacific War.* New York: Pantheon, 1986.

Downing, Bruce T., and Douglas P. Olney, eds. *The Hmong in the West.* Minneapolis: University of Minnesota Center for Urban and Regional Affairs, 1982.

Drinnon, Richard. *Keeper of Concentration Camps: Dillon S. Myer and American Racism.* Berkeley: University of California Press, 1987.

Duus, Masayo Umezawa. *Unlikely Liberators: The Men of the 100th and 442nd.* Translated by Peter Duus. Honolulu: University of Hawaii Press, 1987.

Embrey, Sue Kunitomi, Arthur A. Hansen, and Betty Kulberg Mitson. *Manzanar Martyr: An Interview with Harry Y. Ueno.* Fullerton: California State University, Fullerton, Oral History Program, 1986.

Endo, Russell et al., eds. *Contemporary Perspectives on Asian and Pacific American Education.* South El Monte, Calif.: Pacific Asia Press, 1990.

Espina, Marina E. *Filipinos in Louisiana.* New Orleans: A. F. Laborde and Sons, 1988.

Ethnic Studies Oral History Project and United Okinawan Association of Hawaii, comps. *Uchinanchu: A History of Okinawans in Hawaii.* Honolulu: University of Hawaii Ethnic Studies Program, 1981.

Farber, Don. *Taking Refuge in L.A.: Life in a Vietnamese Buddhist Temple.* New York: Aperture Foundation, 1987.

Fawcett, James T., and Benjamin Carino, eds. *Pacific Bridges: The New Immigration from Asia and the Pacific Islands.* Staten Island: Center for Migration Studies, 1987.

————, Benjamin Carino, and Fred Arnold. *Asia-Pacific Immigration to the United States.* Honolulu: East-West Center, East-West Population Institute, 1985.

Fein, Helen. *Congregational Sponsors of Indochinese Refugees in the United States, 1979–1981.* Cranbury: Farleigh Dickinson University Press, 1987.

Fenton, John Y. *Transplanting Religious Traditions: Asian Indians in America.* New York: Praeger, 1988.

Filipino Oral History Project. *Voices: A Filipino American Oral History.* Stockton: Filipino American Oral History Project, 1984.

Freeman, James A. *Hearts of Sorrow: Vietnamese-American Lives.* Stanford: Stanford University Press, 1989.

Fukuda, Yoshiaki. *My Six Years of Internment: An Issei's Struggle for Justice.* San Francisco: Konko Church of San Francisco, 1990.

Gardiner, C. Harvey. *Pawns in a Triangle of Hate: The Peruvian Japanese and the United States.* Seattle: University of Washington Press, 1981.

Gesensway, Deborah, and Mindy Roseman. *Beyond Words: Images from America's Concentration Camps.* Ithaca: Cornell University Press, 1987.

Gibson, Margaret A. *Accommodation without Assimilation: Sikh Immigrants in an American High School.* Ithaca: Cornell University Press, 1988.

Gillenkirk, Jeff, and James Motlow. *Bitter Melon: Stories from the Last Rural Chinese Town in America.* Seattle: University of Washington Press, 1987.

Glenn, Evelyn Nakano. *Issei, Nisei, War Bride: Three Generations of Japanese American Women in Domestic Service.* Philadelphia: Temple University Press, 1986.

Great Basin Foundation. *Wong Ho Leun: An American Chinatown.* San Diego: Great Basin Foundation, 1988.

Guthrie, Grace Pung. *A School Divided: An Ethnography of Bilingual Education in a Chinese Community.* Hillsdale: Lawrence Erlbaum Associates, 1985.

Haines, David W., ed. *Refugees as Immigrants: Cambodians, Laotians and Vietnamese in America.* Totowa: Rowman and Littlefield, 1989.

Hazama, Dorothy O., and Jane O. Komeji. *Okage Sama de: The Japanese in Hawaii, 1885–1985.* Honolulu: Bess Press, 1986.

Helweg, Arthur W., and Usha M. Helweg. *An Immigrant Success Story: East Indians in America.* Philadelphia: University of Pennsylvania Press, 1990.

Hendricks, Glenn L. et al., eds. *The Hmong in Transition.* Staten Island: Center for Migration Studies, 1986.

Higa, Thomas T. *Memoirs of a Certain Nisei.* Translated by Mitsugu Sakihara. Kaneohe, Hawaii: The author, 1988.

Hirano, Kiyo. *Enemy Alien.* San Francisco: JAM, 1983.

Hohri, William M. *Repairing America: An Account of the Movement for Japanese American Redress.* Pullman: Washington State University Press, 1988.

Hosokawa, Bill. *JACL: In Quest of Justice.* New York: William Morrow, 1982.

Howard, Katsuyo K., comp. *Passages: An Anthology of the Southeast Asian Refugee Experience.* Fresno: California State University, Fresno, Southeast Asian Student Services, 1990.

Hsia, Jayjia. *Asian Americans in Higher Education and at Work.* Hillsdale: Lawrence Erlbaum Associates, 1988.

Hurh, Won Moo, and Kwang Chung Kim. *Korean Immigrants in America: A Structural Analysis of Ethnic Confinement and Adhesive Adaptation.* Cranbury: Farleigh Dickinson University Press, 1984.

Hyun, Peter. *Man Sei! The Making of a Korean American.* Honolulu: University of Hawaii Press, 1986.

Ichinokuchi, Tad. *John Aiso and the M.I.S.: Japanese American Soldiers in the Military Intelligence Service, World War II.* Los Angeles: MIS Club of Southern California, 1988.

Ichioka, Yuji. *The Issei: The World of the First Generation Japanese Immigrants in the United States, 1885–1924.* New York: Free Press, 1988.

———, ed. *Views from Within: The Japanese American Evacuation and Resettlement Study.* Los Angeles: University of California, Los Angeles, Asian American Studies Center, 1989.

Ige, Tom. *Boy from Kahaluu: An Autobiography.* Honolulu: Kin Cho Jin Kai, 1989.

Irons, Peter. *Justice at War: The Story of the Japanese American Internment Cases.* New York: Oxford University Press, 1983.

———, ed. *Justice Delayed: The Record of the Japanese American Internment Cases.* Middletown: Wesleyan University Press, 1989.

Jain, Usha R. *The Gujaratis of San Francisco.* New York: AMS, 1989.

James, Thomas. *Exile Within: The Schooling of Japanese Americans, 1942–1945.* Cambridge: Harvard University Press, 1987.

Jensen, Joan M. *Passage from India: Asian Indian Immigrants in North America.* New Haven: Yale University Press, 1988.

Jiobu, Robert M. *Ethnicity and Assimilation: Blacks, Chinese, Filipinos, Japanese, Koreans, Mexicans, Vietnamese, and Whites.* Albany: SUNY Press, 1988.

———. *Ethnicity and Inequality.* Albany: SUNY Press, 1990.

Kikumura, Akemi. *Through Harsh Winters: The Life of a Japanese Immigrant Woman.* Novato, Calif.: Chandler and Sharp, 1981.

Kim, Elaine H. *Asian American Literature: An Introduction to the Writings and Their Social Context.* Philadelphia: Temple University Press, 1982.

———, with Janice Otani. *With Silk Wings: Asian American Women at Work.* Oakland: Asian Women United of California, 1983.

Kim, Hyung-chan. *Dictionary of Asian American History.* Westport: Greenwood Press, 1986.

Kim, Illsoo. *New Urban Immigrants: The Korean Community in New York.* Princeton: Princeton University Press, 1981.

Kimura, Yukiko. *Issei: Japanese Immigrants in Hawaii.* Honolulu: University of Hawaii Press, 1988.

Kitano, Harry H. L., and Roger Daniels. *Asian Americans: Emerging Minorities.* Englewood Cliffs: Prentice-Hall, 1988, 1994, 2001.

Knoll, Tricia. *Becoming Americans: Asian Sojourners, Immigrants, and Refugees in the Western United States.* Portland: Coast to Coast Books, 1982.

Kodama-Nishimoto, Michi et al. *Hanahana: An Oral History Anthology of Hawaii's Working People.* Honolulu: University of Hawaii Ethnic Studies Oral History Project, 1984.

Koh, Francis M. *Oriental Children in American Homes: How Do They Adjust?* Minneapolis: East-West, 1981.

Kotani, Roland. *The Japanese in Hawaii: A Century of Struggle.* Honolulu: Hawaii Hochi, 1985.

Krauss, Bob, with William P. Alexander. *Grove Farm Plantation: The Biography of a Hawaiian Sugar Plantation,* 2d ed. Palo Alto: Pacific Books, 1984.

Kwik, Greta. *The Indos in Southern California.* New York: AMS, 1989.

Kwong, Peter C. *The New Chinatown.* New York: Hill and Wang, 1988.

LaBrack, Bruce. *The Sikhs of Northern California, 1904–1975.* New York: AMS, 1988.

LaFargue, Thomas E. *China's First Hundred: Educational Mission Students in the United States, 1872–1881.* Pullman: Washington State University Press, 1987.

Larson, Louise Leung. *Sweet Bamboo: A Saga of a Chinese American Family.* Los Angeles: Chinese Historical Society of Southern California, 1989.

Leba, John Kong, with John H. Leba and Anthony T. Leba. *The Vietamese Entrepreneurs in the U.S.A.: The First Decade.* Houston: Zieleks, 1985.

Lee, Mary Paik. *Quiet Odyssey: A Pioneer Korean Woman in America,* edited and with an introduction by Sucheng Chan. Seattle: University of Washington Press, 1990.

Leung, Peter C. Y. *One Day, One Dollar: Locke, California and the Chinese Farming Experience in the Sacramento Delta.* El Cerrito: Chinese/Chinese American History Project, 1984.

Levine, Gene N., and Colbert Rhodes. *The Japanese American Community: A Three-Generation Study.* New York: Praeger, 1981.

Light, Ivan, and Edna Bonacich. *Immigrant Entrepreneurs: Koreans in Los Angeles, 1965–1982.* Berkeley: University of California Press, 1988.

Lim, Shirley G. L., and Mayumi Tsutakawa, eds. *The Forbidden Stitch: An Asian American Women's Anthology.* Corvallis: Calyx Books, 1989.

Ling, Amy. *Between Worlds: Women Writers of Chinese Ancestry.* New York: Pergamon Press, 1990.

Linking Our Lives: Chinese American Women of Los Angeles. Los Angeles: University of California, Los Angeles, Asian American Studies Center and the Chinese Historical Society of Southern California, 1984.

Loescher, Gil, and John A. Scanlan. *Calculated Kindness: Refugees and America's Half-Open Door, 1945–Present.* New York: Free Press, 1986.

Low, Victor. *The Unimpressible Race: A Century of Educational Struggle by the Chinese in San Francisco.* San Francisco: East/West, 1982.

Lueras, Leonard, ed. *Kanyaku Imin: A Hundred Years of Japanese Life in Hawaii.* Honolulu: International Savings and Loan Association, 1985.

Lukes, Timothy, and Gary Y. Okihiro. *Japanese Legacy: Farming and Community Life in California's Santa Clara Valley.* Cupertino: California History Center, 1985.

Lum, Arlene, ed. *Sailing for the Sun: The Chinese in Hawaii, 1789–1989.* Honolulu: University of Hawaii Center for Chinese Studies, 1988.

Lydon, Sandy. *Chinese Gold: The Chinese in the Monterey Bay Region.* Capitola, Calif.: Capitola, 1985.

Lyman, Stanford M. *Chinatown and Little Tokyo: Power, Conflict, and Community among Chinese and Japanese Immigrants in America.* Millwood: Associated Faculty Press, 1986.

Ma, L. Eve Armentrout. *Revolutionaries, Monarchists, and Chinatowns: Chinese Politics in the Americas and the 1911 Revolution.* Honolulu: University of Hawaii Press, 1990.

Malik, Iftikhar H. *Pakistanis in Michigan: A Study of Third Culture and Acculturation.* New York: AMS, 1989.

Mangiafico, Luciano. *Contemporary American Immigrants: Patterns of Filipino, Korean, and Chinese Settlement in the United States.* New York: Praeger, 1988.

Mark, Diane M. L. *Seasons of Light: The History of Chinese Christian Churches in Hawaii.* Honolulu: Chinese Christian Association of Hawaii, 1989.

Masaoka, Mike, with Bill Hosokawa. *They Call Me Moses Masaoka.* New York: William Morrow, 1987.

Masumoto, David M. *Country Voices: The Oral History of a Japanese American Family Farm Community.* Del Rey: Inaka Countryside, 1987.

May, Someth. *Cambodian Witness: The Autobiography of Someth May,* introduction by James Fenton. New York: Random House, 1986.

McCunn, Ruthanne Lum. *Chinese American Portraits: Personal Histories, 1828–1988.* San Francisco: Chronicle, 1988.

McKay, Sandra L., and Sau-ling C. Wong, eds. *Language Diversity: Problem or Resource?* New York: Newbury House, 1988.

Min, Pyong Gap. *Ethnic Business Enterprise: Korean Small Business in Atlanta.* Staten Island: Center for Migration Studies, 1988.

Minnick, Sylvia Sun. *Samfow: The San Joaquin Chinese Legacy.* Fresno: Panorama West, 1988.

Morantte, P. C. *Remembering Carlos Bulosan (His Heart Affair with America).* Quezon City: New Day, 1984.

Moriyama, Alan. *Imingaisha: Japanese Emigration Companies and Hawaii, 1894–1908.* Honolulu: University of Hawaii Press, 1985.

Muir, Karen L. S. *The Strongest Part of the Family: A Study of Lao Refugee Women in Columbus, Ohio.* New York: AMS, 1988.

Murase, Ichiro M. *Little Tokyo: One Hundred Years in Pictures.* Los Angeles: Visual Communications, 1983.

Muthanna, I. M. *People of India in North America: United States, Canada, W. Indies, and Fiji: Immigration History of East Indians up to 1960.* Bangalore, India: Gangarams, 1982.

Nakane, Kazuko. *Nothing Left in My Hand: An Early Japanese American Community in California's Pajaro Valley.* Seattle: Young Pine, 1983.

Nakanishi, Don T., and Marsha Hirano-Nakanishi, eds. *The Education of Asian and Pacific Americans: Historical Perspectives and Prescriptions for the Future.* Phoenix: Oryx, 1983.

Nakano, Mei. *Japanese American Women: Three Generations, 1890–1990.* Berkeley: Mina, 1990.

Ngor, Haing, with Roger Warner. *Haing Ngor: A Cambodian Odyssey.* New York: Macmillan, 1987.

Nguyen-Hong-Nhiem, Lucy, and Joel M. Halpern, eds. *The Far East Comes Near: Autobiographical Accounts of Southeast Asian Students in America.* Amherst: University of Massachusetts Press, 1989.

Noda, Kesa. *Yamato Colony, 1906–1960, Livingston, California.* Merced: JACL Livingston-Merced Chapter, 1981.

Nomura, Gail M. et al., eds. *Frontiers of Asian American Studies: Writing, Research, and Commentary.* Pullman: Washington State University Press, 1989.

Oda, James. *Heroic Struggles of Japanese Americans: Partisan Fighters from America's Concentration Camps.* North Hollywood: The author, 1980.

Odo, Franklin, and Kazuko Sinoto. *A Pictorial History of the Japanese in Hawai'i, 1885–1924.* Honolulu: Bishop Museum, 1985.

Okihiro, Gary Y. et al., eds. *Reflections on Shattered Windows: Promises and Prospects for Asian American Studies.* Pullman: Washington State University Press, 1988.

Okinawa Club of America, ed. *History of the Okinawans in North America.* Los Angeles: University of California, Los Angeles, Asian American Studies Center and the Okinawa Club of America, 1988.

Orleans, Leo A. *Chinese Students in America: Policies, Issues, and Numbers.* Washington: National Academy Press, 1988.

Pai, Margaret K. *The Dreams of Two Yi-min.* Honolulu: University of Hawaii Press, 1989.

Palinkas, L. A. *Rhetoric and Religious Experience: The Discourse of Immigrant Chinese Churches.* Fairfax: George Mason University Press, 1989.

Patterson, Wayne K. *The Korean Frontier in America: Immigration to Hawaii, 1896–1910.* Honolulu: University of Hawaii Press, 1988.

Pido, Antonio J. A. *The Pilipinos in America: Macro/Micro Dimensions of Immigration and Integration.* Staten Island: Center for Migration Studies, 1986.

Quan, Robert S. *Lotus among the Magnolias: The Mississippi Chinese.* Jackson: University Press of Mississippi, 1982.

Riddle, Ronald. *Flying Dragons, Flowing Streams: Music in the Life of San Francisco Chinese.* Westport: Greenwood Press, 1983.

Robertson, Georgia D. *The Harvest of Hate.* Fullerton: California State University, Fullerton, Oral History Program, 1986.

Rutledge, Paul J. *The Role of Religion in Ethnic Self-Identity: A Vietnamese Community.* Lanham: University Press of America, 1985.

Saran, Parmatma. *The Asian Indian Experience in the United States.* Cambridge: Schenkman, 1985.

Sarasohn, Eileen Sunada, ed. *The Issei: Portrait of a Pioneer, an Oral History.* Palo Alto: Pacific, 1983.

Schwendinger, Robert J. *Ocean of Bitter Dreams: Maritime Relations between China and the United States, 1850–1915.* Tucson: Westernlore Press, 1988.

Scott, Joanna C., ed. *Indochina's Refugees: Oral Histories from Laos, Cambodia and Vietnam.* Jefferson, N.C.: McFarland, 1989.

Sheehy, Gail. *Spirit of Survival.* New York: William Morrow, 1986.

Shimada, Shigeo. *A Stone Cried Out: The True Story of Simple Faith in Difficult Days.* Valley Forge: Judson, 1986.

Shimonishi-Lamb, Mili. *And Then a Rainbow.* Santa Barbara: Fithian, 1990.

Siu, Paul C. P. *The Chinese Laundryman: A Study of Social Isolation,* edited by John K. W. Tchen. New York: New York University Press, 1987.

Spickard, Paul R. *Mixed Blood: Intermarriage and Ethnic Identity in Twentieth-Century America.* Madison: University of Wisconsin Press, 1989.

Stannard, David E. *Before the Horror: The Population of Hawaii on the Eve of Western Contact.* Honolulu: University of Hawaii Social Science Research Institute, 1989.

Strand, Paul J., and Woodrow Jones, Jr. *Indochinese Refugees in America: Problems of Adaptation and Assimilation.* Durham: Duke University Press, 1985.

Stuart-Fox, Martin. *The Murderous Revolution: Life and Death in Pol Pot's Kampuchea Based on the Personal Experiences of Bunheang Ung.* Chippendale, Australia: Alternative Publishing Cooperative, 1985.

Sue, Stanley, and James K. Morishima. *The Mental Health of Asian Americans.* San Francisco: Jossey-Bass, 1982.

Sung, Betty Lee. *The Adjustment Experience of Chinese Immigrant Children in New York City.* Staten Island: Center for Migration Studies, 1987.

———. *Chinese American Intermarriage.* Staten Island: Center for Migration Studies, 1990.

Sutter, Valerie O. *The Indochinese Refugee Dilemma.* Baton Rouge: Louisiana State University Press, 1990.

Szymusiak, Molyda. *The Stones Cry Out: A Cambodian Childhood, 1975–1980.* Translated by Linda Coverdale. New York: Hill and Wang, 1986.

Takaki, Ronald. *Pau Hana: Plantation Life and Labor in Hawaii.* Honolulu: University of Hawaii Press, 1983.

———. *Strangers from a Different Shore.* Boston: Little, Brown, 1989.

Tanaka, Chester. *Go for Broke: A Pictorial History of the Japanese American 100th Infantry Battalion and the 442nd Regimental Combat Team.* Richmond, Calif.: Go for Broke, 1982.

Tanaka, Richard K. *America on Trial.* New York: Carlton, 1987.

Tateishi, John. *And Justice for All: An Oral History of the Japanese American Detention Camps.* New York: Random House, 1984.

Taylor, Sandra C. *Advocate of Understanding: Sidney Gulick and the Search for Peace with Japan.* Kent: Kent State University Press, 1984.

Teodoro, Luis V., Jr., ed. *Out of This Struggle: The Filipinos of Hawaii.* Honolulu: University Press of Hawaii, 1981.

Tollefson, James W. *Alien Winds: The Reeducation of America's Indochinese Refugees.* New York: Praeger, 1989.

Trueba, Henry T., Lila Jacobs, and Elizabeth Kirton. *Cultural Conflict and Adaptation: The Case of Hmong Children in American Society.* New York: Falmer, 1990.

Tsai, Shih-shan H. *China and the Overseas Chinese in the United States, 1868–1911.* Fayetteville: University of Arkansas Press, 1983.

———. *The Chinese Experience in America.* Bloomington: Indiana University Press, 1986.

Tsuchida, Nobuya, ed. *American Justice: Japanese American Evacuation and Redress Cases.* Minneapolis: University of Minnesota, Asian/Pacific American Learning Resource Center, 1988.

———. *Asian and Pacific American Experiences: Women's Perspectives.* Minneapolis: University of Minnesota, Asian/Pacific American Learning Resource Center, 1982.

Tsutakawa, Mayumi, and Alan C. Lau, eds. *Turning Shadows into Light: Art and Culture of the Northwest's Early Asian/Pacific Community.* Seattle: Young Pine Press, 1982.

Uchida, Yoshiko. *Desert Exile: The Uprooting of a Japanese American Family.* Seattle: University of Washington Press, 1982.

Vallanga, Caridad C. *The Second Wave: Pinay and Pinoy (1945–1960).* San Francisco: Strawberry Hill, 1987.

Wain, Barry. *The Refused: The Agony of the Indochinese Refugees.* New York: Simon and Schuster, 1981.

Walls, Thomas K. *The Japanese Texans.* San Antonio: University of Texas Institute of Texan Cultures, 1987.

Williams, Raymond B. *Religions of Immigrants from India and Pakistan: New Threads in the American Tapestry.* New York: Cambridge University Press, 1988.

Wong, Bernard. *Chinatown: Economic Adaptation and Ethnic Identity of the Chinese.* New York: Holt, Rinehart, and Winston, 1982.

———. *Patronage, Brokerage, Entrepreneurship and the Chinese Community of New York.* New York: AMS, 1988.

Wu, William F. *The Yellow Peril: Chinese Americans in American Fiction, 1850–1940.* Hamden: Archon, 1982.

Yanagisako, Sylvia J. *Transforming the Past: Tradition and Kinship among Japanese Americans.* Stanford: Stanford University Press, 1985.

Yap, Stacy F. H. *Gather Your Strength, Sisters: The Emerging Role of Chinese Women Community Workers.* New York: AMS, 1989.

Yathay, Pin, with John Man. *Stay Alive, My Son.* New York: Free Press, 1987.

Yoneda, Karl. *Ganbatte: Sixty-Year Struggle of a Kibei Worker.* Los Angeles: University of California, Los Angeles, Asian American Studies Center, 1983.

Yoshina, Shizue, ed. *Nisei Christian Journey (Its Promise and Fulfillment).* N.p.: Nisei Christian Oral History Project, 1988.

Yu, Eui-Young et al., eds. *Koreans in Los Angeles: Prospects and Promises.* Los Angeles: California State University Center for Korean-American and Korean Studies, Los Angeles, 1982.

———, and Earl H. Phillips, eds. *Korean Women in Transition: At Home and Abroad.* Los Angeles: California State University Center for Korean-American and Korean Studies, Los Angeles, 1987.

Yung, Judy. *Chinese Women of America: A Pictorial History.* Seattle: University of Washington Press, 1986.

Yoshitsu, Masao. *My Moments in the Twentieth Century: An Immigrant's Story.* New York: Vintage, 1987.

Books, since 1991

Aarim-Heriot, Najia. *Chinese Immigrants, African Americans, and Racial Anxiety in the United States, 1848–82.* Urbana: University of Illinois Press, 2003.

Abelman, Nancy, and John Lie. *Blue Dreams: Korean Americans and the Los Angeles Riots.* Cambridge: Harvard University Press, 1995.

Abraham, Margaret. *Speaking the Unspeakable: Marital Violence among South Asian Immigrants in the United States.* New Brunswick: Rutgers University Press, 2000.

Aguilar-San Juan, Karen, ed. *The State of Asian America: Activism and Resistance in the 1990s.* Boston: South End, 1994.

Ancheta, Angelo N. *Race, Rights, and the Asian American Experience.* New Brunswick: Rutgers University Press, 1998.

Aoudé, Ibrahim, ed. *The Ethnic Studies Story: Politics and Social Movements in Hawaii.* Honolulu: Distributed for Social Process in Hawaii by the University of Hawaii Press, 1999.

Argawal, Priya. *Passage from India: Post-1965 Indian Immigrants and Their Children.* Palos Verdes: Yuvati, 1991.

Asante, Molefi K., and Eungjun Min, eds. *Socio-Cultural Conflict between African American and Korean American.* Lanham: University Press of America, 2000.

Asian Pacific American Public Policy Institute. *The State of Asian Pacific America: Policy Issues to the Year 2020.* Los Angeles: Leadership Education for Asian Pacifics and University of California, Los Angeles, Asian American Studies Center, 1993.

Austin, Allan W. *From Concentration Camp to Campus: Japanese American Students and World War II.* Urbana: University of Illinois Press, 2005.

Azuma, Eiichiro. *Between Two Empires: Race, History, and Transnationalism in Japanese America.* New York: Oxford University Press, 2005.

Bacon, Jean. *Life Lines: Community, Family, and Assimilation among Asian Indian Immigrants.* New York: Oxford University Press, 1996.

Bahri, Deepika, and Mary Vasudeva, eds. *Between the Lines: South Asians and Postcoloniality.* Philadelphia: Temple University Press, 1996.

Bao, Xiaolan. *Holding Up Half the Sky: Chinese Women Garment Workers in New York City, 1948–92.* Urbana: University of Illinois Press, 2001.

Barkan, Elliott R. *Asian and Pacific Islander Migration to the United States: A Model of New Global Patterns.* Westport: Greenwood Press, 1992.

Barringer, Herbert R., Robert W. Gardner, and Michael J. Levin. *Asians and Pacific Islanders in the United States.* New York: Russell Sage Foundation, 1993.

Bautista, Veltisezar. *The Filipino Americans from 1763 to the Present: Their History, Culture, and Traditions.* Farmington Hills: Bookhaus, 1998.

Becker, Jules. *The Course of Exclusion, 1882–1924: San Francisco Newspaper Coverage of the Chinese and Japanese in the United States.* Lewiston: Edwin Mellen Press, 1991.

Beechert, Alice M., and Edward D. Beechert, eds. *From Kona to Yenan: The Political Memoir of Koji Ariyoshi.* Honolulu: University of Hawaii Press, 2000.

Belden, Elionne L. W. *Claiming Chinese Identity.* New York: Garland, 1997.

Birchall, Diana. *Onoto Watanna: The Story of Winnifred Eaton.* Urbana: University of Illinois Press, 2001.

Bishoff, Tonya, and Jo Rankin, eds. *Seeds from a Silent Tree: An Anthology by Korean Adoptees.* Glendale: Pandal Press, 1997.

Bonner, Arthur. *Alas! What Brought Thee Hither? The Chinese in New York, 1800–1950.* Cranbury: Associated University Press, 1997.

Bonus, Rick. *Locating Filipino Americans: Ethnicity and the Cultural Politics of Space.* Philadelphia: Temple University Press, 2000.

Bow, Leslie. *Betrayal and Other Acts of Subversion: Feminism, Sexual Politics, Asian American Women's Literature.* Princeton: Princeton University Press, 2001.

Caplan, Nathan, Marcella H. Choy, and John K. Whitmore. *Children of the Boat People: A Study of Educational Success.* Ann Arbor: University of Michigan Press, 1991.

Cargill, Mary Terrel, and Jade Q. Huynh, eds. *Voices of Vietnamese Boat People: Nineteen Narratives of Escape and Survival.* Jefferson, N.C.: McFarland, 2000.

Cassel, Susie L., ed. *The Chinese in America: A History from the Gold Mountain to the New Millennium.* Walnut Creek, Calif.: AltaMira Press, 2002.

Chan, Jachinson W. *Chinese American Masculinities: From Fu Manchu to Bruce Lee.* New York: Routledge, 2001.

Chan, Sucheng. *Asian Americans: An Interpretive History.* Boston: Twayne, 1991.

———. *Asian Californians.* San Francisco: Boyd and Fraser, 1991.

———. *Survivors: Cambodian Refugees in the United States.* Urbana: University of Illinois Press, 2004.

———, ed. *Chinese American Transnationalism: The Flow of People, Resources, and Ideas between China and America during the Exclusion Era, 1882–1943.* Philadelphia: Temple University Press, 2005.

———, ed. *Entry Denied: Exclusion and the Chinese Community in America, 1882–1943.* Philadelphia: Temple University Press, 1991.

———, ed. *Hmong Means Free: Life in Laos and America.* Philadelphia: Temple University Press, 1994.

———, ed. *Not Just Victims: Conversations with Cambodian Community Leaders in the United States.* Urbana: University of Illinois Press, 2003.

———, ed. *Remapping Asian American History.* Walnut Creek, Calif.: AltaMira Press, 2003.

Chang, Edward T., and Jeannette Diaz-Veizades. *Ethnic Peace in the American City: Building Community in Los Angeles and Beyond.* New York: New York University Press, 1999.

Chang, Gordon H., ed. *Asian Americans and Politics: Perspectives, Experiences, Prospects.* Washington: Woodrow Wilson Center Press, and Stanford: Stanford University Press, 2001.

———, ed. *Morning Glory, Evening Shadow: Yamato Ichihashi and His Internment Writings, 1942–1945.* Annotated and with a biographical essay. Stanford: Stanford University Press, 1997.

———, Purnima Mankekar, and Akhil Gupta, eds. *Caste and Outcast* by Dhan Gopal Mukerji. Stanford: Stanford University Press, 2002.

Chang, Kou, and Sheila Pinkel. *Kou Chang's Story: The Journey of a Laotian Hmong Refugee Family.* Rochester: Visual Studies Workshop Press, 1993.

Chang, Robert S. *Disoriented: Asian Americans, Law, and the Nation-State.* New York: New York University Press, 1999.

Chang, Thelma. *"I Can Never Forget": Men of the 100th/442nd.* Honolulu: Sigi Productions, 1991.

Charr, Easurk E. *The Golden Mountain: The Autobiography of a Korean Immigrant, 1985– 1960,* edited and with an introduction by Wayne Patterson. 2d ed. Urbana: University of Illinois Press, 1996.

Chen, Hsiang-shui. *Chinatown No More: Taiwan Immigrants in Contemporary New York.* Ithaca: Cornell University Press, 1992.

Chen, Shehong. *Being Chinese, Becoming Chinese American.* Urbana: University of Illinois Press, 2002.

Chen, Yong. *Chinese San Francisco, 1850–1943: A Trans-Pacific Community.* Stanford: Stanford University Press, 2000.

Cheung, King-Kok, ed. *Articulate Silences: Hisaye Yamamoto, Maxine Hong Kingston, Joy Kogawa.* Ithaca: Cornell University Press, 1993.

———. *The Cambridge Companion to Asian American Literature.* New York: Cambridge University Press, 1995.

———. *"Seventeen Syllables"—Hisaye Yamamoto.* New Brunswick: Rutgers University Press, 1994.

———. *Words Matter: Conversations with Asian American Writers.* Honolulu: University of Hawaii Press in association with the UCLA Asian American Studies Center, Los Angeles, 2000.

Chew, Ron, ed. *Reflections of Seattle's Chinese Americans: The First Hundred Years.* Seattle: University of Washington Press and Wing Luke Asian Museum, 1994.

Chin, Frank. *Born in the USA: A Story of Japanese Americans, 1889–1947.* Lanham: Rowman and Littlefield, 2002.

Chin, Jean L. et al. *Transference and Empathy in Asian American Psychotherapy: Cultural Values and Treatment Needs.* New York: Praeger, 1993.

Chin, Ko-Lin. *Chinatown Gangs: Extortion, Enterprise, and Ethnicity.* New York: Oxford University Press, 1996.

———. *Smuggled Chinese: Clandestine Immigration to the United States.* Philadelphia: Temple University Press, 1999.

Chin, Soo-Young. *Doing What Had to Be Done: The Life Narrative of Rosa Yum Kim.* Philadelphia: Temple University Press, 1999.

Chin, Tung Pok, with Winifred C. Chin. *Paper Son: One Man's Story,* introduction by K. Scott Wong. Philadelphia: Temple University Press, 2000.

Chiu, Monica. *Filthy Fictions: Asian American Literature by Women.* Walnut Creek, Calif.: AltaMira Press, 2004.

Chong, Denise. *The Concubine's Children: The Story of a Chinese Family Living on Two Sides of the Globe.* New York: Penguin Books, 1994.

Choy, Catherine C. *Empire of Care: Nursing and Migration in Filipino American History.* Durham: Duke University Press, 2003.

Choy, Philip P., Lorraine Dong, and Marlon K. Hom. *The Coming Man: Nineteenth-Century American Perceptions of the Chinese.* Hong Kong: Joint Publications, 1994.

Chu, Patricia P. *Assimilating Asians: Gendered Strategies of Authorship in Asian America.* Durham: Duke University Press, 2000.

Chuh, Kandice, and Karen Shimakawa, eds. *Orientations: Mapping Studies in the Asian Diaspora.* Durham: Duke University Press, 2001.

Chun, Gloria H. *Of Orphans and Warriors: Inventing Chinese American Culture and Identity.* New Brunswick: Rutgers University Press, 2000.

Chuong, Chung H., and Le Van. *The Amerasians from Vietnam: A California Study.* Folsom: Southeast Asia Community Resource Center, 1994.

Coward, Howard et al. *The South Asian Religious Diaspora in Britain, Canada, and the United States.* Albany: SUNY Press, 2000.

Criddle, JoAn D. *Bamboo and Butterflies: From Refugee to Citizen.* Dixon, Calif.: East/West Bridge Publishing House, 1992.

Crost, Lyn. *Honor by Fire: Japanese Americans at War in Europe and the Pacific.* Novato, Calif.: Presidio Press, 1994.

Danico, Mary Yu. *The 1.5 Generation: Becoming Korean American in Hawaii.* Honolulu: University of Hawaii Press, 2004.

Daniels, Roger. *Prisoners without Trial: Japanese Americans in World War II.* New York: Hill and Wang, 1993.

Dasgupta, Shamita D., ed. *A Patchwork Shawl: Chronicles of South Asian Women in America.* New Brunswick: Rutgers University Press, 1998.

Davidson, Sue. *A Heart in Politics: Jeannette Rankin and Patsy T. Mink.* Seattle: Seal Press, 1994.

Davis, Leonard. *Hong Kong and the Asylum-Seekers from Vietnam.* New York: St. Martin's Press, 1991.

DeBonis, Steven. *Children of the Enemy: Oral Histories of Vietnamese Amerasians and Their Mothers.* Jefferson, N.C.: McFarland, 1994.

Detzner, Daniel F. *Elder Voices: Southeast Asian Families in the United States.* Walnut Creek, Calif.: AltaMira Press, 2004.

Dionisio, Juan C., Stu Glauberman, and Carl H. Zimmerman, eds. *From Mabuhay to Aloha: The Filipinos in Hawaii.* Honolulu: Filipino Association of University Women, 1991.

Dirlik, Arif, ed. *Chinese on the American Frontier.* Lanham: Rowman and Littlefield, 2001.

Dith Pran, comp. *Children of Cambodia's Killing Fields: Memoirs by Survivors,* edited by Kim DePaul, introduction by Ben Kiernan. New Haven: Yale University Press, 1997.

Donnolly, Nancy D. *Changing Lives of Refugee Hmong Women.* Seattle: University of Washington Press, 1994.

Duus, Masayo U. *The Japanese Conspiracy: The Oahu Sugar Strike of 1920.* Berkeley: University of California Press, 1999.

Dye, Bob. *Merchant Prince of the Sandalwood Mountains: Afong and the Chinese in Hawai'i.* Honolulu: University of Hawaii Press, 1997.

Ebaugh, Helen R., and Janet S. Chafetz. *Religion and the New Immigrants: Continuities and Adaptations in Immigrant Congregations.* Walnut Creek, Calif.: AltaMira Press, 2000.

———, eds. *Religion across Borders: Transnational Immigrant Networks.* Walnut Creek, Calif.: AltaMira Press, 2002.

Ebihara, May M., Carol A. Mortland, and Judy Ledgerwood, eds. *Cambodian Culture since 1975: Homeland and Exile.* Ithaca: Cornell University Press, 1994.

Endo, Russell et al., eds. *Current Issues in Asian and Pacific American Education.* South El Monte, Calif.: Pacific Asia Press, 1998.

Eng, Alvin, ed. *Tokens? The New York City Asian American Experience on Stage.* New York: Asian American Writers' Workshop, 1999.

Eng, David L. *Racial Castration: Managing Masculinity in Asian America.* Durham: Duke University Press, 2001.

———, and Alice Y. Hom, eds. *Q & A: Queer in Asian America.* Philadelphia: Temple University Press, 1998.

English, T. J. *Born to Kill: America's Most Notorious Vietnamese Gang and the Changing Face of Organized Crime.* New York: William Morrow, 1995.

Espiritu, Yen L. *Asian American Panethnicity: Bridging Institutions and Identities*. Philadelphia: Temple University Press, 1992.

———. *Asian American Women and Men: Labor, Laws, and Love*. Thousand Oaks: Sage, 1997.

———. *Filipino American Lives*. Philadelphia: Temple University Press, 1995.

———. *Home Bound: Filipino American Lives across Cultures, Communities, and Countries*. Berkeley: University of California Press, 2003.

Faderman, Lillian, with Ghia Xiong. *I Begin My Life All Over: The Hmong and the American Immigrant Experience*. Boston: Beacon Press, 1993.

Fadiman, Anne. *The Spirit Catches You and You Fall Down: A Hmong Child, Her American Doctors, and the Collision of Two Cultures*. New York: Farrar, Straus, and Giroux, 1997.

Feng, Peter X. *Identities in Motion: Asian American Film and Video*. Durham: Duke University Press, 2002.

———, ed. *Screening Asian Americans*. New Brunswick: Rutgers University Press, 2002.

Ferens, Dominika. *Edith and Winnifred Eaton: Chinatown Missions and Japanese Romances*. Urbana: University of Illinois Press, 2002.

Fiffer, Sharon S. *Imagining America: Paul Thai's Journel from the Killing Fields to Freedom in the U.S.A.* New York: Paragon House, 1991.

Fiset, Louis. *Imprisoned Apart: The World War II Correspondence of an Issei Couple*. Seattle: University of Washington Press, 1997.

Flewelling, Stan. *Shirakawa: Stories from a Pacific Northwest Japanese American Community*. Auburn, Wash.: White River Valley Museum, 2002.

Flynn, James R. *Asian Americans: Achievement beyond IQ*. Hillsdale: Lawrence Erlbaum Associates, 1991.

Foner, Philip S., and Daniel Rosenberg, eds. *Racism, Dissent, and Asian Americans from 1850 to the Present: A Documentary History*. Westport: Greenwood Press, 1993.

Fong, Timothy P. *The Contemporary Asian American Experience: Beyond the Model Minority*. Upper Saddle River: Prentice-Hall, 1998.

———. *The First Suburban Chinatown: The Remaking of Monterey Park, California*. Philadelphia: Temple University Press, 1994.

———, and Larry H. Shinagawa, eds. *Asian Americans: Experiences and Perspectives*. Upper Saddle River: Prentice-Hall, 2000.

Fong-Torres, Ben. *The Rice Room: Growing Up Chinese-American—From Number Two Son to Rock 'n' Roll*. New York: Plume Books, 1994.

Forbes, David W. *Encounters with Paradise: Views of Hawaii and Its People, 1778–1941*. Honolulu: Honolulu Academy of Arts, 1992.

Foster, Jenny R., Frank Stewart, and Heinz I. Fenkl, eds. *Century of the Tiger: One Hundred Years of Korean Culture in America, 1903–2003*. Honolulu: *Manoa Journal,* Centennial Committee of Korean Immigration to the United States, and the University of Hawaii Press, 2003.

Freedman, Amy L. *Political Participation and Ethnic Minorities: Overseas Chinese in Malaysia, Indonesia, and the United States*. New York: Routledge, 2000.

Freeman, James M. *Changing Identities: Vietnamese Americans, 1975–1995*. Boston: Allyn and Bacon, 1995.

Friday, Chris. *Organizing Asian American Labor: The Pacific Coast Canned-Salmon Industry, 1870–1942.* Philadephia: Temple University Press, 1994.

Fugita, Stephen S., and Marilyn Fernandez. *Altered Lives, Enduring Community: Japanese Americans Remember Their World War II Incarceration.* Seattle: University of Washington Press, 2004.

——, and David J. O'Brien. *Japanese American Ethnicity: The Persistence of Community.* Seattle: University of Washington Press, 1991.

Fujino, Diane C. *Heartbeat of Struggle: Revolutionary Practice of Yuri Kochiyama.* Minneapolis: University of Minnesota Press, 2005.

Fujita-Rony, Dorothy. *American Workers, Colonial Power: Philippine Seattle and the Transpacific West, 1919–1941.* Berkeley: University of California Press, 2003.

Furuto, Sharlene M. et al., eds. *Social Work Practice with Asian Americans.* Newbury Park, Calif.: Sage, 1992.

Ghymn, Esther M. *The Shapes and Styles of Asian American Prose Fiction.* New York: Peter Lang, 1992.

Gold, Steven J. *Refugee Communities: A Comparative Field Study.* Newbury Park, Calif.: Sage, 1992.

Gupta, Sangeeta R., ed. *Emerging Voices: South Asian American Women Redefine Self, Family, and Community.* Thousand Oaks: Sage, 1999.

Gyory, Andrew. *Closing the Gate: Race, Politics, and the Chinese Exclusion Act.* Chapel Hill: University of North Carolina Press, 1998.

Ha, Kim. *Stormy Escape: A Vietnamese Woman's Account of Her 1980 Flight.* Jefferson, N.C.: McFarland, 1997.

Haddad, Yvonne Y., and Jane I. Smith. *Mission to America: Five Islamic Sectarian Communities in North America.* Gainesville: University Press of Florida, 1993.

——, eds. *Muslim Communities in North America.* Albany: SUNY Press, 1994.

Haines, David W., ed. *Case Studies in Diversity: Refugees in America in the 1990s.* New York: Praeger, 1997.

Hall, Bruce E. *Tea That Burns: A Family Memoir of Chinatown.* New York: Free Press, 1998.

Hall, Patricia W., and Victor M. Hwang, eds. *Anti-Asian Violence in North America: Asian American and Asian Canadian Reflections on Hate, Healing, and Resistance.* Walnut Creek, Calif.: AltaMira Press, 2001.

Hamamoto, Darrell Y. *Monitored Peril: Asian Americans and the Politics of TV Representation.* Minneapolis: University of Minnesota Press, 1994.

——, and Sandra Liu, eds. *Countervisions: Asian American Film Criticism.* Philadelphia: Temple University Press, 2000.

Hansen, Arthur A., ed. *Japanese American World War II Evacuation History Project.* 5 vols. Westport: Meckler, 1991–93.

Harris, Catherine E. *Dusty Exile: Looking Back at Japanese Relocation during World War II.* Honolulu: Mutual, 1999.

Hatamiya, Leslie T. *Righting a Wrong: Japanese Americans and the Passage of the Civil Liberties Act of 1988.* Stanford: Stanford University Press, 1993.

Hawaii Nikkei History Editorial Board. *Japanese Eyes, American Heart: Personal Reflections of Hawaii's World War II Nisei Soldiers.* Honolulu: Tendai Educational Foundation, 1998.

Hayashi, Brian M. *Democratizing the Enemy: The Japanese American Internment.* Princeton: Princeton University Press, 2004.

———. *"For the Sake of Our Japanese Brethren": Assimilation, Nationalism, and Protestantism among the Japanese in Los Angeles, 1895–1942.* Stanford: Stanford University Press, 1995.

Hein, Jeremy. *Ethnic Origins: History, Politics, Culture, and the Adaptation of Cambodian and Hmong Refugees in American Cities.* New York: Russell Sage Foundation, 2005.

———. *From Vietnam, Laos, and Cambodia: A Refugee Experience in America.* New York: Twayne, 1995.

———. *States and International Migrants: The Incorporation of Indochinese Refugees in the United States and France.* Boulder: Westview Press, 1993.

Heuterman, Thomas H. *The Burning Horse: Japanese American Experience in the Yakima Valley, 1920–1942.* Cheney: Eastern Washington University Press, 1995.

Higa, Karin M. *The View from Within: Japanese American Art from the Internment Camps, 1942–1945.* Los Angeles: Japanese American Museum, 1992.

Hill, Kimi K., ed. *Topaz Moon: Chiura Obata's Art of the Internment.* Berkeley: Heyday Books, 2000.

Him, Chanrithy. *When Broken Glass Floats: Growing Up under the Khmer Rouge.* New York: W. W. Norton, 2000.

Hing, Bill O. *Defining America through Immigration Policy.* Philadelphia: Temple University Press, 2004.

———. *Making and Remaking Asian America through Immigration Policy, 1850–1990.* Stanford: Stanford University Press, 1993.

Hirabayashi, Lane R. *Nishimoto of Poston: Daily Life and Popular Resistance in an American Concentration Camp.* Tucson: University of Arizona Press, 1995.

———. *The Politics of Fieldwork: Research in an American Concentration Camp.* Tucson: University of Arizona Press, 1999.

———, ed. *Teaching Asian America: Diversity and the Problem of Community.* Lanham: Rowman and Littlefield, 1998.

———, Akemi Kikumura-Yano, and James A. Hirabayashi. *New Worlds, New Lives: Globalization and People of Japanese Descent in the Americas and from Latin America in Japan.* Stanford: Stanford University Press, 2002.

Hirobe, Uzumi. *Japanese Pride, American Prejudice: Modifying the Exclusion Clause of the 1924 Immigration Act.* Stanford: Stanford University Press, 2001.

Hmong Youth Cultural Awareness Project. *A Free People: Our Stories, Our Voices, Our Dreams.* Minneapolis: Hmong Youth Cultural Awareness Project, 1994.

Ho, Wendy. *In Her Mother's House: The Politics of Asian American Mother-Daughter Writing.* Walnut Creek, Calif.: AltaMira Press, 1999.

Horton, John. *The Politics of Diversity: Immigration, Resistance, and Change in Monterey Park, California.* Philadelphia: Temple University Press, 1995.

Hsu, Madeline Y. *Dreaming of Gold, Dreaming of Home: Transnationalism and Migration between the United States and South China, 1882–1943.* Stanford: Stanford University Press, 2000.

Hu-DeHart, Evelyn, ed. *Across the Pacific: Asian Americans and Globalization.* Philadelphia: Temple University Press, 1999.

Hune, Shirley, and Gail M. Nomura, eds. *Asian/Pacific American Women: A Historial Anthology.* New York: New York University Press, 2003.
—— et al., eds. *Asian Americans: Comparative and Global Perspectives.* Pullman: Washington State University Press, 1991.
Hurh, Won Moo. *The Korean Americans.* Westport: Greenwood Press, 1998.
Huynh, Jade N. *South Wind Changing.* St. Paul: Greywolf Press, 1994.
Hyun, Peter. *In the New World: The Making of a Korean American.* Honolulu: University of Hawaii Press, 1995.
Ichioka, Yuji. *Beyond Internment: Essays in Prewar Japanese-American History.* Stanford: Stanford University Press, 2005.
Inada, Lawson F., ed. *Only What We Could Carry: The Japanese American Internment Experience.* Berkeley: Heyday Books and San Francisco: California Historical Society, 2000.
Ishikawa, Yoshimi. *Strawberry Road: A Japanese Immigrant Discovers America.* Tokyo: Kodansha International, 1991.
Ishimura, Stone S. *Military Intelligence Service Language School, U.S. Army, Fort Snelling, Minnesota.* Los Angeles: TecCom Productions, 1991.
Iwamura, Jane, and Paul Spickard, eds. *Revealing the Sacred in Asian and Pacific America.* New York: Routledge, 2003.
Iwata, Masakazu. *Planted in Good Soil: A History of the Issei in United States Agriculture.* New York: Peter Lang, 1992.
Kalita, S. Mitra. *Suburban Sahibs: Three Immigrant Families and Their Passage from India to America.* New Brunswick: Rutgers University Press, 2003.
Kang, K. Connie. *Home Was the Land of Morning Calm: A Saga of a Korean-American Family.* Reading, Mass.: Addison-Wesley, 1995.
Kang, Laura H. Y. *Compositional Subjects: Enfiguring Asian/American Women.* Durham: Duke University Press, 2002.
Kashima, Tetsuden. *Judgment without Trial: Japanese American Imprisonment during World War II.* Seattle: University of Washington Press, 2003.
Kawakami, Barbara F. *Japanese Immigrant Clothing in Hawaii, 1885–1941.* Honolulu: University of Hawaii Press, 1993.
Keller, Nora O. et al., eds. *Yobo: Korean American Writing in Hawai'i.* Honolulu: Bamboo Ridge Press, 2003.
Kerkvliet, Melinda Tria. *Unbending Cane: Pablo Manlapit, a Filipino Labor Leader in Hawaii.* Honolulu: University of Hawaii Office of Multicultural Student Services, 2002.
Kessler, Lauren. *Stubborn Twig: Three Generations in the Life of a Japanese American Family.* New York: Random House, 1993.
Khalidi, Omar, ed. *Indian Muslims in North America.* Watertown, Mass.: South Asia Press, 1991.
Khandelwal, Madhulika S. *Becoming American, Being Asian: An Immigrant Community in New York City.* Ithaca: Cornell University Press, 2002.
Kibria, Nazli. *The Family Tightrope: The Changing Lives of Vietnamese Americans.* Princeton: Princeton University Press, 1993.
Kikuchi, Shigeo. *Memoirs of a Buddhist Woman Missionary in Hawaii.* Honolulu: Buddhist Center Press, 1991.

Kikumura, Akemi. *Issei Pioneers, Hawaii and the Mainland, 1885 to 1924*. Los Angeles: Japanese American National Museum, 1992.

———. *Promises Kept: The Life of an Issei Man*. Novato, Calif.: Chandler and Sharp, 1991.

Kim, Ai Ra. *Women Struggling for a New Life*. Albany: SUNY Press, 1996.

Kim, Claire J. *Bitter Fruit: The Politics of Black-Korean Conflict in New York City*. New Haven: Yale University Press, 2000.

Kim, Elaine H., and Eui-Young Yu, eds. *East to America: Korean American Life Stories*. New York: New Press, 1996.

———, and Lisa Lowe, eds. *New Foundations, New Questions, Asian American Studies*. Durham: Duke University Press, 1997.

———, Margo Machida, and Sharon Mizota. *Fresh Talk, Daring Gazes: Conversations on Asian American Art*. Berkeley: University of California Press, 2003.

———, and Norma Alarcon, eds. *Writing Self, Writing Nation: A Collection of Essays on Dictée by Theresa H. K. Cha*. Berkeley: Third Woman Press, 1994.

——— et al., eds. *Making More Waves: New Writing by Asian American Women*. Boston: Beacon Press, 1997.

Kim, Hyung-chan, ed. *Asian Americans and the Supreme Court: A Documentary History*. Westport: Greenwood Press, 1992.

———, ed. *Distinguished Asian Americans: A Biographical Dictionary*. Westport: Greenwood Press, 1999.

Kim, Jung Ha. *Bridge-Makers and Cross-Bearers: Korean-American Women and the Church*. Atlanta: Scholars Press, 1997.

Kim, Kwang Chung, ed. *Koreans in the Hood: Conflict with African Americans*. Baltimore: Johns Hopkins University Press, 1999.

Kinkead, Gwen. *Chinatown: A Portrait of a Closed Society*. New York: HarperCollins, 1992.

Kitano, Harry H. L. *Generations and Identity: The Japanese American*. Needham Heights, Mass.: Ginn Press, 1993.

Kiyosaki, Wayne S. *A Spy in Their Midst: The World War II Struggle of a Japanese-American Hero*. Lanham: Madison Books, 1995.

Kiyota, Minoru. *Beyond Loyalty: The Story of a Kibei*. Translated by Linda K. Keenan. Honolulu: University of Hawaii Press, 1997.

Knaefler, Tomi K. *Our House Divided: Seven Japanese American Families in World War II*. Honolulu: University of Hawaii Press, 1991.

Koltyk, Jo Ann. *New Pioneers in the Heartland: Hmong Life in Wisconsin*. Needham Heights, Mass.: Allyn and Bacon, 1998.

Koshy, Susan. *Desiring Orientals: Race, Sex, and the American Imaginary*. Stanford: Stanford University Press, 2005.

Kurashige, Lon. *Japanese American Celebration and Conflict: A History of Ethnic Identity and Festival in Los Angeles, 1934–1990*. Berkeley: University of California Press, 2002.

———, and Alice Yang Murray, eds. *Major Problems in Asian American History*. Boston: Houghton Mifflin, 2003.

Kwon, H. Y., and S. Kim, eds. *The Emerging Generation of Korean Americans*. Seoul: Kyoung Hee University Press, 1993.

Kwong, Peter. *Forbidden Workers: Illegal Chinese Immigrants and American Labor.* New York: New Press, 1997.

Lafreniere, Bree. *Music through the Dark: A Tale of Survival in Cambodia.* Honolulu: University of Hawaii Press, 2000.

Lai, Him Mark. *Becoming Chinese American: A History of Communities and Institutions.* Walnut Creek, Calif.: AltaMira Press, 2004.

Lal, Brij V., Doug Munro, and Edward D. Beechert, eds. *Planation Workers: Resistance and Accommodation.* Honolulu: University of Hawaii Press, 1993.

Lebra, Joyce C. *Women's Voices in Hawaii.* Niwot: University Press of Colorado, 1991.

Lee, Bill. *Chinese Playground: A Memoir.* San Francisco: Rhapsody Press, 1999.

Lee, Erika. *At America's Gates: Chinese Immigration during the Exclusion Era, 1882–1943.* Chapel Hill: University of North Carolina Press, 2003.

Lee, Helie. *Still Life with Rice: A Young American Woman Discovers the Life and Legacy of Her Korean Grandmother.* New York: Touchstone, 1996.

Lee, James K. *Urban Triage: Race and the Fictions of Multiculturalism.* Minneapolis: University of Minnesota Press, 2004.

Lee, Jennifer. *Civility in the City: Blacks, Jews, and Koreans in Urban America.* Cambridge: Harvard University Press, 2002.

Lee, Joann F. J., ed. *Asian American Experiences in the United States: Oral Histories of First to Fourth Generation Americans from China, the Philippines, Japan, India, the Pacific Islands, Vietnam and Cambodia.* Jefferson, N.C.: McFarland, 1991.

Lee, Josephine. *Performing Asian America: Race and Ethnicity in the Contemporary Stage.* Philadelphia: Temple University Press, 1997.

———, Imogene L. Lim, and Yuko Matsukawa, eds. *Re-Collecting Early Asian America: Essays in Cultural History.* Philadelphia: Temple University Press, 2002.

Lee, Lee C., and Nolan W. S. Zane, eds. *Handbook of Asian American Psychology.* Thousand Oaks: Sage, 1998.

Lee, Rachel C. *The Americas of Asian American Literature: Gendered Fictions of Nation and Transnation.* Princeton: Princeton University Press, 1999.

———, and Sau-ling C. Wong, eds. *Asian America.Net: Ethnicity, Nationalism, and Cyberspace.* New York: Routledge, 2003.

Lee, Robert G. *Orientals: Asians in Popular Culture.* Philadelphia: Temple University Press, 1999.

Lee, Stacy J. *Unraveling the Model Minority Stereotype: Listening to Asian American Youth.* New York: Columbia University Teachers College Press, 1996.

Leonard, Karen I. *Making Ethnic Choices: California's Punjabi Mexican Americans.* Philadelphia: Temple University Press, 1992.

———. *Muslims in the United States: The State of Research.* New York: Russell Sage Foundation, 2003.

———. *The South Asian Americans.* Westport: Greenwood Press, 1997.

Leong, Russell, ed. *Asian American Sexualities: Dimensions of the Gay and Lesbian Experience.* New York: Routledge, 1996.

———, ed. *Moving the Image: Independent Asian Pacific American Media Arts.* Los Angeles: University of California, Los Angeles, Asian American Studies Center and Visual Communications, 1991.

Lessinger, Johann. *From the Ganges to the Hudson: Indian Immigrants in New York City.* Boston: Allyn and Bacon, 1995.

Levine, Ellen. *A Fence away from Freedom: Japanese Americans and World War II.* New York: G. P. Putnam's Sons, 1995.

Levitt, Peggy, and Mary C. Waters, eds. *The Changing Face of Home: The Transnational Lives of the Second Generation.* New York: Russell Sage Foundation, 2002.

Li, David L. *Imagining the Nation: Asian American Literature and Cultural Consent.* Stanford: Stanford University Press, 1998.

Lien, Pei-te. *The Making of Asian America Through Political Participation.* Philadelphia: Temple University Press, 2001.

———. *The Political Participation of Asian Americans: Voting Behavior in Southern California.* New York: Garland, 1997.

Lim, Christina M., and Sheldon H. Lim. *In the Shadow of the Tiger: The 407th Air Service Squadron, 14th Air Service Group, 14th Air Force, World War II.* N.p.: Veterans of the 407th Air Service Squadron, 1993.

Lim, Shirley G. L., ed. *Approaches to Teaching Kingston's* The Woman Warrior. New York: Modern Language Association of America, 1991.

———, and Amy Ling, eds. *Reading the Literatures of Asian America.* Philadelphia: Temple University Press, 1992.

———, Larry E. Smith, and Wimal Dissanayake, eds. *Transnational Asia Pacific: Gender, Culture, and the Public Sphere.* Urbana: University of Illinois Press, 1999.

Lim-Hing, Sharon, ed. *The Very Inside: An Anthology of Writing by Asian and Pacific Islander Lesbian and Bisexual Women.* Toronto: Sister Vision Press, 1994.

Lin, Jan. *Reconstructing Chinatown: Ethnic Enclave, Global Change.* Minneapolis: University of Minnesota Press, 1998.

Ling, Amy, ed. *Yellow Light: The Flowering of Asian American Arts.* Philadelphia: Temple University Press, 1999.

Ling, Huping. *Chinese St. Louis: From Enclave to Cultural Community.* Philadelphia: Temple University Press, 2004.

———. *Surviving on Gold Mountain: A History of Chinese American Women and Their Lives.* Albany: SUNY Press, 1998.

Ling, Jinqi. *Narrating Nationalisms: Ideology and Form in Asian American Literature.* New York: Oxford University Press, 1998.

Liu, Eric. *The Accidental Asian: Notes of a Native Speaker.* New York: Random House, 1998.

Long, Lynellyn D. *Ban Vinai: The Refugee Camp.* New York: Columbia University Press, 1993.

Long, Patrick D. P., with Laura Richard. *The Dream Shattered: Vietnamese Gangs in America.* Boston: Northeastern University Press, 1996.

Loo, Chalsa M. *Chinatown: Most Time, Hard Time.* New York: Praeger, 1992.

Lott, Juanita T. *Asian Americans: From Racial Category to Multiple Identities.* Walnut Creek, Calif.: AltaMira Press, 1997.

Louie, Miriam C. Y. *Sweatshop Warriors: Immigrant Women Workers Take on the Global Factory.* Boston: South End Press, 2001.

Louie, Steve, and Glenn Omatsu. *Asian Americans: The Movement and the Moment.* Los

Angeles: University of California, Los Angeles, Asian American Studies Center Press, 2001.

Louie, Vivian S. *Immigration, Education, and Opportunity among Chinese Americans.* Stanford: Stanford University Press, 2004.

Lowe, Lisa. *Immigrant Acts: On Asian American Cultural Studies.* Durham: Duke University Press, 1996.

Lundell, I. G. Kim. *Bridging the Gaps: Contextualization among Korean Nazarene Churches in America.* New York: Peter Lang, 1995.

Ma, Laurence J. C., and Carolyn Cartier. *The Chinese Diaspora: Space, Place, Mobility, and Identity.* Lanham: Rowman and Littlefield, 2003.

Ma, Sheng-mei. *Immigrant Subjectivities in Asian American and Asian Diaspora Literatures.* Albany: SUNY Press, 1998.

MacDonald, Jeffrey L. *Transnational Aspects of Iu-Mien Refugee Identity.* New York: Garland, 1997.

Machida, Margo, Vishakha N. Desai, and John K. W. Tchen. *Asia/America: Identities in Contemporary Asian American Art.* New York: New Press, 1994.

Mackey, Mike. *Heart Mountain: Life in Wyoming's Concentration Camp.* Powell: Western History, 2000.

———, ed. *Remembering Heart Mountain: Essays on Japanese American Internment in Wyoming.* Powell: Western History, 1998.

Maira, Sunaina M. *Desis in the House: Indian American Youth Culture in New York City.* Philadelphia: Temple University Press, 2002.

———, and Rajini Srikanth, eds. *Contours of the Heart: South Asians Map North America.* New York: Asian American Writers' Workshop, 1996.

Maki, Mitchell T., Harry H. L. Kitano, and S. Megan Berthold. *Achieving the Impossible Dream: How Japanese Americans Obtained Redress.* Urbana: University of Illinois Press, 1999.

Manalansan, Martin F., IV. *Global Divas: Filipino Gay Men in the Diaspora.* Durham: Duke University Press, 2003.

———, ed. *Cultural Compass: Ethnographic Explorations of Asian America.* Philadelphia: Temple University Press, 2000.

Mar, M. Elaine. *Paper Daughter: A Memoir.* New York: HarperCollins, 1999.

Marchetti, Gina. *Romance and the "Yellow Peril": Race, Sex, and Discursive Strategy in Hollywood Fiction.* Berkeley: University of California Press, 1994.

Mast, Robert H., and Anne B. Mast. *Autobiography of Protest in Hawai'i.* Honolulu: University Press of Hawaii, 1996.

Matsumoto, Valerie. *Farming the Home Place: A Japanese American Community in California, 1919–1982.* Ithaca: Cornell University Press, 1993.

Matsuoka, Fumitaka. *Out of Silence: Emerging Themes in Asian American Churches.* Cleveland: United Church Press, 1995.

McAdoo, Harriette P., ed. *Family Ethnicity: Strength in Diversity.* Newbury Park: Sage, 1993.

McClain, Charles J. *In Search of Equality: The Chinese Struggle against Discrimination in Nineteenth-Century America.* Berkeley: University of California Press, 1994.

McKelvey, Robert S. *The Dust of Life: America's Children Abandoned in Vietnam.* Seattle: University of Washington Press, 1999.

———. *A Gift of Barbed Wire: America's Allies Abandoned in South Vietnam.* Seattle: University of Washington Press, 2002.

McKeown, Adam. *Chinese Migrant Networks and Cultural Change: Peru, Chicago, Hawaii, 1900–1936.* Chicago: University of Chicago Press, 2001.

Min, Pyong Gap. *Caught in the Middle: Korean Communities in New York and Los Angeles.* Berkeley: University of California Press, 1996.

———. *Changes and Conflicts: Korean Immigrant Families in New York.* Boston: Allyn and Bacon, 1998.

———, ed. *Asian Americans: Contemporary Trends and Issues.* Newbury Park: Sage, 1995.

———, ed. *The Second Generation: Ethnic Identity among Asian Americans.* Walnut Creek, Calif.: AltaMira Press, 2002.

———, and Jung Ha Kim, eds. *Religions in Asian America: Building Faith Communities.* Walnut Creek, Calif.: AltaMira Press, 2002.

———, and Rose Kim, eds. *Struggle for Ethnic Identity: Narratives by Asian American Professionals.* Walnut Creek, Calif.: AltaMira Press, 1999.

Mokuau, Noreen, ed. *Handbook of Social Services for Asian and Pacific Islanders.* Westport: Greenwood Press, 1991.

Monrayo, Angeles. *Tomorrow's Memories: A Diary, 1924–1928.* Honolulu: University of Hawaii Press, 2003.

Moore, Brenda L. *Serving Our Country: Japanese American Women in the Military during World War II.* New Brunswick: Rutgers University Press, 2003.

Morimoto, Toyotomi. *Japanese Americans and Cultural Continuity: Maintaining Language and Heritage.* New York: Garland, 1997.

Morrison, Gayle L. *Sky Is Falling: An Oral History of the CIA's Evacuation of the Hmong from Laos.* Jefferson, N.C.: McFarland, 1999.

Moy, James S. *Marginal Sights: Staging the Chinese in America.* Iowa City: University of Iowa Press, 1993.

Muntarbhorn, Vitit. *The Status of Refugees in Asia.* New York: Oxford University Press, 1992.

Murata, Kiyoaki. *An Enemy among Friends.* Tokyo: Kodansha International, 1991.

Nagata, Donna K. *Legacy of Injustice: Exploring the Cross-Generational Impact of the Japanese American Internment.* New York: Plenum, 1993.

Nakane, Kazuko. *Nothing Left in My Hand: An Early Japanese American Community in California's Pajaro Valley.* Seattle: Young Pine, 1983.

Nakasone, Ronald Y., ed. *Okinawan Diaspora.* Honolulu: University of Hawaii Press, 2002.

Nakayama, Thomas K., ed. *Asian Pacific American Genders and Sexualities.* Tempe: Arizona State University Press, 1999.

Nelson, Emmanuel S. *Bharati Mukherjee: Critical Perspectives.* New York: Garland, 1993.

———, ed. *Reworlding: The Literature of the Indian Diaspora.* New York: Greenwood Press, 1992.

Ng, David. *People on the Way: Asian North Americans Discovering Christ, Culture, and Community.* Valley Forge: Judson Press, 1996.

Ng, Franklin. *The Taiwanese Americans.* Westport: Greenwood Press, 1998.

———, ed. *Adaptation, Acculturation, and Transnational Ties among Asian Americans.* New York: Garland, 1998.

———, ed. *The Asian American Encyclopedia.* New York: M. Cavendish, 1995.

———, ed. *Asian American Family Life and Community.* New York: Garland, 1998.

———, ed. *Asian American Interethnic Relations and Politics.* New York: Garland, 1998.

———, ed. *Asian American Issues Relating to Labor, Economics, and Socioeconomic Status.* New York: Garland, 1998.

———, ed. *Asian American Women and Gender.* New York: Garland, 1998.

———, ed. *Asians in America: The Peoples of East, Southeast, and South Asia in American Life and Culture.* New York: Garland, 1998.

———, ed. *The History and Immigration of Asian Americans.* New York: Garland, 1998.

——— et al., eds. *New Visions in Asian American Studies: Diversity, Community, Power.* Pullman: Washington State University Press, 1994.

Ngai, Mae M. *Impossible Subjects: Illegal Aliens and the Making of Modern America.* Princeton: Princeton University Press, 2004.

Nguyen, Kien. *The Unwanted: A Memoir.* Boston: Little, Brown, 2001.

Nguyen, Viet Thanh. *Race and Resistance: Literature and Politics in Asian America.* New York: Oxford University Press, 2002.

Niiya, Brian, ed. *Japanese American History: An A-to-Z Reference from 1868 to the Present.* New York: Facts on File, 1993.

Nomura, Gail M., and Louis Fiset, eds. *Nisei in the Pacific Northwest: Japanese Americans and Japanese Canadians in the Twentieth Century.* Seattle: Center for the Study of the Pacific Northwest in association with the University of Washington Press, 2005.

O'Brien, David J., and Stephen S. Fugita. *The Japanese American Experience.* Bloomington: Indiana University Press, 1991.

Odo, Franklin. *No Sword to Bury: Japanese Americans in Hawaii during World War II.* Philadelphia: Temple University Press, 2004.

———, ed. *Columbia Documentary History of the Asian American Experience.* New York: Columbia University Press, 2003.

Okamura, Jonathan Y. *Imagining the Filipino American Diaspora: Transnational Relations, Identities, and Communities.* New York: Garland, 1998.

———, Amefil R. Agbayani, and Melinda T. Kerkvliet, eds. *The Filipino American Experience in Hawai'i: In Commemoration of the Eighty-fifth Anniversary of Filipino Immigration to Hawaii.* Vol. 33 of *Social Process in Hawaii.* Honolulu: University of Hawaii Sociology Department, 1991.

Okihiro, Gary Y. *Cane Fires: The Anti-Japanese Movement in Hawaii, 1865–1945.* Philadelphia: Temple University Press, 1991.

———. *Margins and Mainstreams: Asians in American History and Culture.* Seattle: University of Washington Press, 1994.

———. *Storied Lives: Japanese American Students and World War II.* Seattle: University of Washington Press, 1996.

———. *Teaching Asian American History.* Washington: American Historical Association, 1997.

——— et al., eds. *Privileging Positions: The Sites of Asian American Studies.* Pullman: Washington State University Press, 1995.

Ong, Aihwa. *Buddha Is Hiding: Refugees, Citizenship, the New America.* Berkeley: University of California Press, 2003.

———. *Flexible Citizenship: The Cultural Logics of Transnationality.* Durham: Duke University Press, 1999.

Ong, Paul, and Suzanne Hee. *Losses in the Los Angeles Civil Unrest, April 29–May 1, 1992: Lists of the Damaged Properties.* Los Angeles: University of California, Los Angeles, Center for Pacific Rim Studies, 1993.

Ong, Paul M., ed. *Impacts of Affirmative Action: Policies and Consequences in California.* Walnut Creek, Calif.: AltaMira Press, 1999.

———, ed. *The State of Asian Pacific America: Economic Diversity, Issues and Policies.* Los Angeles: Asian American Public Policy Institute and University of California, Los Angeles, Asian American Studies Center, 1994.

———, ed. *Transforming Race Relations: A Public Policy Report.* Los Angeles: Asian Pacific American Public Policy Institute and University of California, Los Angeles, Asian American Studies Center, 2000.

———, Lucie Cheng, and Edna Bonacich, eds. *The New Asian Immigration in Los Angeles and Global Restructuring.* Philadelphia: Temple University Press, 1994.

——— et al. *Beyond Asian American Poverty: Community Economic Development Policies and Strategies.* Los Angeles: Leadership Education for Asian Pacifics, Asian American Public Policy Institute, 1993.

Origins and Destinations: Forty-one Essays on Chinese America. Los Angeles: Chinese Historical Society of Southern California and University of California, Los Angeles, Asian American Studies Center, 1994.

Ouk, Vibol, and Charles M. Simon. *Goodnight Cambodia: Forbidden History.* Santa Cruz: Charles Martin Simon, 1997, 1998.

Palumbo-Liu, David. *Asian/American: Historical Crossings of a Racial Frontier.* Stanford: Stanford University Press, 1999.

Park, Clara C., and Marilyn M. Y. Chi, eds. *Asian American Education: Prospects and Challenges.* Granby, Mass.: Bergin and Garvey, 1999.

Park, John S. W. *Elusive Citizenship: Immigration, Asian Americans, and the Paradox of Civil Rights.* New York: New York University Press, 2004.

———, and Edward J. W. Park. *Contemporary Immigration Policies and the Shaping of Asian American Communities.* New York: Routledge, 2004.

Park, Kyeyoung. *The Korean American Dream: Immigrants and Small Business in New York City.* Ithaca: Cornell University Press, 1997.

Parreñas, Rhacel S. *Children of Global Migrations: Transnational Families and Gendered Woes.* Stanford: Stanford University Press, 2005.

———. *Servants of Globalization: Women, Migration, and Domestic Work.* Stanford: Stanford University Press, 2001.

Patterson, Wayne. *The Ilse: First-Generation Korean Immigrants in Hawai'i, 1903–1973.* Honolulu: University of Hawaii Press, 2000.

Peffer George A. *"If They Don't Bring Their Women Here": Chinese Female Immigration before Exclusion.* Urbana: University of Illinois Press, 1999.

Pfaff, Tim. *Hmong in America: Journey from a Secret War.* Eau Claire: Chippewa Valley Museum Press, 1995.

Posadas, Barbara M. *The Filipino Americans.* Westport: Greenwood Press, 1999.

Prashad, Vijay. *The Karma of Brown Folk.* Minneapolis: University of Minnesota Press, 2000.

Prebish, Charles S., and Kenneth K. Tanaka, eds. *The Faces of Buddhism in America.* Berkeley: University of California Press, 1998.

Quincy, Keith. *Harvesting Pa Chay's Wheat: The Hmong and America's Secret War in Laos.* Spokane: Eastern Washington University Press, 2000.

Rafael, Vicente, ed. *Discrepant Histories: Translocal Essays on Filipino Cultures.* Philadelphia: Temple University Press, 1995.

Ratliff, Sharon K. *Caring for Cambodian Americans: A Multidisciplinary Resource for the Helping Professions.* New York: Garland, 1997.

Reineke, John E. *The Filipino Piecemeal Sugar Strike of 1924–1925.* Honolulu: University of Hawaii Social Research Institute, 1996.

Revilla, Linda A. et al., eds. *Bearing Dreams, Shaping Visions: Asian Pacific American Perspectives.* Pullman: Washington State University Press, 1993.

Reyes, Adelaida. *Songs of the Caged, Songs of the Free: Music and the Vietnamese Refugee Experience.* Philadelphia: Temple University Press, 1999.

Rhee, Helen C. *The Korean-American Experience: A Detailed Analysis of How Well Korean-Americans Adjust to Life in the United States.* New York: Vantage Press, 1995.

Rhodes, Daisy C. *Passages to Paradise: Early Korean Immigrant Narratives from Hawai'i.* Los Angeles: Academica Koreana, 1998.

Robinson, Greg. *By Order of the President: FDR and the Internment of Japanese Americans.* Cambridge: Harvard University Press, 2001.

Robinson, W. Courtland. *Terms of Refuge: The Indochinese Exodus and the International Response.* London: Zed Books, 1998.

Root, Maria P. P., ed. *Filipino Americans: Transformation and Identity.* Thousand Oaks: Sage, 1997.

———, ed. *Racially Mixed People in America.* Newbury Park, Calif: Sage, 1992.

Rudrappa, Sharmila. *Ethnic Routes to Becoming American: Indian Immigrants and the Cultures of Citizenship.* New Brunswick: Rutgers University Press, 2004.

Rustomji-Kerns, Roshni, ed. *Encounters: People of Asian Descent in the Americas.* Lanham: Rowman and Littlefield, 1999.

Rutledge, Paul J. *The Vietnamese Experience in America.* Bloomington: Indiana University Press, 1992.

Saiki, Patsy S. *Early Japanese Immigrants in Hawaii.* Honolulu: University of Hawaii Press, 1993.

Saito, Leland T. *Race and Politics: Asian Americans, Latinos, and Whites in a Los Angeles Suburb.* Urbana: University of Illinois Press, 1998.

Salyer, Lucy E. *Laws Harsh as Tigers: Chinese Immigrants and the Shaping of Modern Immigration Law.* Chapel Hill: University of North Carolina Press, 1995.

San Juan, Epifanio, Jr. *From Exile to Diaspora: Versions of the Filipino Experience in the United States.* Boulder: Westview Press, 1998.

———. *The Philippine Temptation: Dialectics of Philippines–U.S. Literary Relations.* Philadelphia: Temple University Press, 1996.

———, ed. *On Becoming Filipino: Selected Writings of Carlos Bulosan.* Philadelphia: Temple University Press, 1995.

Sarasohn, Eileen S. *Issei Women: Echoes from Another Frontier.* Palo Alto: Pacific Books, 1998.

Sawada, Mitziko. *Tokyo Life, New York Dreams: Urban Japanese Visions of America, 1890–1924.* Berkeley: University of California Press, 1996.

Scharlin, Craig, and Lilia V. Villaneuva. *Philip Vera Cruz: A Personal History of Filipino Immigrants and the Farmworkers Movement.* Los Angeles: University of California, Los Angeles, Labor History Center and Asian American Studies Center, 1992.

Schmidt, Garbi. *Islam in Urban America: Sunni Muslims in Chicago.* Philadelphia: Temple University Press, 2004.

See, Lisa. *On Gold Mountain: The One-Hundred-Year Odyssey of a Chinese-American Family.* New York: St. Martin's Press, 1995.

Shah, Nayan. *Contagious Divides: Epidemics and Race in San Francisco's Chinatown.* Berkeley: University of California Press, 2001.

Shah, Nita. *The Ethnic Strife: A Study of Asian Indian Women in the United States.* New York: Pinkerton and Thomas, 1993.

Shah, Sonia, ed. *Dragon Ladies: Asian American Feminists Breathe Fire.* Boston: South End Press, 1997.

Shankar, Lavina D., and Rajini Srikanth, eds. *A Part, Yet Apart: South Asians in Asian America.* Philadelphia: Temple University Press, 1998.

Shimabukuro, Robert S. *Born in Seattle: The Campaign for Japanese American Redress.* Seattle: University of Washington Press, 2001.

Shimakawa, Karen. *National Abjection: The Asian American Body Onstage.* Durham: Duke University Press, 2002.

Shimizu, Celine P. *The Hypersexuality of Race: Screening Asian Women in the United States.* Durham: Duke University Press, 2005.

Simpson, Caroline C. *An Absent Presence: Japanese Americans in Postwar American Culture, 1945–1960.* Durham: Duke University Press, 2001.

Smith, Susan L. *Japanese American Midwives: Culture, Community, and Health Politics.* Urbana: University of Illinois Press, 2005.

Smith-Hefner, Nancy. *Khmer American: Identity and Moral Education in a Diasporic Community.* Berkeley: University of California Press, 1999.

Spickard, Paul R. *Japanese Americans: The Formation and Transformation of an Ethnic Group.* Boston: Twayne, 1996.

———, Joanne L. Rondilla, and Debbie H. Wright, eds. *Pacific Diaspora: Island Peoples in the United States and Across the Pacific.* Honolulu: University of Hawaii Press, 2002.

Srikanth, Rajini. *The World Next Door: South Asian American Literature and the Idea of America.* Philadelphia: Temple University Press, 2004.

Storti, Craig. *Incident at Bitter Creek: The Story of the Rock Springs Chinese Massacre.* Ames: Iowa State University Press, 1991.

Streed, Sarah. *Leaving the House of Ghosts: Cambodian Refugees in the American Midwest.* Jefferson, N.C.: McFarland, 2002.

Suh, Sharon A. *Being Buddhist in a Christian World: Gender and Community in a Korean American Temple.* Seattle: University of Washington Press, 2004.

Sumida, Stephen H. *And the View from the Shore: Literary Traditions of Hawai'i.* Honolulu: University of Hawaii Press, 1991.

Takabuki, Matsuo. *An Unlikely Revolutionary: Matsuo Takabuki and the Making of Modern Hawai'i.* Honolulu: University of Hawaii Press, 1998.

Takagi, Dana Y. *The Retreat from Race: Asian-American Admissions and Racial Politics.* New Brunswick: Rutgers University Press, 1992.

Takahashi, Jerrold. *Nisei/Sansei: Shifting Japanese American Identities and Politics.* Philadelphia: Temple University Press, 1997.

Takaki, Ronald T. *A Different Mirror: A History of Multicultural America.* Boston: Little, Brown, 1993.

———. *Double Victory: A Multicultural History of America in World War II.* Boston: Little, Brown, 2000.

Takezawa, Yasuko I. *Breaking the Silence: Redress and Japanese American Ethnicity.* Ithaca: Cornell University Press, 1995.

Tamura, Eileen H. *Americanization, Acculturation, and Ethnic Identity: The Nisei Generation in Hawaii.* Urbana: University of Illinois Press, 1994.

Tamura, Linda. *The Hood River Issei: An Oral History of Japanese Settlers in Oregon's Hood River Valley.* Urbana: University of Illinois Press, 1993.

Tatla, Darshan S. *The Sikh Diaspora: The Search for Statehood.* Seattle: University of Washington Press, 1999.

Taylor, Sandra C. *Jewel of the Desert: Japanese American Internment at Topaz.* Berkeley: University of California Press, 1993.

Tchen, John K. W. *New York before Chinatown: Orientalism and the Shaping of American Culture, 1776–1882.* Baltimore: Johns Hopkins University Press, 1999.

Tenhula, John, ed. *Voices from Southeast Asia: The Refugee Experience in the United States.* New York: Holmes and Meier, 1991.

Thao, Paoze. *Mong Education at the Crossroads.* Lanham, Md.: University Press of America, 1999.

Tomita, Mary K. *Dear Miye: Letters Home from Japan, 1936–1946,* edited and with an introduction by Robert G. Lee. Stanford: Stanford University Press, 1995.

Tong, Benson. *The Chinese Americans.* Westport: Greenwood Press, 2000.

———. *Unsubmissive Women: Chinese Prostitutes in Nineteenth-Century San Francisco.* Norman: University of Oklahoma Press, 1994.

Trask, Haunani K. *From a Native Daughter: Colonialism and Sovereignty in Hawai'i.* Monroe, Me.: Common Courage Press, 1993.

Trueba, Henry T., Lilly Cheng, and Kenji Ima. *Myth or Reality: Adaptive Strategies of Asian Americans in California.* Washington: Falmer Press, 1993.

———, and Yali Zou. *Power in Education: The Case of Miao University Students and Its Significance for American Education.* Washington: Falmer Press, 1994.

Tsuchida, J. Nobuya. *Reflections: Memoirs of Japanese American Women in Minnesota.* Covina, Calif.: Pacific Asia Press, 1994.

Tsukakawa, Mayumi, ed. *They Painted from Their Hearts: Pioneer Asian American Artists.* Seattle: Wing Luke Asian Museum, 1994.

Tuan, Mia. *Forever Foreigners or Honorary Whites? The Asian Ethnic Experience Today.* New Brunswick: Rutgers University Press, 1998.

Uba, Laura. *Asian Americans: Personality Patterns, Identity, and Mental Health.* New York: Guilford Press, 1994.

Ung, Luong. *First They Killed My Father: A Daughter of Cambodia Remembers.* New York: HarperCollins, 2000.

Uyeda, Clifford I. *Suspended: Growing Up Asian in America.* San Francisco: National Japanese American Historical Society, 2000.

———, and Barry Saiki, eds. *The Pacific War and Peace: Americans of Japanese Ancestry in Military Intelligence Service, 1941 to 1952.* San Francisco: Military Intelligence Service Association of Northern California and the National Japanese American Historical Society, 1991.

Van Sant, John. *Pacific Pioneers: Japanese Journeys to America and Hawaii, 1850–80.* Urbana: University of Illinois Press, 2000.

Van Valkenblurg, Carol B. *An Alien Place: The Fort Missoula, Montana, Detention Camp, 1941–1944.* Missoula: Pictorial Histories, 1995.

Vo, Linda T. *Mobilizing an Asian American Community.* Philadelphia: Temple University Press, 2004.

———, and Marian Sciachitano, eds. *Asian American Women: The "Frontiers" Reader.* Lincoln: University of Nebraska Press, 2004.

———, and Rick Bonus, eds. *Contemporary Asian American Communities: Intersections and Divergences.* Philadelphia: Temple University Press, 2002.

Wakamatsu, Jack K. *Silent Warriors: A Memoir of America's 442nd Regimental Combat Team.* New York: Vantage Press. 1995.

Walker-Moffat, Wendy. *The Other Side of the Asian American Success Story.* San Francisco: Jossey-Bass, 1995.

Wang, Ling-chi, and Wang Gungwu, eds. *The Chinese Diaspora: Selected Essays.* 2 vols. Singapore: Times Academic Press, 1998.

Wang, Xinyang. *Surviving the City: The Chinese Immigrant Experience in New York City, 1890–1970.* Lanham, Md.: Rowman and Littlefield, 2001.

Warner, R. Stephen, and Judith G. Wittner, eds. *Gatherings in Diaspora: Religious Communities and the New Immigration.* Philadelphia: Temple University Press, 1998.

Wegars, Priscilla, ed. *Hidden Heritage: Historical Archaeology of the Overseas Chinese.* Amityville: Baywood, 1993.

Wei, William. *The Asian American Movement.* Philadelphia: Temple University Press, 1993.

Welaratna, Usha. *Beyond the Killing Fields: Voices of Nine Cambodian Survivors in America.* Stanford: Stanford University Press, 1993.

Whelchel, Toshio. *From Pearl Harbor to Saigon: Japanese American Soldiers and the Vietnam War.* London: Verso Press, 1999.

White-Parks, Annette. *Sui Sin Far/Edith Maude Eaton: A Literary Biography.* Urbana: University of Illinois Press, 1995.

Williams, Raymond B. *Christian Pluralism in the United States: The Indian Immigrant Experience.* New York: Cambridge University Press, 1996.

Williams-Leon, Teresa K., and Cynthia L. Nakashima, eds. *The Sum of Our Parts: Mixed Heritage Asian Americans.* Philadelphia: Temple University Press, 2001.

Wilson, Rob, and Arif Dirlik, eds. *Asia/Pacific as Space of Cultural Production.* Durham: Duke University Press, 1995.

Women of South Asian Descent Collective, eds. *Our Feet Walk the Sky: Women of the South Asian Diaspora.* San Francisco: Aunt Lute Books, 1993.

Wong, K. Scott. *Americans First: Chinese Americans and the Second World War.* Cambridge: Harvard University Press, 2005.

———, and Sucheng Chan, eds. *Claiming America: Constructing Chinese American Identities during the Exclusion Era.* Philadelphia: Temple University Press, 1998.

Wong, Marie R. *Sweet Cakes, Long Journey: The Chinatowns of Portland, Oregon.* Seattle: University of Washington Press, 2004.

Wong, Sau-ling C. *Reading Asian American Literature: From Necessity to Extravagance.* Princeton: Princeton University Press, 1993.

———, ed. *Maxine Hong Kingston's* The Woman Warrior: *A Casebook.* New York: Oxford University Press, 1999.

Woo, Deborah. *Glass Ceilings and Asian Americans: The New Face of Workplace Barriers.* Walnut Creek, Calif.: AltaMira Press, 2000.

Wu, Diana T. L. *Asian Pacific Americans in the Workplace.* Walnut Creek, Calif.: AltaMira Press, 1997.

Wu, Jean Y. W., and Min Song, eds. *Asian American Studies: A Reader.* New Brunswick: Rutgers University Press, 2000.

Wyman, Nona M. *Chopstick Childhood: In a Town of Silver Spoons.* San Francisco: China Book and Periodicals, 1999.

Xing, Jun. *Asian America Through the Lens: History, Representations, and Identity.* Walnut Creek, Calif.: AltaMira Press, 1998.

———, and Lane R. Hirabayashi, eds. *Reversing the Lens: Ethnicity, Race, Gender, and Sexuality through Film.* Niwot: University Press of Colorado, 2003.

Yamamoto, Traise. *Masking Selves, Making Subjects: Japanese American Women, Identity, and the Body.* Berkeley: University of California Press, 1999.

Yee, Alfred. *Shopping at Giant Foods: Chinese American Supermarkets in Northern California.* Seattle: University of Washington Press, 2003.

Yin, Xiao-huang. *Chinese American Literature since the 1850s.* Urbana: University of Illinois Press, 2000.

———, and Peter H. Koehn, eds. *The Expanding Roles of Chinese Americans in U.S.-China Relations: Transnational Networks and Trans-Pacific Interactions.* Armonk: M. E. Sharpe, 2002.

Yoo, David K. *Growing Up Nisei: Race, Generation, and Culture among Japanese Americans of California, 1924–49.* Urbana: University of Illinois Press, 2000.

———, ed. *New Spiritual Homes: Religion and Asian Americans.* Honolulu: University of Hawaii Press, 1999.

Yoon, In-Jin. *On My Own: Korean Businesses and Race Relations in America.* Chicago: University of Chicago Press, 1997.

Yu, Diana. *Winds of Change: Korean Women in America.* Silver Spring: Women's Institute Press, 1991.

Yu, Henry. *Thinking Orientals: Migration, Contact, and Exoticism in Modern America.* New York: Oxford University Press, 2001.

Yu, Renqiu. *To Save China, to Save Ourselves: The Chinese Hand Laundry Alliance of New York.* Philadelphia: Temple University Press, 1992.

Yuh, Ji-Yeon. *Beyond the Shadow of Camptown: Korean Military Brides in America.* New York: New York University Press, 2002.

Yung, Judy. *Unbound Feet: A Social History of Chinese Women in San Francisco.* Berkeley: University of California Press, 1995.

———, ed. *Unbound Voices: A Documentary History of Chinese Women in San Francisco.* Berkeley: University of California Press, 1999.

Zane, Nolan W. S., David T. Takeuchi, and Kathleen N. J. Young, eds. *Confronting Critical Health Issues of Asian and Pacific Islander Americans.* Thousand Oaks: Sage, 1994.

Zelko, Frank. *Generation, Culture, and Prejudice: The Japanese American Decision to Cooperate with Evacuation and Internment during World War II.* Monash, Australia: Monash Publications in History, 1992.

Zhao, Xiaojian. *Remaking Chinese America: Immigration, Family, and Community, 1940–1965.* New Brunswick: Rutgers University Press, 2002.

Zhou, Min. *Chinatown: The Socioeconomic Potential of an Urban Enclave.* Philadelphia: Temple University Press, 1992.

———, and Carl L. Bankston III. *Growing Up American: Vietnamese Children Adapt to Life in the United States.* New York: Russell Sage Foundation, 1998.

———, and James V. Gatewood, eds. *Contemporary Asian America: A Multidisciplinary Reader.* New York: New York University Press, 2000.

Zhu, Luping. *A Chinaman's Chance: The Chinese on the Rocky Mountain Mining Frontier.* Niwot: University Press of Colorado, 1997.

Zia, Helen. *Asian American Dreams: The Emergence of an American People.* New York: Farrar, Straus, and Giroux, 2000.

Bibliographies

Alcantara, Ruben R., and Nancy S. Alconcel. *The Filipinos in Hawaii: An Annotated Bibliography.* Honolulu: University of Hawaii Social Science Research Institute, 1972.

Amerasia Journal. Annual bibliographies, 1977 to present.

Ashmun, Lawrence F. *Resettlement of Indochinese Refugees in the United States: A Selective and Annotated Bibliography.* DeKalb: Northern Illinois University Center for Southeast Asian Studies, 1983.

Asian American Studies Program, comp. *Asians in America: A Selected Annotated Bibliography—An Expansion and Revision.* Davis: University of California, Davis, Asian American Studies Program, 1983.

Chan, Sucheng. "Asian American Historiography." *Pacific Historical Review* 65, no. 3 (1996): 363–400.

———. "Asian Americans: A Selected Bibliography of Writings Published Since the 1960s." In *Reflections on Shattered Windows: Promises and Prospects for Asian American Studies,* edited by Gary Y. Okihiro et al., 214–37. Pullman: Washington State University Press, 1988.

———. "A Selected Bibliography and List of Films on the Vietnamese, Cambodian, and Laotian Experience in Southeast Asia and the United States," in *New Visions in Asian American Studies: Diversity, Community, Power,* edited by Franklin Ng et al., 63–110. Pullman: Washington State University Press, 1994.

———. "Selected Bibliography," in *Hmong Means Free: Life in Laos and America,* edited by Sucheng Chan, 247–64. Philadelphia: Temple University Press, 1994.

———. "Selected Bibliography," in *Survivors: Cambodian Refugees in the United States,* by Sucheng Chan, 277–311. Urbana: University of Illinois Press, 2004.

Cheung, King-Kok, and Stan Yogi. *Asian American Literature: An Annotated Bibliography.* New York: Modern Language Association of America, 1988.

Ebio, Raul et al. *Filipino Americans at the Crossroads—One Hundred Years of United States–Philippines Relations.* Los Angeles: University of California, Los Angeles, Asian American Studies Center, 1998.

Endo, Russell. "Asian American Bibliographic Resources, 1968–1988," in *Frontiers of Asian American Studies: Writing, Research, and Commentary,* edited by Gail M. Nomura et al., 317–38. Pullman: Washington State University Press, 1989.

Espiritu, Yen Le. *Vietnamese in America: An Annotated Bibliography of Materials in Los Angeles and Orange County Libraries.* Los Angeles: University of California, Los Angeles, Asian American Studies Center, 1988.

Felsman, J. Kirk et al. *Selected Bibliography on Indochinese Refugee Children and Adolescents.* Hanover, N.H.: Amerasian Project, 1985.

Frankel, Robert. *The Resettlement of Indochinese Refugees in the United States: A Selected Bibliography.* Washington: Indochina Refugee Action Center, 1980.

Friday, Chris. "Asian American Labor and Historical Interpretation." *Labor History* 35, no. 4 (1994): 524–46.

Fujimoto, Isao et al. *Asians in America: A Selected Annotated Bibliography.* Davis: University of California, Davis, Asian American Studies Program, 1983.

Gardner, Arthur L. *The Koreans in Hawaii: An Annotated Bibliography.* Honolulu: University of Hawaii Social Science Research Institute, 1970.

Hammond, Ruth E., and Glenn L. Hendricks, comps. *Southeast Asian Refugee Youth: An Annotated Bibliography.* Minneapolis: University of Minnesota Center for Urban and Regional Affairs, 1988.

Hansen, Gladys, and William F. Heintz. *The Chinese in California: A Bibliographic History.* Portland: Richard Abel, 1972.

Hoang, Trang et al. *Emergence of the Vietnamese American Communities: A Working Bibliography of Works Including Selected Annotated Citations.* Los Angeles: University of California, Los Angeles, Asian American Studies Center, 1996.

Hune, Shirley. "Asian American and Pacific Islander American Women as Historical Subjects: A Bibliographic Essay," in *Asian/Pacific Islander Women: A Historical Anthology,* edited by Shirley Hune and Gail M. Nomura, 385–400. New York: New York University Press, 2003.

———. *Pacific Migration to the United States: Trends and Themes in Historical and Sociological Literature.* Washington: Smithsonian Institution, 1977.

———. *Teaching Asian American Women's History.* Washington: American Historical Association, 1997.

Ichioka, Yuji et al. *A Buried Past: An Annotated Bibliography of the Japanese American Research Project Collection.* Berkeley: University of California Press, 1974.

Kim, Hyung-chan, ed. *Asian American Studies: An Annotated Bibliography and Research Guide.* Westport: Greenwood Press, 1989.

Kim, Nancy I. Y. "'In Her Eyes': An Annotated Bibliography of Video Documentaries on Asian/Pacific Islander American Women," in *Asian/Pacific Islander American Women:*

A Historical Anthology, edited by Shirley Hune and Gail M. Nomura, 401–16. New York: New York University Press, 2003.

Kitano, Harry H. L. *Asians in America: A Selected Bibliography for Use in Social Work Education.* New York: Council on Social Work Education, 1971.

Lai, Him Mark. *A History Reclaimed: An Annotated Bibliography of Chinese Language Materials on the Chinese of America.* Los Angeles: University of California, Los Angeles, Asian American Studies Center, 1986.

Liu, Kwang-Ching. *Americans and Chinese: A Historical Essay and a Bibliography.* Cambridge: Harvard University Press, 1962.

Lowe, C. H. *The Chinese in Hawaii: A Bibliographic Survey.* Taipei: China Printing, 1972.

Marston, John. *An Annotated Bibliography of Cambodia and Cambodian Refugees.* Minneapolis: University of Minnesota, Center for Urban and Regional Affairs, 1987.

Matsuda, Mitsugu. *The Japanese in Hawaii: An Annotated Bibliography of Japanese Americans,* revised by Dennis M. Ogawa with Jerry Y. Fujioka. Honolulu: University of Hawaii Social Science and Linguistics Institute, 1975.

Morishima, James K. et al. *Handbook of Asian American/Pacific Islander Mental Health.* Washington: U.S. Department of Health, Education and Welfare, 1979.

Ng, Pearl. *Writings on the Chinese in California.* San Francisco: R and E Research Associates, 1971.

Norell, Irene P. *Literature of the Filipino-American in the United States: A Selective and Annotated Bibliography.* San Francisco: R and E Research Associates, 1976.

Okihiro, Gary Y. *The Columbia Guide to Asian American History.* New York: Columbia University Press, 2001.

———. *Teaching Asian American History.* Washington: American Historical Association, 1997.

Peterson, S. C. et al. *An Annotated Bibliography on Refugee Mental Health.* Minneapolis: University of Minnesota Mental Health Technical Assistance Center, 1989.

Saito, Shiro. *Filipinos Overseas: A Bibliography.* Staten Island: Center for Migration Studies, 1977.

Sakata, Yasuo. *Fading Footsteps of the Issei: An Annotated Check List of the Manuscript Holdings of the Japanese American Research Project Collection.* Los Angeles: University of California, Los Angeles, Asian American Studies Center, 1992.

Singh, Jane et al., eds. *South Asians in North America: An Annotated and Selected Bibliography.* Berkeley: University of California, Berkeley, Center for South and Southeast Asian Studies, 1988.

Smith, Christina J., comp. *The Hmong: An Annotated Bibliography.* Minneapolis: University of Minnesota Southeast Asian Refugee Studies Project, 1988.

Southeast Asian Refugee Studies Project. *Bibliography of the Hmong,* 2d ed. Minneapolis: University of Minnesota Southeast Asian Refugee Studies Project, 1983.

Spickard, Paul R., and Debbie Hippolite Wright. *Pacific Islander Americans: An Annotated Bibliography of the Social Sciences.* Laie, Hawaii: Brigham Young University Institute for Polynesian Studies, 1995.

Tamura, Eileen H. "Using the Past to Inform the Future: An Historiography of Hawaii's Asian and Pacific Islander Americans." *Amerasia Journal* 26, no. 1 (2000): 55–85.

Tatla, Darshan S. *Sikhs in North America: An Annotated Bibliography.* Westport: Green-wood Press, 1991.

U.S. Department of Health and Human Services. *An Annotated Bibliography on Refugee Mental Health.* Washington: Government Printing Office, 1989.

Williams, C. L. *An Annotated Bibliography on Refugee Mental Health.* Rockville: National Institutes of Mental Health, 1987.

Wong, Sau-ling C., and Stephen H. Sumida, eds. *A Resource Guide to Asian American Literature.* New York: Modern Language Association of America, 2001.

Yang, Eun Sik, and Gary Wanki Park, comps. *Korean Americans: An Annotated Bibliography of Korean and English Language Materials.* Los Angeles: University of California, Los Angeles, Asian American Studies Center, 1992.

Yoshitomi, Joan et al. *Asians in the Northwest: An Annotated Bibliography.* Seattle: University of Washington Northwest Asian American Studies Research Group, 1978.

Young, Nancy Foon. *The Chinese in Hawaii: An Annotated Bibliography.* Honolulu: University of Hawaii Social Science Research Institute, 1973.

Zimmerman, Diana. *Refugees: Holdings of the Center for Migration Studies Library/Archives.* Staten Island: Center for Migration Studies, 1987.

Index

academic: culture, 54; discourse, 83, 86, 88, 102, 117, 129; establishment, 166, 187; freedom, 30, 154, 168; legitimacy or legitimization, 29, 35, 154; standards, 84; training, 176. *See also* graduate degree/s, education, school/s, study/studies, or training; professional/s, training; work, 16

acculturation, 50

activism or activist/s, political or social, 7, 30, 50, 54, 56–57, 59, 120, 147, 166, 170, 173, 175, 183, 189, 191–94, 196, 201–2. *See also* student/s, activism or activist/s

administrator/s, 21, 25, 31, 40, 45, 56–57, 81, 119, 135, 138, 149, 152, 154–57, 159, 161, 167, 170, 172, 174–75, 185–86, 192

affirmative action, 151, 153, 155, 157, 159, 163, 186

Africa, 54, 69, 139

African/s, 53

African American/s, 3, 48, 50, 54, 74, 78, 107, 122, 134, 172, 190, 194, 201–2; student/s, 74. *See also* student/s, minority

African American or Afro-American studies, 5, 40, 57, 121

agency/agents, 37, 55–56, 148–49

Alamaguer, Tomas, 54

Almirol, Edwin B., 36

Altbach, Philip G., 151

Althusser, Louis, 182

Amerasian, 171

Amerasia Journal, 39, 119, 134

America Is in the Heart, 8

American Friends Service Committee, 202

American/s, 31, 52–53, 71, 83, 113, 134, 137, 139–41, 177, 182, 189, 192–93, 196; creed, 196; dream, 140; studies, 177, 182, 192–93; West, 52. *See also* United States, all entries

the Americas, 54

analytical, conceptual, or theoretical framework/s, 1, 41, 55, 147, 176, 185, 193

Anglo-American/s. *See* Euro or European American/s

anti-Asian environment, movements, or sentiments, 32, 37, 53

anti-Chinese movement, 7

anti-Filipino movement, 7

anti-immigrant groups, 64

anti-Indian movement, 7

anti-intellectual/ism, 16, 189

anti-Japanese movement, 7

anti-racist critique, 194

anti-Vietnam War movement, 54, 56, 166, 202

articulate or articulation, 127–28

Asia, 16, 42, 54, 66, 75, 97–98, 104, 126, 188–89. *See also* East Asia; Southeast Asia

Asian/s, 4, 7–8, 12, 24, 32, 37–38, 41, 44–45, 47, 49–50, 53–54, 59–60, 70–75, 77–79, 82, 84, 89–91, 96–100, 102–7, 109–111, 113–14, 126, 129, 131, 139, 182, 188, 190, 193–94, 201–2

Asian American/s, 1–8, 10–14, 16–17, 19–20,

SUCHENG CHAN retired from teaching in 2001. She continues to write despite her many ailments because she has not yet said everything she wants to say. The recipient of two Distinguished Teaching Awards (1978 and 1998), her most recent books are *Not Just Victims: Conversations with Cambodian Community Leaders in the United States, Remapping Asian American History,* and *Survivors: Cambodian Refugees in the United States.*

The Asian American Experience

The University of Illinois Press
is a founding member of the
Association of American University Presses.

———————————————————

Composed in 10.5/3 Adobe Minion
by Jim Proefrock
at the University of Illinois Press
Manufactured by Maple-Vail
Book Manufacturing Group

University of Illinois Press
1325 South Oak Street
Champaign, IL 61820-6903
www.press.uillinois.edu